Underst
US Presidency

Malcolm Walles

University of Leeds

PHILIP ALLAN

New York   London   Toronto   Sydney   Tokyo   Singapore

First published 1991 by
Philip Allan,
66 Wood Lane End, Hemel Hempstead,
Hertfordshire, HP2 4RG
A division of
Simon & Schuster International Group

Typeset by MHL Typesetting Ltd, Coventry
Printed and bound in Great Britain by
Billings and Sons Ltd, Worcester

British Library Cataloguing in Publication Data

Walles, Malcolm
  Understanding the US presidency.
  I. Title
  321.80973

  ISBN 0-86003-830-0
  ISBN 0-86003-872-6 pbk

---

1 2 3 4 5 95 94 93 92 91

Contents

To Mark, Christopher and Anne

Introduction

Constitution, law and custom combine to make the presidency of the United States what it is today. It is a post which combines so many elements that it defies easy description or simple understanding. The titles of just a few volumes taken from the vast list of books which have been written about the institution hint at the problem: *Twilight of the Presidency* (1970); *The Imperial Presidency* (1973); *The Illusion of Presidential Government* (1981); *The Impossible Presidency* (1984); *The Elusive Executive* (1988).[1] For some commentators the President is, or can be, too powerful, free of the limitations which the Founding Fathers in their wisdom had imposed upon the office. For others he is too often constrained by parochial politicians seeking narrow, short-term advantage at the expense of expansive, longer-term programmes. For yet others the manner whereby people have reached the White House represents either anarchy rampant or democracy triumphant. With such an array of apparently contradictory opinions, it does appear that the presidency is, as the title to Godfrey Hodgson's book suggests, all things to all men.[2]

The American President, who has at times been described as 'imperial', is more often than not at the mercy of other forces at work in the nation, to the extent that while he is the only nationally elected figure (pace the Vice-President), and the one from whom leadership is expected, many will accept that leadership only if it accords with their own political goals or desires. The twentieth-century President is, in part, a victim of the eighteenth century, of the fears and prejudices of the Founding Fathers as expressed in the Constitution. As we note in the chapter on the creation of the presidency, fear by some of a monarchical dominance by the executive, and by others of a radical assertiveness by the legislature, led to the adoption of

1

a system in which powers were separated, a separation which today still constrains Congress and President alike, and militates against the emergence of coherent policy and responsible government. But the eighteenth century is not totally responsible for the current situation, for had united political parties developed, with a commitment to the attainment of national goals under the leadership of the President, then the gulf between legislature and executive which the Founding Fathers created might have been bridged.

Even here, however, we must recognize that that other construct central to the Constitution, the federal system, has played an important part, for the emphasis in party building has come to be placed much more on state and locality than on nation. Consequently, as the President is a nationally elected figure, while Congressmen and Senators are elected from districts and states, the ground is set for possible conflict between the two branches of the government, even though the same nominal party may control both, for they answer to different constituencies. Furthermore, while in the past party regulars have performed the highly significant role of determining who should carry the party banner in the presidential election, in more recent years this function, as we discuss in more detail later, has been lost. The spread of the primary system as a means of selecting the delegates to the parties' national conventions has meant that professionals have been replaced by amateurs whose criteria for preferring one candidate to another may have little to do with ability to govern. The nominations are open to any who can persuade registered party members to support them in sufficient numbers. While the break from the more traditional links between candidates and party leaders may mean that those who capture the nomination may feel little obligation towards the party, on the other side of the coin it may also mean that co-operation between Congressional members of the President's party and *their* President may be further weakened. It is probably too simple to suggest, as some have done, that the President's only power is the power to persuade, but it is, none the less, quite apparent that presidential leadership is not a function of the emergence of a party leader after a period of apprenticeship which has persuaded fellow party members to accept his commands. No President is blessed with the position a Prime Minister in the

British system faces when taking office. He has no united, majority party in the legislature ready to accept the leads he offers.

When one bears in mind the massive responsibilities which are attached to the presidency of the United States, one might reasonably expect that most careful consideration would go into the selection of the person to provide the leadership and to assume those responsibilities. And yet the two-tier process whereby the post is filled has been described by J.M. Burns as 'one of the worst top-leadership recruitment systems in the democratic societies of the world'.[3] It militates against thoughtful and informed choice, for few relevant criteria are available to the electorate. The candidates for leadership emerge through the television screen rather than through a hard climb up through the ranks of a party hierarchy. The opportunities that Americans possess to participate in candidate selection as well as in the election itself — and America is by far the largest country in the world to elect its chief executive through a system of universal adulthood suffrage — do appear to exemplify the democratic ethos at work. However, the means whereby someone ultimately becomes President, and the suitability of the successful candidate, seem to suggest a warning against an excess of democracy, while the long-drawn-out campaigns of recent years, which have concentrated on personality rather than on issues, on media projection rather than on policy discussion, on denigration rather than on affirmation, speak more of anarchy than of order.

To the outside observer there are two particular but interrelated aspects of the American electoral process that stand in sharp contrast to systems elsewhere. First, there is the length of the two-tier campaigns, which may dominate the political horizon for a couple of years or more before the actual polling day. Secondly, and undoubtedly a contributor to the first, there is the absence, as we have suggested above, of the idea of party, except in the most nominal sense, or of a person being elevated to the highest post in the nation as leader of a united, like-minded group of people with a commitment to the enactment of a policy programme upon which they are all more or less agreed.

The first part of the electoral process makes quite different demands upon the candidates from the second. In the scramble to secure the party nomination, the aspirants are contending with fellow party members while seeking the support of the registered voters of their own party. This imposes constraints upon the type of electioneering in which they indulge, with discussion of issues largely confined by the spectrum of concerns usually associated with their particular party, as they try to establish themselves as the true Democrat or the true Republican. Yet at the same time, no candidate can afford to ignore the fact that what may be said during the primary season may be brought up and used by opponents in the election proper. Thus, the effort to establish an image distinct from that of other hopefuls of one's own party can involve liabilities for the future.

After the national convention, when the task is increasingly one of persuading independent voters to give support, serious discussion of issues, while attracting some, may drive others away; the impulse is, then, to avoid specifics and to indulge in bland generalities. (At times, of course, politicians will hit upon a theme to which they will pledge commitment because it appears to be a vote winner — for example, George Bush's 'no new taxes' — but even this may prove ultimately to be a liability, as Bush found when, as President, he had to abandon the promise, thereby alienating many of his nominal supporters in the Congress.) As a consequence, the American voters are offered, in classical terms, a choice between Scylla and Charybdis or, in more modern American jargon, between a rock and a hard place. In the specific context of the 1988 election, Eric Hobsbawm has written: 'Two colourless gentlemen . . . pretended for weeks to be as dumb and as ignorant as they supposed the American voters to be, the one advised by competent professional cynics, the other not. Neither said a word about what both knew to be the central problems of the U.S.A. and what to do about them'.[4] This analysis of the campaign catches the complaints of many observers at the time, but it does not, in itself, provide sufficient support for Hobsbawm's conclusion that 'neither deserved to be elected'. The campaign was not edifying, it stooped to what appeared to be new lows, but, until America takes MacGregor Burns's strictures to heart and does adopt a better system for the recruitment of its leaders, judgement of the suitability of the candidates who emerge under the present arrangements is best related to performance in office rather than to the tactics that they feel required to adopt in order to attain that office.

Despite the excesses of the campaign, the election over, the politician is translated into the statesman. As Rossiter has put it, when the Founding Fathers created the office of President they 'fused the dignity of a king and the power of a prime minister in one elective office'.[5] While we may disagree about the prime ministerial power aspect of this description — it might have been more accurate to talk of prime ministerial responsibilities — it does nevertheless point to a conjunction of roles which are separate, for instance, in the United Kingdom. For the world at large, as for the Americans themselves, the President is the embodiment (albeit temporarily) of the nation. He symbolizes the state in a fashion which, in some respects, is above or beyond the crude political battle which put him into the White House. Once elected, he is expected to act not just as a Democratic President or as a Republican President but as the American President. His policy goals and proposals will, of course, have a political tinge, while members of his party will expect, and receive, most of the prestigious appointments to be made. But there is an aura about the presidency which has little or nothing to do with the overtly political activity in which he must at times engage but which, rather, attracts support from all sections of the society. In this particular mode, to attack the President is as un-American as attacking the flag or revealing a dislike of apple pie, for, to many, such an attack is seen not as just an attack upon an individual politician but much more as an attack upon the nation itself. In the United Kingdom, where monarch, the symbolic head of the nation, and Prime Minister, the political head, are separate, onslaughts may be launched upon the politician without suggestion that the state itself is being challenged. In the United States, however, this fusion of the two roles can at times create a certain ambivalence in some people, as was perhaps best illustrated at the time of the investigations into President Nixon's involvement in what has become known as the Watergate affair. In spite of the most damaging revelations and accusations that were being made, there were those who argued that the investigations should be halted, and that the President's assurances that he had done no wrong should be accepted because of the harm that was being done to the nation through the attacks on the man in the White House. For some, it would appear that, as the symbolic and the political leadership of the country were united in the one person, the flag should always be wrapped around the politician, and letters to this effect appeared at that time in the press, including the prestigious *New York Times*. Fortunately for America, this attitude of 'my President right or wrong' is by no means universal and a healthy ability to see the warts does prevail; although it may be worth recording that in the highly Christian society that is America (according to church membership and attendance figures), a Gallup poll of 1945 'revealed that 28 per cent of Americans thought Franklin Roosevelt was "the greatest person living or dead in world history" compared with 15 per cent for Jesus'.[6]

The fusion of monarch and Prime Minister into a President with a limited term of office brings dignity to the politician and a certain common touch to the aristocrat. Thus, the politician who reaches the White House is in some sense immediately raised above the political battle field, while the monarchical role he inherits is tempered by the expectations of the people and the demands of political circumstance. He must be prepared to perform all those ceremonies usually associated with the leadership of the state — to receive ambassadors and visiting heads of state; to preside at state functions; to deliver State of the Union addresses; to speak for the nation as a nation. But he is also expected to engage in activities which bring the office and its occupant down to mere mortal size — to receive groups visiting Washington, whether they be scouts, firemen, or astronauts; to travel the country to join in community celebrations for this or that local hero; to inaugurate grand new developments, or to open the baseball season by pitching the first baseball. All have been demanded of Presidents in the past and at different times Presidents have responded to all. Rossiter may have been guilty of some overstatement when he wrote that the people think of the President as 'a combination of scoutmaster, Delphic oracle, hero of the silver screen, and father of the multitudes',[7] but he does capture something of the range of expectations associated with the post in its non-party-political aspects. The nation does look to the President for both moral and political leadership.

We should not, of course, be so naive as to imagine that, while these actions may be projected in non-party terms, they have no political intent or pay-off. Quite obviously, a President who builds up a fund of goodwill around the country, through his skilful use of the potential this particular aspect of the office provides, may well reap some reward when he turns his attention to matters more distinctly political — whether it be in the legislative or the electoral field. Thus, the constant identification, by Presidents in their utterances, of the presidency and the nation is geared towards the establishment in the eyes of citizens of a link between the President's best interests and the nation's best interests which transcends mere party considerations. Barbara Hinckley has reminded us of Gerald Ford's comment during his inaugural address that he had 'not subscribed to any partisan programme',[8] and this attempt to separate the political and the ritual aspects of the post has been attempted by most Presidents, although few have gone as far as Ford in denying any partisan subscription. (We must remember, however, that Ford was in the unique position of never having campaigned on a presidential ticket. He had been appointed Vice-President, under the terms of the Twenty-fifth Amendment, when Vice-President Spiro Agnew resigned, and then reached the presidency upon the resignation of President Richard Nixon.) But there is a limit to the extent to which these monarchical functions can enhance a President's reputation or power. Even should he wish it, no chief executive can stand long outside the political arena. He will have goals which derive from his own political beliefs, from past commitments and from present circumstance. Their attainment will require that he engage in activities which are quite distinctly political and partisan.

Herein, for the American President, is the difficulty. Most chief executives of other nations, if not leaders of the majority party in their legislatures, are at least heads of a major grouping in the political arena. From such positions they draw a strength which eases their pursuit of their political goals. The American President only nominally heads such a group, and the support he receives is more likely to be accorded individually by members of his party rather than collectively by the party acting as a unit. The federal system, as we have noted, provided a setting which was conducive to the development of localized, fragmented parties owing and according little to a national leadership. Nevertheless, quadrennial opportunities for party activists to select a presidential candidate and, if the candidate were successful, to ride the coattails of the President's popularity and to partake of presidential spoils did induce a kind of marriage of convenience which could prove beneficial to both sides.

A number of developments in the twentieth century, however,

have tended to undermine those factors which had encouraged the loose alliance between President and the congressional members of his party. The democratization of the selection process has lessened the role of party, minimizing as it does the role of party professionals, while the reform of the campaign finance laws has deprived them of yet another sphere of influence, for, as we shall see, candidates now draw most of their contributions from political action committees or from the state rather than from their party. The increase in the number of congressional seats which are safe for one party or the other decreases the importance of the coat-tail effect and, hence, the number of Congressmen who feel any obligation to the President for their election. A decline in party identification and the consequent increase in the number of Americans calling themselves 'independents' requires presidential candidates to be less openly partisan in their appeal to a less committed electorate. Finally, the growth of large personal staffs has freed candidates from dependence upon the resources the parties once offered. The President can no longer rely upon his party, for the party no longer relies upon him.

Some Presidents have sought to strengthen the idea, and the reality, of party. John F. Kennedy, Gerald Ford, Ronald Reagan all stressed the importance they attached to their political party. As Ford said: 'As President and as a member of the Republican Party and the leader of the Republican Party, I have an obligation to try and strengthen and rebuild the Republican Party organisation in many, many states'.[9] When Ronald Reagan became the Republican candidate, letters went out over his name 'seeking support for the GOP [Grand Old Party: nickname of the Republican Party] Victory Fund' — money which was to be used to help congressional aspirants and to sponsor training schools — in the effort to develop a sense of party leadership and ideological and programmatic commitment.[10] But the norm appears to be that while Presidents do wish to promote their own party, they are fully aware that they must work with Congressmen of both political parties. Consequently, they tend to avoid too much emphasis on party label as that might jeopardize their efforts at putting together the bipartisan coalitions which are likely to be essential if they are to achieve their goals.

In this chapter I have pointed to some, but by no means all, of the paradoxes and problems associated with the post of President of the United States. Although political parties appear to dominate the scene, the President achieves his office, it would seem, almost despite rather than because of party. Endowed with responsibilities, he is denied many of the appropriate powers for translating proposals into policy. While he may be a lion abroad, at home he is forced to be a fox. To understand the office one needs to understand how it was conceived, how it has developed over the last two hundred years, and how it relates to the countervailing agencies of the state — the Congress, the bureaucracy, and the courts. The following pages seek to offer such an understanding.

Notes

1. George Reedy (New York: World); Arthur Schlesinger Jr (New York: Popular Library); Hugh Heclo and Lester M. Salamon, eds (Boulder, Col.: Westview Press); Harold M. Barger (Glenview, Ill.: Scott, Foresman); Gary King and Lyn Ragsdale (Washington, DC: Congressional Quarterly Press).
2. Godfrey Hodgson, *All Things To All Men* (Harmondsworth: Penguin Books, 1980).
3. J.M. Burns, *The Power To Lead* (New York: Simon & Schuster, 1984), p.43.
4. Eric Hobsbawm, 'Bush by Default', *Marxism Today*, December 1988, p.19.
5. Clinton Rossiter, *The American Presidency*, 2nd edn (Ithaca, NY: Harvest Books, 1960), p.19.
6. Quoted by Robert J. Sickels, *The Presidency* (Englewood Cliffs, NJ: Prentice Hall, 1980), p.45.
7. Although in light of the election of Ronald Reagan, ex-film actor, as President some twenty years after he wrote, Rossiter did perhaps show some persipience when he talked of the 'hero of the silver screen'. Rossiter, op. cit., p.17.
8. Barbara Hinckley, *Problems of the Presidency* (Glenview, Ill.: Scott, Foresman, 1985), p.29.
9. *Presidency 1975* (Washington, DC: Congressional Quarterly, 1976), p.87-A, quoted by Roger Brown and David Welborn, 'Presidents and their Parties', in Harry Bailey Jr and Jay Shafritz (eds), *The American Presidency* (Chicago: The Dorsey Press, 1988), p.293.
10. Burns, op. cit., pp.70–71.

The making of the presidency

A proper understanding of the American presidency today requires an understanding of the circumstances of its creation, of the contending pressures and philosophies that combined to produce the document — the Constitution of the United States — that Gladstone described as the 'most wonderful work ever struck off at a given time by the brain and purpose of man'.

America in the late eighteenth century was a territory of thirteen colonies (states) spread along 1,300 miles of the Atlantic seaboard of the North American continent. The population, estimated at between 2.5 and 3 million, was largely rural in character with 80 per cent dependent on the land for their living and 95 per cent dwelling in isolated farms or in villages of less than 2,500 inhabitants. Communications among the constituent parts were poor, and travel was slow, uncomfortable and often hazardous. The colonies, while each subject to British domination, had never been a united group, but had rather been independent one of the other, and their people thought of themselves not so much as Americans but as New Yorkers or Virginians or whatever. Only the common desire to secure release from that domination had occasioned a temporary sense of unity during the War of Independence. The surrender of General Cornwallis at Yorktown in 1781 and the subsequent Treaty of Paris in 1783 destroyed that centripetal force, and most Americans reverted to thinking in state rather than national terms.

During the conflict, Articles of Confederation had been drawn up which provided for a quasi-national government but the League of Friendship thus established soon proved inadequate for the growth and expansion of thirteen disunited states. The Articles reflected the suspicions of their creators towards the establishment of a strong central government at the time they were fighting such a government in Britain. The absence of a common legal structure and of a common currency, the continued existence of tariff barriers among the states, the failure to provide for a national executive which might offer some kind of national leadership, all heightened the centrifugal forces at work once the war was over. Schlesinger has suggested that the Articles established 'in effect parliamentary government without a prime minister'[1] but, while to a certain extent true, this judgment is limited, for it was also a system lacking the potential for leadership which may derive from united parties (or groups) operating within a unitary as opposed to a confederal system.

Inflation, rebellion and fear of foreign powers all ultimately combined to convince a number of Americans that the Articles were inadequate for the secure development of the region. Shay's rebellion of 1786 — an armed revolt by farmers in Massachusetts seeking relief from debts and foreclosures brought about by the economic depression which followed the war — demonstrated congressional impotence when faced with a request for assistance from the state governor, and provided the final spur for action to remedy the defects. In 1787 a convention was convened in Philadelphia for the ostensible purpose of revising the Articles. In the event, the outcome was not revision but replacement.

The convention met, in Carl Van Doren's words, under 'the dread of future tyranny as well as of immediate anarchy'[2] — of the tyranny (legislative or executive) that might spring from an overbearing central government or the anarchy into which the country might slide if steps were not taken to remedy the patent defects of the Articles. Such dread was never far from the surface of the discussions of the Founding Fathers. By and large, there was agreement that central powers and responsibilities had to be increased at the expense of the states, but there was considerable disagreement about the extent of that expansion and the degree to which checks would exist to curb legislative or executive excess.

The Declaration of Independence having ascribed so many evils to the monarch, George III — 'the history of the present King of Great Britain is a history of repeated injustices and usurpations

all having in direct object the establishment of an absolute
Tyranny over these states' — the creation of an executive for the
new nation was attended by many disagreements. The different
state constitutions, written during or after the war, had generally
sought to guard against executive predominance through a careful
separation of the legislative, executive and judicial powers of
government.[3] The outcome, however, was largely to substitute
legislative supremacy for executive supremacy. While, in the early
days of independence, this new order of things was welcome,
many Americans soon came to recognize the weaknesses inherent
in such a style of government and to agree with the tenor of
Madison's comment at the convention that the 'executives of the
states are in general little more than cyphers; the legislatures
omnipotent. If no effective check can be devised for restraining
the instability and encroachment of the [legislatures], a revolution
of some kind or other would be inevitable.' Further, a number
of the delegates were acquainted with John Locke's Second
Treatise on Government and ready to accept his analysis that:

> the good of the society requires that several things should be left
> to discretion of him that has the executive power. ... For the
> legislators, not being able to foresee and provide by laws for all
> that may be useful to the community, the executor of the laws,
> having the power in his hands, has by the common law of Nature
> a right to make use of it for the good of society.

The debate at Philadelphia concerning the creation of an
executive branch encompassed a number of aspects which
reflected different fears and different theories about the nature
of government and of man, and ranged from calls for a powerful,
monarchical type figure to appeals for an officer who would be
merely concerned with the implementation of the will of an
omnipotent legislative branch. The issues raised, then, concerned
the questions of whether there should be a single or plural
executive; the tenure which would be attached to the post; the
manner whereby the office would be filled; the possibility of
reappointment or re-election; and the duties, responsibilities and
powers of the 'chief magistrate(s)'.

The first proposals considered by the convention were those
advanced in what is known as the Virginia plan. These called for
a national executive which would be elected by the national
legislature for a single term, which would have the authority to

execute the national laws and which would 'enjoy the executive rights vested in Congress by the confederation'. James Wilson of Pennsylvania called for a single executive arguing that, while the idea of a monarchy might be conjured up, energy, dispatch and responsibility demanded the single head. Such an executive, he added, had been successful in both New York and Massachusetts. He was supported in this by John Rutledge of South Carolina who, although recognizing the fears of many of the delegates, still wanted a single executive, although he would deny to the post powers with regard to war and peace.

A counter-argument was put by Roger Sherman of Connecticut, who thought the 'Executive magistracy' should be the mere agent of the legislature which 'should be at liberty to appoint one or more as experience might dictate'. The executive, in his view, should be absolutely dependent on the legislature, as it was the will of the latter which was to be executed. An 'independence of the Executive ... was in his opinion the very essence of tyranny'.[4] Edmund Randolph, a member of the Virginia delegation, expressed yet another view. While not wishing to see the executive dependent upon the legislature, he took issue with Wilson's proposal for a single executive. He 'strongly opposed a unity in the executive magistracy' regarding it as 'the foetus of monarchy' which people would oppose. He had 'no motive to be governed by the British government as our prototype' and could not see why vigour, dispatch and responsibility could not be found in three men as well as in one. The executive, he thought, should be independent 'and in order to support that independence should consist of more than one'. A single executive would, in his view, never attract the necessary confidence, would favour those near the centre of the community and would leave the remote parts on an unequal footing.

Pierce Butler of South Carolina in putting his case for a single executive argued that:

> if one man should be appointed he would be responsible to the whole and would be impartial to its interests. If three or more should be taken from as many districts there would be a constant struggle for local advantages. In military matters this would be particularly mischievous.

Wilson supported this line of argument, saying that 'among three equal members he foresaw nothing but uncontrolled, continued and violent animosities'. When, as we discuss later, Roger Sherman, still seeking to contain the executive, pushed the proposal, also favoured by Elbridge Gerry, for a council of advice without which the first magistrate could not act (a condition in most of the states), Wilson contended that such a council 'oftener serves to cover than to prevent malpractices'.

The most extreme argument for a single executive came from Alexander Hamilton. He stated that he had 'no scruple in declaring ... that the British government was the best in the world: and that he doubted much whether any thing short of it would do in America', uniting, as it did, 'public strength with individual security'. Doubting that there could be good government without a good executive, he continued:

> the English model was the only good one on this subject. The hereditary interest of the King was so interwoven with that of the Nation, and his personal emoluments so great, that he was placed above the danger of being corrupted from abroad — and at the same time was both sufficiently independent and sufficiently controuled, to answer the purpose of the institution at home'.[5]

Hamilton proposed, then, an executive for life, but an elected monarch such as he sought was not to the taste of the delegates and his proposals were never discussed.

On 17 July, in spite of the disagreements that had been expressed during discussions, a resolution 'that the National Executive consist of a single person' was agreed without dissent, undoubtedly, in part, because most delegates believed that the president of the convention, George Washington, would be the first executive. But agreement on a single executive was a relatively simple task compared with that of determining the method of filling the post. Wilson described it as 'in truth the most difficult of all on which we have had to decide',[6] and John P. Roche characterized the debates as a game of 'three-dimensional chess' because of two other variables involved, length of tenure and re-eligibility.[7]

The Virginia Plan had called for the executive to be elected by the national legislature for a fixed term of years with no possibility of re-election. George Mason of Virginia argued that a single seven-year term would remove the need to intrigue with the legislature for re-election or reappointment. Roger Sherman, as we have already noted, supported the idea of the executive being chosen by the legislature but thought the term of office should be shorter — three years — and that incumbents should be eligible to serve for more than one term. These two proposals would, of course, have helped Sherman to attain his goal of making the executive dependent upon the legislative branch. James Wilson supported the idea of a three-year term and possible re-election but wanted to keep both the national legislature and the states out of the process. His plan was for the states to:

> be divided into districts: and that the persons qualified to vote in each district for members of the first branch of the national legislature elect . . . members for their respective districts to be electors of the Executive magistracy, that the said electors . . . shall proceed to elect by ballot, but not out of their own body [the] person in whom the executive authority of the National Government shall be vested.

Elbridge Gerry also opposed election by the national legislature, fearing that 'there would be a constant intrigue kept up for the appointment. The legislature and the candidates would bargain and play into one another's hands, votes would be given by the former under promises or expectations from the latter.' On the other hand, he was not prepared to involve the electorate to the extent that Wilson proposed in his plan. He thought 'the Community not yet ripe for stripping the States of their powers' and the people 'too little informed of personal characters in large districts and liable to deceptions'.[8] While the plan advanced by Wilson was a close forerunner of the scheme which was ultimately to be adopted, on this early day in the life of the convention it was rejected in favour of election by the national legislature for a single term.

The vote on 2 June did not, quite obviously, close the debate on the subject. Thus, on 19 July, Gouverneur Morris of Pennsylvania, taking a stand diametrically opposed to that of Roger Sherman, argued that:

> one great object of the Executive is to control the legislature. The legislature will continually seek to aggrandise and perpetuate themselves. . . . It is necessary then that the Executive Magistrate should be the guardian of the people, even of the lower classes, against legislative tyranny, against the Great and the wealthy who in the course of things will necessarily compose the legislative body.

He proposed then that 'if he is to be the guardian of the people' he should 'be appointed by the people'. He suggested biennial elections but argued strongly for re-eligibility:

if the Executive is not to be re-eligible ... (1) it will destroy the great incitement to merit public esteem by taking away the hope of being rewarded with a reappointment. ... The love of fame is the great spring to noble and illustrious actions. Shut the Civil road to glory and he may be compelled to seek it by the sword. (2) It will tempt him to make the most of the short space of time allotted him, to accumulate wealth and provide for his friends.

Edmund Randolph thought eligibility for re-election would create 'a temptation to court a re-appointment' and was of the opinion that 'election by the legislature with an incapacity to be elected a second time' was preferable to the Morris plan. Rufus King, on the other hand, 'did not like the ineligibility. He thought ... he who had proved himself to be most fit for an office ought not to be excluded by the Constitution from holding it.' He was of the opinion that 'the people at large would choose wisely' and 'that an appointment by electors chosen by the people for the purpose would be liable to fewest objections'. Gerry, however, asserted that 'the people are uninformed and would be misled by a few designing men' and urged election by electors chosen by state executives, while Oliver Ellsworth thought such electors should be appointed by the legislatures of the States.

On 25 July James Madison advanced his objections to the idea of election of the executive by the state legislatures as they 'had betrayed a strong propensity to a variety of pernicious measures'. 'One object of the National Legislature was to control this propensity. One object of the National Executive ... was to control the National Legislature, so far as it might be infected with similar propensity.' Appointment by electors chosen by the people, he argued, would be better than appointment by the national legislature, but believed that 'election by the people or rather by the qualified part of them, at large,' would, despite all its imperfections, be the best. The following day, Benjamin Franklin offered further support to the popular election argument:

it seems to have been imagined by some that the returning to the mass of the people was degrading the magistrate. This he thought was contrary to Republican principles. In free governments the rulers are the servants and the people their supporters and sovereigns. For the former therefore to return among the latter was not to *degrade* but to *promote* them.

George Mason, however, in a speech reviewing the various proposals that had been advanced for selection of the executive, concluded that 'election by the national legislature . . . was the best' and argued for a seven-year term and ineligibility for a second term.[9] His proposals were carried.

But even this reaffirmation of the earlier vote did not dispose of the matter. A failure to settle the question of *how* the legislature would elect the executive led to the matter being referred to a Committee on Unfinished Parts which reported to the convention on 4 September. The proposal which was then advanced followed closely Mr Wilson's plan from early June. Election of the President, by electors chosen by the states, for a four-year term was called for and the question of re-eligibility was left open. Should the electors fail to give a majority to one candidate the election was to be left to the Senate. Reasons for the changes were given by Gouverneur Morris. He argued that if appointment were made by the legislature there was a danger of intrigue and faction, and pointed to the inconvenience of an ineligibility which would be required by that mode of appointment in order to lessen that danger. He asserted that nobody appeared satisfied with legislative appointment and raised the spectre (for some) that many (including himself) would prefer an immediate choice by the people. (George Mason had 'conceived it would be as unnatural to refer the choice of a proper character for chief magistrate to the people as it would to refer a trial of colours to a blind man'.) Morris also argued that it was an indispensible necessity to make the executive independent of the legislature. Further, 'as the Electors would vote at the same time throughout the U.S. and at so great a distance from each other, the great evil of cabal was avoided'.[10]

A number of objections were raised to the committee proposals. Some of Mason's fears had been allayed by the introduction of indirect election, but he was convinced that there would be so many candidates for the presidency that the electors would give a majority to any one person in only about one election in twenty. Thus, for 95 per cent of the time it would be the Senate which would choose the president, and he considered this 'an improper body for the purpose'. Charles Pinkney added his weight to this particular objection and, indeed, expanded it, pointing out that it made 'the same body of men which will in fact elect the President his Judges in case of an impeachment'.[11] Pinkney also raised fears that the electors would 'be strangers to the several candidates and . . . unable to decide on their comparative merits', and that re-eligibility would 'endanger the public liberty'.

While the point that the electors might know little of the respective candidates had undoubted validity for the early years of the Republic (although few would have been unaware of Washington's merits), Wilson argued that 'Continental Characters will multiply as we more and more coalesce, so as to enable the electors in every part of the Union to know and judge of them'. Wilson was also opposed to just the Senate having a role in the election process and proposed that the task be assigned to the legislature. In a vote on 5 September this idea was rejected, Madison having argued that the large States would predominate in such an arrangement. The next day, in an attempt to minimize the influence of the large states, Hugh Williamson suggested that the choice should be made by the legislature voting by states and not per capita. Opposition to Senate involvement was still strong, however, and when Roger Sherman moved that the appropriate clause should now read 'The House of Representatives shall immediately choose by ballot one of them for President, the members from each State having one vote', the motion was carried with only one dissentient.

At the same time as deliberations were continuing over the nature and appointment of the executive, there was also concern about how an incumbent might be removed from office. The first proposal came on 2 June from John Dickinson of Delaware who wanted the national legislature to have the power of removal on the request of a majority of the legislatures of the individual states. Madison and Wilson were both opposed to giving the states a role in this regard and argued that to give equality of weight to the legislatures of the small and the large states could lead to a situation in which a minority of the people might be able 'to prevent ye. removal of an officer who had rendered himself justly criminal in the eyes of a majority'. They both thought it inappropriate that the state authorities should have a role in this matter. George Mason recognized the need for removal of an executive who had become unfit to hold office but was worried that if the power were put into the hands of the legislature, it would make the executive the creature of the legislature — 'a violation of the fundamental principle of good government'. Dickinson's plan was rejected by all the states except Delaware.

On 13 June a report of the Committee of the Whole called for executives to be removable on impeachment and conviction of malpractices or neglect of duty, but did not specify the mechanics of instituting or implementing the procedures. Two days later William Patterson introduced the New Jersey Plan which was aimed largely at strengthening the Articles. A single-term executive was called for who would be removable by Congress on application by a majority of the executives in the states. In July, Gouverneur Morris argued that the possibility of impeachment would render the executive dependent upon the legislature, and as he was concerned, as we have seen, that the executive should control the legislature, he therefore opposed impeachment proposals. To meet any dangers which might arise from an unimpeachable executive he suggested biennial elections by the people at large. The ever-practical Benjamin Franklin, however, made the point that lack of power to impeach might well necessitate recourse to assassination.

Opinion, in general, held that there should be some means of removing from office an executive who had proven himself unfit, and when the Committee on detail reported in August it provided for removal from office on impeachment by the House of Representatives and conviction in the Supreme Court of treason, bribery or corruption. By the time the final document was submitted in September, the Senate, chaired by the Chief Justice, had been substituted for the Supreme Court, but the sanction otherwise remained intact.

While it would appear that debate over the methods by which an executive might be chosen overshadowed discussion of the functions and limitations of the office, there can be little doubt that the former was greatly influenced by conceptions of what those functions and limitations should be. All of the delegates had experienced state government and had observed the working relations between legislatures and executives. Those observations, often allied with political philosophies derived from European writers, served to inform the debate over the distribution of powers in this new constitution, and the fears already alluded to, of either excessive legislative or executive predominance, provided the backcloth against which the discussions took place.

One particular question which was raised at different times throughout the convention concerned the matter of a council of advice which would be attached to the presidency. Roger Sherman, who was opposed to a strong executive, argued for such a council, 'without which the first magistrate could not act', as this would 'make the establishment acceptable to the people'. He was supported in this by Elbridge Gerry who thought such a body would 'give weight and inspire confidence'. However, as we have noted earlier, James Wilson thought the proposed council might well have negative value.

The idea of an executive council, which was to be found in most of the states, was often associated with the proposed veto power of the president. Thus, in the Virginia Plan the proposal was made to associate a number of the national judiciary with the executive in a Council of Revision which would pass on all laws emerging from the legislature. Debate on a veto ranged from those, like Sherman, who were opposed to giving such a power to a single executive, to those, such as Hamilton and Wilson, who believed the executive should have an absolute veto over all laws. Sherman was against 'enabling any one man to stop the will of the whole. No one man could be found so far above all the rest in wisdom. ... [W]e ought to avail ourselves of his wisdom in revising the laws, but not permit him to overrule the decided and cool opinions of the Legislature.' Benjamin Franklin called upon his experiences in Pennsylvania — where 'the negative of the Governor was constantly made use of to extort money'; where 'no good law whatever could be passed without a private bargain with him' — to oppose an absolute veto unless the executive were accompanied by a council. Wilson and Hamilton argued that the executive ought to have an absolute negative, for without 'such a self-defense the Legislature can at any moment sink it into non-existence'. They believed that the importance of the power would derive not from its frequent use but from knowledge of its existence.

Those who favoured the absolute power of veto for the Executive found little support among the other delegates and on 4 June the idea was rejected, in the Committee of the Whole, by ten votes to none. However, a conditional veto, which could be overridden by a two-thirds vote in each branch of the legislature, was passed without objection. The proposal to associate the judiciary with the revising power was overruled on this occasion but Wilson did not let it die here. If he could not have an absolute veto for his executive acting alone, he sought to revise it in association with the judiciary. Thus, on 21 July, three days after the convention had voted to give the executive the qualified veto power, Wilson moved an amendment that 'the supreme National Judiciary should be associated with the Executive in the Revisionary power.' Support for the proposal came from both Ellsworth and Madison. Ellsworth argued that 'the aid of the Judges will give more wisdom and fairness to the Executive. They will possess a systematic and accurate knowledge of the laws, which the Executive cannot be expected always to possess.' Madison thought the association would be useful to the Executive, by inspiring additional confidence and firmness in exerting the revisionary power'. In reply to the suggestion that such a link would give too much power either to the executive or to the judiciary, he argued that the legislature 'would still be an over-match for them. Experience in all the States had evinced a powerful tendency in the Legislature to absorb all power into its vortex' and 'this was the real source of danger to the American Constitutions'.

Luther Martin and Nathaniel Gorham put the case against this particular role for the judiciary. Martin considered the association 'a dangerous innovation' which would give the judges two opportunities to negate laws — when acting with the executive and when acting in their proper, judicial role. Gorham objected on the ground that he thought 'Judges ought to carry into the exposition of the laws no prepossessions with regard to them.' Association at the prior stage would undoubtedly compromise attitudes at the latter. The motion was lost, and the convention again voted to give the executive the qualified veto.

Debate concerning the election, tenure and eligibility of Presidents occupied considerably more of the delegates' time than did discussion of the functions the new officers would perform. Leaving aside the veto power already discussed, the Virginia plan, which set the tone for the early debates, simply called for the national executive to have a general authority to execute the national laws and to enjoy the executive rights vested in Congress by the Confederation. The New Jersey plan, which, less ambitiously than that from Virginia, sought to revise and extend the Articles, proposed that the executive, in addition to the general authority to execute the federal acts, ought to appoint all federal officers not otherwise provided for, and should also direct all military operations, although without taking personal command of any troops. Alexander Hamilton, with his plan for a strong executive with life tenure (subject to good behaviour), proposed giving the office the direction of war when authorized or begun; the power of making all treaties, with the advice and consent of the Senate; the sole appointment of the heads of the departments of Finance, War, and Foreign Affairs, and the nomination of all other officers, subject to Senatorial concurrence.

A committee on detail, established to produce a constitution based on the various resolutions which had been passed by the convention, reported on 6 August. According the style *President* to the executive, the committee proposed that, in addition to the authority to execute the laws, the President 'shall, from time to time, give information to the Legislature, of the state of the Union' and 'may recommend to their consideration such measures as he shall judge necessary and expedient'. He was to have the sole power to commission all officers of the United States, and to appoint officers in all cases not otherwise provided for. He was to be Commander-in-Chief of the army and navy of the United States and of the militia of the various states. He was authorized to receive ambassadors but was not, however, given the treaty-making power which was vested, rather, in the Senate, along with the right to appoint ambassadors and judges of the Supreme Court. At the end of August, those matters which had not been resolved — among them, the power to make treaties and to appoint ambassadors and judges — were referred to a committee on unfinished business. After bargaining between representatives of the large and the small states (the latter seeing the Senate, where they had equality of representation, as their bastion), the President was given the treaty-making power, subject to the approval of two-thirds of the Senate, and the appointing power, subject to the approval of a majority of the Senate. With this agreement, the creation of the presidency was virtually complete, and on Saturday, 15 September the full Constitution was agreed by all the participating states.

Unanimous acceptance by the state delegations did not necessarily involve unanimous acceptance by the delegates themselves and, indeed, a number were prepared to speak out firmly against certain aspects of the completed document. Thus,

Charles Pinkney objected to the 'contemptible weakness and dependence' of the executive, while George Mason, on the other hand, was concerned that the president would be unsupported by a constitutional council, and was worried that, as all treaties were to be supreme laws of the land, the executive and the Senate together would have an exclusive power of legislation.

The different fears which beset the delegates when they arrived in Philadelphia were still in evidence, then, as they departed, and were to form a major part of the heated debate over ratification when the Constitution was put to the states for their agreement. Pinkney's complaint, for instance, was matched by Patrick Henry's assertion in the debate in Virginia that the 'mighty President' was to have 'the powers of a King'.[12]

The most notable battleground over ratification was to be found, however, in the pages of New York newspapers. George Clinton, governor of New York, and a strong anti-Federalist, under the pseudonym 'Cato' published a number of essays which set forth his strong, even vitriolic objections to what he considered the dangers inherent in the post of President. He warned that 'the great powers of the President . . . would lead to oppression and ruin', that the presidential 'court' 'would be the asylum of the base, idle, avaricious and ambitious', and that 'the President, possessed of the power given him by this frame of government differs but very immaterially from the establishment of monarchy in Great Britain'. With this in mind, he suggested to the New Yorkers that 'your posterity will find that great power connected with ambition, luxury and flattery, will as readily produce a Caesar, Caligula, Nero and Domitian in America, as the same causes did in the Roman Empire'.[13]

To counter these objections of those who feared the Constitution concentrated too much power, the Letters of Publius, better known as *The Federalist*, were written by Hamilton, Madison and Jay, 'to the people of New York'. In this classic of American political thought, strength checked by balance represents a dominant theme: 'ambition must be made to counter ambition' (No. LI). Hamilton wrote that 'energy in the executive is a leading character in the definition of good government' (No. LXX), but had, in the previous letter, taken pains to demonstrate the limitations under which a president, unlike a king, would operate: he is elected for a limited term; is liable to impeachment; has only a qualified right of veto; may make treaties and appointments only with Senatorial consent; and may not declare war. Of the arguments of those like Henry or Clinton, he wrote: 'the image of Asiatic despotism and voluptuousness have scarcely been wanting to crown the exaggerated scene', (LXVII) and went on to make the case for a unity in the executive which he considered 'one of the best of the distinguishing features' of the Constitution. Allied to competent powers, this would make for the energetic government he thought necessary for America.

The arguments in the Publius letters prevailed. New York ratified the Constitution. In 1789 George Washington was unanimously elected first President of the United States.

Notes

1. Arthur Schlesinger Jr., *The Imperial Presidency* (New York: Popular Library, 1974), p.14.
2. Carl Van Doren, *The Great Rehearsal* (London: The Cresset Press, 1948), p.62.
3. I.W. Blackstone's *Commentaries on the Laws of England* were well known in the colonies and many agreed with his diagnosis that 'in all tyrannical governments, the supreme magistracy, or the right both of *making* and *enforcing* the laws is vested in one and the same man, or one and the same body of men; and wherever these two powers are united together, there can be no public liberty.' (T. Cooley edition, 2nd edn 1872, p.146.)
4. Madison's Notes of the Debates, 1 June, as edited by Winton U. Solberg in *The Federal Convention and the Formation of the Union of the American States* (Indianapolis: Bobbs-Merrill, 1958). All future references to Madison's Notes relate to this edition.
5. Notes, 18 June.
6. Notes, 4 September.
7. J.P. Roche, 'The Founding Fathers: A Reform Caucus in Action', *American Political Science Review*, December 1961.
8. Notes, 2 June.
9. Notes, 26 July.
10. Notes, 4 September.
11. See the Constitution.
12. Quoted by Broadus Mitchell and Louise Mitchell, *A Biography of the Constitution of the United States* (New York: Oxford University Press, 1964), p.151.
13. Letter of 'Cato', *New York Journal*, 22 November 1787, reproduced in Harry A. Bailey Jr and Jay M. Shafritz (eds) *The American Presidency* (Chicago, Ill.: The Dorsey Press, 1988), pp.18–19.

Selection and election

The Presidency of George Washington represented a link, as it were, between the weak, decentralized form of government under the Articles and the more structured, centralized institutions of the Constitution. His unanimous election gave Americans time to adjust to the new order, free from the immediate clash of contending candidates for the post of chief executive. But contest and confrontation were not long in coming. The differences at the convention were reflected in political life generally. Advocates of a strong federal government were soon ranged against those concerned to keep the functions of central government to a minimum. Federalists faced anti-Federalists and while Washington, a Federalist, was unchallenged in the second presidential election, his Vice-President, John Adams, was opposed by a Democratic-Republican (anti-Federalist). So organized did these factions become that when Washington left office after his second term[1] his Farewell Address (in the composition of which Alexander Hamilton had played a considerable part) contained a warning against the 'baneful effects of the spirit of party'.

Cynics would suggest that the Federalists were less worried about party than they were about an *opposition* party. Certainly such a worry would have been well founded, for, in 1796, in the first real contest for the Presidency, Thomas Jefferson came within three electoral college votes of John Adams and was duly elected Vice-President to his Federalist opponent. Four years later, with both sides voting as blocs, Jefferson and Aaron Burr, the Democratic-Republican candidates, defeated the Federalist ticket of Adams and Pinckney.

The development of political factions thus quickly demonstrated a sharp divide between the theory which lay behind the 'jerry-rigged improvisation'[2] that is the Electoral College and the realities of political life. As Carl Becker has written, the College could only work in the manner its creators sought if 'politicians would cease to be politicians, would divest themselves of party prejudice and class and sectional bias, and be ... inspired solely by pure love of liberty and the public good'.[3] Far from such Olympian detachment, once the uncontested elections of George Washington were past, the Electoral College electors were seen to be full members of their political environment, reflecting the desires of those who had chosen them rather than providing objective evaluation of the merits of the candidates.

The election of 1800 also demonstrated a difficulty which the Founding Fathers had not foreseen. The Constitution required the electors to vote for two people and, assuming that one received a majority of the votes, the candidate with the most votes would become President, the runner-up Vice-President. If there were a tie, however, as that produced by the bloc voting of 1800, there was no mechanism for determining the preferred choice of the electors. Thus, in 1800 it was recognized that Jefferson was sought as President, Burr as Vice-President, but the wording of the Constitution provided no means of translating wish into reality. The election had to go to the House of Representatives which, after thirty-six ballots occasioned by some intense factional disputes, ultimately gave victory to Jefferson. As a consequence of this impasse the Twelfth Amendment to the Constitution was rapidly introduced and ratified, providing that the electoral college would first vote for the presidential candidate and then, separately, for the vice-presidential candidate. The confusion of 1800 could not then be repeated.

Despite the considerable time spent on the subject at the Constitutional Convention, the Constitution is remarkably quiet about factors which are central to the election of Presidents. For instance, apart from age, citizenship and residency requirements, it has nothing to say about the emergence of candidates for the post of chief executive. This is, of course, hardly surprising in light of the Founding Fathers' expectations (or hopes) that the Electoral College would make its choice from a 'field narrowed to those with pre-existing reputations' and would 'exclude those who sought to make their name during the campaign by issue arousal'.[4] As Hamilton wrote: 'The choice of *several* to form an intermediate body of electors will be much less apt to convulse the community with any extraordinary or violent movements than the choice of *one* who was himself to be the final object of the public wishes'.[5]

Further, while the Constitution does give to the states' legislatures the right to determine how Electoral College voters shall be chosen — 'Each state shall appoint, in such manner as the legislature thereof may direct, a number of electors' — it says nothing about the way in which the electoral votes should be allocated among the different candidates. The processes whereby Presidents have emerged and Electoral College votes have been distributed are, then, much more a product of operational politics than of abstract theory, and they are processes which have continued to evolve in varying degrees throughout the history of the Republic.

The very first elections in which the presidency was contested demonstrated how little the deliberations and resolutions of the Founding Fathers had to do with the reality of the political situation that was soon to arise. Thus, in the years to 1824 candidates for the presidency were chosen by congressional caucus — the parties in Congress — thereby establishing a link between the legislature and the executive that the Constitutional Convention had sought to avoid. (We noted, however, in the chapter on the making of the presidency, that some of the Founding Fathers were of the opinion that the Electoral College would fail as often as nineteen times out of twenty to provide a majority for one candidate, thus giving to the House of Representatives the determinant voice in the election of the President.)

There was much to be said for 'King Caucus', as it came, disparagingly, to be called, for it did provide a mechanism whereby elected representatives of a party could bring some kind of order to an unstructured situation. In the early days of the Republic no other mechanisms existed whereby candidates with a national backing could easily emerge. Indeed, some Americans, when faced with the almost anarchic practices of present-day candidate selection, look back with a degree of nostalgia to the days of those links between presidential candidates and the elected members of their parties in Congress.

However, while it provided an early and useful service in

making presidential elections more manageable by simplifying
the choices for the electorate, the caucus was soon under attack.
Some were offended on the constitutional grounds, referred to
above, that the carefully planned doctrine of the separation of
powers was thereby undermined. Others, more significantly,
complained that such a selection process put too much power into
the hands of a small elite who could, and did, ignore grassroot
sentiment within the party. When, in 1824, such elitist practices
led to the rejection of the popular Andrew Jackson and the
selection of William Crawford, and when Crawford was well
beaten in the election (last in popular votes, third in Electoral
College votes, in a field of four), the days of the caucus were
numbered. Jackson went on to win the 1828 election, promising
to democratize the selection process. Four years later, the
candidates of all three parties contesting the presidential election
owed their nominations to national conventions (the anti-
Masonic party having instituted the first such convention in
September 1831).

The failure of the Constitution to prescribe a common method
of allocation of the Electoral College votes within the states meant
that a number of different practices developed. At the outset, in
a majority of the states it was the state legislature which played
the dominant role, but six states did move immediately to involve
the people and by 1804 most provided for direct, popular election
of the electors. By 1828 only one state left the choice to the state
legislature. However, while the involvement of the electorate was
soon all but universal, there were still different practices with
regard to the actual allocation of the electoral votes. Thus, initially
most of the states providing for popular election required the
electors to be chosen from districts. The electoral votes from a
state were then allocated among the various candidates according
to their success in the districts. This proportionate distribution
of the votes, while democratic in its operation, weakened the
power of the party bosses in the states and there was soon a move
away from the 'district rule' to the 'unit rule' whereby the
candidate who secured the majority of popular votes across the
state received all of the state's electoral votes. The 'unit rule'
rapidly displaced the 'district rule' which by 1836 had largely been
abandoned. Since then, with very few exceptions, the 'unit rule'
has applied.

By 1836, considerable flesh had been put on to the skeletal framework of the Constitution, although the figure thereby produced bore little resemblance to the model the Founding Fathers had envisaged. Parties and party bosses dominated the selection system and party allegiance the election process. Electors were not chosen for their statesmanlike ability to pick the best person for the post of president but for their adherence to a particular party candidate. Demonstrations by electors of an independence of the party vote which elected them came to be frowned on as a denial of democratic processes rather than welcomed as an affirmation of the intentions of those who created the Constitution.

The national convention, which replaced the congressional caucus, is still with the Americans today, although considerable change during the twentieth century has modified its functions. Its introduction undoubtedly extended the opportunities for party supporters around the country to involve themselves in the candidate selection process: the congressional caucus had denied such opportunities to a party's supporters who lived in districts represented by another party. The party conventions provided for delegate representation of the various party constituencies — congressional district, city, town, rural area — as well as involving the elected office-holders and officials of the party.[6] Initially, the conventions tended to be arenas in which front-running candidates were confirmed as party standard-bearers. It was not long, however, before the delegates became the kingmakers. Those who would be President had to bargain with those who had the power to bestow the accolade of 'party candidate'. Delegates (or at least the party leaders among them) did not, of course, arrive at the convention city with no knowledge of the respective claims of the aspirants. Contenders and their supporters would have been busy for some time prior to the meeting seeking to establish their reputations. But few were so well established in the public eye that they could forgo the bargaining processes which became a central part of convention activity. The era of the 'smoke-filled room' had arrived.

For the remainder of the century, the national convention was the arena in which state party 'bosses' (rather than the party rank and file) played the dominant role in deciding who should represent them in the presidential race. It was not a period noted for the quality of the presidents who thereby emerged, as a roll-call of those who attained the White House demonstrates. With one or two notable exceptions (this was, after all, the period which produced Lincoln) they were very ordinary men. This change in the nature of the men who became President was noted by Lord Bryce. Until 1828, he wrote, 'all the Presidents had been statesmen in the European sense of the word, men of education, of administrative experience, of a certain largeness of view and dignity of character.' After that period, until the Lincoln presidency, they 'were either mere politicians ... or else successful soldiers. ... They were intellectual pygmies beside the real leaders of that generation ...'. 'The only thing remarkable about them is that being so commonplace they should have climbed so high'.[7] Much of this assessment could equally well be applied to the Presidents who came after the Civil War.

Towards the end of the century, adverse criticism of these boss-dominated conventions became rife, with Ostrogorski's comments perhaps best catching the mood of the critics. He described the convention as 'a colossal travesty of popular institutions', a meeting at which a 'greedy crowd of office-holders, or of office-seekers, disguised as delegates of the people, ... indulged in ... intrigues and manoeuvres, the object of which was the chief magistracy of the greatest Republic of the two hemispheres ...'. In 1924 H.L. Mencken, satirist of the American political and social scene, offered an equally unprepossessing picture when he wrote:

> There is something about a national convention that makes it as fascinating as a revival or a hanging. It is vulgar, it is ugly, it is stupid, it is tedious, it is hard upon both the cerebral centers and the gluteus maximus. ... One sits through long sessions wishing heartily that all the delegates were dead in Hell.

And yet he did suggest that it had a certain charm, for 'suddenly there comes a show so gaudy, so hilarious, so melodramatic, so unimaginably exhilirating and preposterous that one lives a gorgeous year in an hour'.[8] Even Ostrogorski had acknowledged that while those who became President as a result of such intrigue by greedy men were not great men in the mould of a Washington or a Jefferson, they were, at least, 'honourable men', thus lending credence to the saying that 'God takes care of drunkards, of little children, and of the United States'.[9] As a response to the criticisms, some weakening of party ties took place and the kingmakers at the conventions were forced to pay more attention to the personal popularity of contenders, while, from the other side, some contenders came to recognize the political advantages such popularity could bring. Thus, for example, as Ceaser has written, as early as 1896 the candidacy of William McKinley 'relied heavily on image techniques and mass persuasion'.[10]

At about the same time as reaction to the boss-controlled conventions was setting in, both Populists and Progressives started to call for the introduction of presidential primaries which would elect delegates to the national conventions and thereby diminish the influence of the 'smoke-filled rooms'. While Florida may claim 'to be the first state to have enacted a presidential primary law',[11] in 1901, it was Wisconsin which really pioneered the shift with its Act of 1905 which provided for the first direct election of delegates to national conventions (although nothing was said about the presidential preferences of the delegates). Wisconsin was followed in fairly quick order by Pennsylvania in 1906 and South Dakota in 1909. But it was an Oregon law of 1910 that paved the way for most of the modern primaries, for it 'allowed voters to register their preference for president and vice-president and allow[ed] them the opportunity to directly choose the national convention delegates'.[12] The movement spread and by 1912 'twelve states had primary laws providing for direct election of delegates, a preference vote, or both'.[13] Another three states had laws providing for optional primaries.

The election of 1912 has been characterized by Key as 'one of the fabulous chapters of American politics'.[14] The Progressives within the Republican party sought to overthrow the 'tyranny' of the party bosses by capturing enough delegates through the primary states to demonstrate a strength which might persuade some of the party regulars to join them. Indeed, Theodore Roosevelt, as the Progressive flag-bearer, did achieve a commanding majority over President Taft in the primaries. However, the President held on to the delegates from the non-primary states and secured re-nomination 'in one of the most acrimonious of national gatherings'.[15] The Progressives, including Roosevelt, left the Republican party and ran a third-party campaign which, while failing to win, pushed the regular Republicans under Taft into third place. The 1912 campaign within the Republican party demonstrated, according to Ceaser, 'the potential threat to party unity that the new system could create',[16] and was a harbinger of developments later in the century.

The number of states using the primary system continued to rise for a time, and by 1916 had reached some two dozen, and it began to look as though the new procedures were becoming a firmly established part of the American selection process. In fact, progress towards the Progressives' goal of opening up the processes of selection and nomination was soon to be checked. Once the First World War was over, America lapsed into a conservatism which, when allied with the high costs and relatively low turnout associated with the primaries, occasioned a reaction and a return by many states to the more traditional, boss-dominated selection processes. By 1935 only fifteen states retained the primary.

From the point of view of those concerned with the health of the political parties, the return of the selection processes to the hands of the party professionals was a welcome and salutary development. Primaries militated against party regularity, promoted factionalism, put a premium on the colourful as opposed to the thoughtful candidate, and generally helped to undermine the parties as meaningful, national organizations.

However, while many states reverted to pre-primary practices, thereby instituting a mixed system in which some delegates to the national conventions were chosen in primaries but in which the bulk were chosen by state party conventions or caucuses, the new arrangements still provided opportunities for contenders to establish themselves despite either hostility or indifference on the part of the party regulars. Thus, those who could not be sure of winning sufficient backing through the conventions and caucuses at state level, were able to follow a primary trail which might demonstrate their popular appeal, their ability to win votes. It was, nevertheless, a hazardous trail for it could also demonstrate an absence of popularity and thereby put an end to presidential aspirations. Indeed, conventional wisdom had it that to enter a primary was like a drowning man grasping at straws. For example, Wendell Willkie, the Republican candidate in 1940, sought a comeback in 1944 by entering the Wisconsin primary, and came last in a field of four. While he continued on in other primary races, his candidacy was effectively at an end. (We must, however, beware of attributing too much to the primaries, for in that same year Douglas MacArthur polled approximately 400,000 more primary votes than Thomas Dewey, and yet, at the national convention Dewey received all but one vote on the first ballot.) In 1948, Harold Stassen offered an exciting primary challenge to the Republican party regulars; although he failed to win the nomination he rekindled interest in the primary as a technique for delegate selection, and in the next few years a number of states re-introduced primaries.

Keech and Matthews have suggested that 'the evolution of the modern selection system can be traced to the Goldwater candidacy of 1964' which produced 'the most effective and elaborate candidate organization seen in presidential politics up to that time'.[17] However, the candidacy of John F. Kennedy in 1960 (documented so well in the first of Theodore White's books entitled *The Making of the President*), in which, through primary victories, he demonstrated to the party's power brokers that his youth and particularly his Roman Catholicism were not insuperable handicaps, surely ranks as the campaign which set the pattern for the future. In the words of James Davis, it 'marked a breakthrough in presidential nominating politics'.[18] The personal visits, the extensive use of the electronic media, the campaign teams put together, all betokened the shift to candidate-oriented campaigns which would present the national conventions with a *fait accompli*.

In 1960, the bulk of delegates were still chosen by non-primary methods and Kennedy could not, therefore, merely rely on his primary victories to secure the nomination. They may ultimately have been the deciding factors but they had to be accompanied by astute groundwork among the party leaders around the country. Since then, particularly under the spur of reaction to the happenings of 1968, the balance has changed dramatically. The Democratic national convention of that year, held in Chicago, was marked by a rift between the forces of the older order and those of the new. On the one side were ranged those who sought, as far as possible, to keep the convention and the nominating processes in their own hands, while on the other stood those seeking reforms which would permit the involvement of those who felt excluded from those processes, in particular the young, blacks, housewives and professionals. The old guard found their strength in the non-primary states, while the challengers were much more powerful in those which held primaries: Hubert Humphrey, who had not entered a single primary, received the nomination. Such was the division that clashes broke out between delegates within the convention hall, and between police and demonstrators outside. This was, in Croty's view, 'the ugliest and most violent [convention] either party had experienced'.[19]

Following the shocks of 1968, a number of reforms were instituted, starting with the McGovern–Fraser Commission report of 1970, and were accompanied by an increase in the number of states using primaries. These had a dramatic and immediate effect upon the nature of the candidate selection process. Thus, as early as 1972, 84 per cent of the delegates to the Democratic convention had never been to a convention before, while today more than 70 per cent of delegates are chosen as a result of primary elections. Furthermore, McGovern–Fraser was concerned that state delegations' should fairly reflect the division of preferences expressed by those who participate in the presidential nominating process', and consequently the Democrats abolished the unit rule whereby the candidate who received the most votes in the primary received all the delegates from that state; proportional allocation was introduced in its place. Later in the decade, the Winograd Commission provided for delegates to be bound to their stated preferences for the first ballot at the convention.

During the 1980s, the Democrats engaged in what was labelled a 'quadrennial post-election rite' in which they consistently tinkered with their selection rules. Thus, they lowered the percentage of votes a candidate had to receive in a primary or caucus to qualify for a proportion of the state's delegates from 20 per cent to 15 per cent, and following the 1988 election they barred the winner-reward system (whereby the winner in a primary was rewarded with more delegates than his percentage of the votes entitled him to). Most inconsistently, they have played around with their new creation, the super-delegates. These super-delegates, created to enhance the role of the party in the candidate-selection process, are made up of representatives of the Democratic members of Congress, of the Democratic National Committee, and of the party in the states. After the 1984 election the number of such delegates was increased by a hundred to more than 650, but in 1988 super-delegate places for most of the DNC were eliminated, and then the following year they were restored. While behind some of the changes there undoubtedly lay the desire to restore a more important role to the party machine, many of the changes appear to have originated in inter-factional wrangling, the price to be paid by one group for support by another.

The Democrats have been more concerned to establish national rules for delegate selection than the Republicans who have been relatively content to leave these matters in the hands of the state parties. Thus, the Republicans still permit the unit rule if state laws permit it; Democratic delegates must express their preferences, or their uncommitted status, while the Republicans are not so required; Republican delegates are not bound by the first ballot requirement, unless state law so ordains; Democratic party rules do not permit primary crossover voting — that is, registered Republicans are not allowed to vote in Democratic primaries — while the Republicans are more open.[20] (Although the Democrats have introduced some national rules, there does still exist a variety of practices within the different states, too numerous to discuss in detail here, but one or two examples will provide an illustration of some of those practices. In Texas, in 1988, 119 of the Democratic delegates to the national convention were chosen by primary vote, the other 64 by separate caucus action. In Virginia, the Republicans operate a non-binding primary, a so-called 'beauty contest' which demonstrates a candidate's popular appeal, but all of the delegates are selected later by caucus. This practice is also followed by the Democrats in Idaho and Vermont.)

The outcome of the attempt by reformers to 'democratize' the parties, to offer delegate representation to a wide range of societal groups, has contributed significantly to the undermining of the party system. Much power has now passed from the hands of the party professionals into the hands of the rank and file, and persons often outside the mainstream of the parties. Candidates must now gear their efforts directly to the persuasion of that rank and file and those 'outsiders'. In addition, they no longer have the luxury, most recently enjoyed by Hubert Humphrey, of deciding whether or not to enter the primary circuit: only by so entering will they be in a position to take the nomination. It is true that a deadlocked convention might turn to someone who had not entered the primaries, but no serious contender could rely upon such an eventuality. Only twice since 1924, and not once since the number of primary states increased dramatically, have the conventions of either party required more than one ballot: 1932 and 1952 for the Democrats; 1940 and 1948 for the Republicans. The Democratic Party's super-delegates have not yet had a significant role to play as, since their introduction, the majority needed to take the nomination has been achieved before the convention has met.

Once the national conventions have ratified the decisions of the primaries and the caucus/conventions, the election proper can get under way. After the almost internecine struggle for the nomination, the inter-party battle seems almost anticlimactic. Certainly, in recent years the campaign has degenerated into a clash in which policy proposals come a poor second to personal invective. Negativism now seems to prevail, as the candidates and their teams strive to demonstrate the weaknesses of their opposition rather than the strength of their own case, seeking thereby to secure a victory almost, as it were, by default. The Bush–Dukakis contest of 1988 was a classic of this kind, with Dukakis, the Democrat, demonstrating an inability or an unwillingness to respond in kind to the very personal attacks launched by Bush.

By the time election day finally arrives, Americans have been exposed, as we have noted, to nearly a year of formal campaigning and often to several years of informal campaigning before that. It is, perhaps, not too surprising then, that nearly 50 per cent of the electorate, wearied by the processes and rendered cynical by the tactics, do not bother to vote. (We should note that while this is a very low voting percentage it is not, in comparative terms, quite as low as it might appear. The American percentage is taken from a base of the total eligible population, while in the United Kingdom, for instance, the base is that part of the eligible population which has registered to vote.)

It is at this stage of the electoral process that the eighteenth-century anachronism, the Electoral College, comes into play. Technically, Americans still do not vote for a presidential candidate but instead vote for slates of electors who will decide who should be president. Of course, as already indicated, this is now myth. In reality, the public votes for electors committed to one particular candidate or another: indeed, in some states the myth is ignored entirely, no mention is made of the electors on the ballot and only the names of the presidential and vice-presidential candidates appear. So, although the Electoral College voters do not meet in their respective states until December to perform their ritual, the result of the election is known almost as soon as the polls close. (In some instances, given the time differentials across the United States, the result may be apparent before the west coast has finished polling.)

We have noted how, in a very short time, party-line voting in the Electoral College largely nullified the intentions of the Founding Fathers when they created the College, and the question has long been asked, why should the College be preserved? While, over the years, it could be said that the College has generally worked well enough, a number of valid criticisms have been raised.

First, and foremost in many critics eyes, the fact that a candidate could become President with fewer popular votes than his opponent is a glaring denial of democratic majoritarian principles. This has, in fact, happened only three times in American history (1824, 1876, 1888), but there have been several other elections when relatively small shifts in popular votes could have produced other 'minority' presidents. For example, in 1960, Kennedy received 49.7 per cent of the popular vote compared to Nixon's 49.5 per cent, and in 1968 Nixon won with 43.4 per cent to Humphrey's 42.7 per cent.

A second major criticism derives from the development of the unitary rule. There is no evidence to suggest that the Founding Fathers ever intended that all of a state's electoral votes should go to the candidate receiving the majority of the popular vote. The original district rule ensured that minority candidates in states would receive electoral votes if they won any districts. The adoption of the unit rule, therefore, strongly disadvantaged minor groupings. It also had the added effect of removing any incentive for increased voter turnout in safe seats.

A third, and relatively minor complaint has been raised against the potential role of the individual College electors — that they may cast their vote for a candidate other than the one to whom they were pledged, thus denying the electorate's wishes. While this has happened on one or two occasions in the past, it has never had an effect upon the outcome of an election. The possibility is, nevertheless, a real one, and it is probably desirable that the opportunities for such maverick behaviour should be removed.

Finally, the procedures for dealing with a situation in which no candidate receives an absolute majority of the Electoral College vote are, it is argued, totally unrepresentative. If the selection does go to the House of Representatives, under the terms of the Constitution, each state has one vote regardless of the size of its delegation. In such an instance, several scenarios are possible. First, the candidate with the most popular votes is given the election because his party happens to control a majority of the state delegations. This would probably be regarded as the most desirable outcome, but there is no guarantee that this would occur. A second scenario could have the Democrats, say, with a majority in the House but with the Republicans controlling a majority of the delegations (because the Democrats find their strength in large, industrialized states and the Republicans theirs in more, but less populated, states). Thus, a minority of the House could be in a position to give the presidency perhaps to the candidate who polled the fewer popular votes. Thirdly, the situation could arise where the House having picked a President of one party, the Senate picks a Vice-President of another party. Finally, should the House fail to secure a majority for one of the candidates, the person chosen by the Senate as Vice-President would become acting-President. Such possibilities would hardly enhance the prestige or status of the presidential office. Fortunately, no recourse to the Congress has been necessary since 1824, but undoubtedly George Wallace with his third-party candidacy in 1968 hoped to create such an eventuality.

Apart from the comment that it has generally worked, those who defend the Electoral College do so on three grounds. First, they argue that it continues to put stress on the states as units and thereby emphasizes the continued importance of the federal principle. Secondly, the unit rule, far from being criticized for failing to give adequate representation to minority groupings, is praised for discouraging the growth of splinter groups, which might otherwise have led to much more deadlock in the College and subsequent use of the House of Representatives to pick the President. Finally, it is claimed that the exaggeration of the winner's popular majority when it is translated into electoral votes helps to give added legitimacy to the presidency. In 1960, for instance, the narrow popular vote margin became a 303–219 Electoral College vote majority for Kennedy, while in 1968 Nixon's slight popular advantage became a 301–191 majority in the College.

Proposals for reform of the electoral system have been numerous and frequent. Some have sought abolition of the Electoral College and the introduction of a direct vote, while others have argued for the replacement of the unit rule by some form of proportionality. We consider below three representative examples of those proposals.

The direct vote, it is claimed, would have the great merit of simplicity. All votes would be of equal value and would count in the final tally. The discouragement to vote which arises when some districts, or states, are generally dominated by one particular party would vanish, and politicians would thereby be encouraged to spread their campaigns more evenly. Of course, a direct vote method would encourage more candidates to enter the field and, as a consequence, it might be that no candidate would receive an absolute majority of the votes, thus, perhaps, diminishing the legitimacy of the result. To counter this, it has been proposed that if no candidate should receive more than 40 per cent of the vote, there should be a run-off election between the two leading candidates two weeks later. The arguments arrayed against the direct vote generally take refuge in claims about the importance of the Electoral College to the preservation of the federal principle, and of the slight advantage accorded the small states by the allocation of electoral votes.[21] Such arguments are difficult to sustain. The federal system would hardly collapse were the Electoral College to disappear, and the advantage that accrues to the small states under the present system is as nothing compared to the over-representation they receive in the Senate.

Another proposal for reform was advanced in the 1950s by two staunch Republicans, Congressman Frederick Coudert and Senator Karl Mundt. Their 'district plan' called for the Electoral College votes in a state to be distributed on a congressional district-by-district basis, with the candidate gaining the plurality in the state receiving the extra two votes which each state receives because of its Senate representation. If no candidate received a majority in the College, the new House and Senate members would sit jointly and, each voting as individuals, choose from among the leading three candidates. Such a plan, it was argued, would return the system to something like that envisaged by the Founding Fathers, would not discriminate against minority parties, and would ensure 'that both the President and the Congress should have the same "constituency"' and 'lead to more harmony in relation between the executive and legislative branches of government'.[22] Those opposed to the Mundt–Coudert plan pointed out, in particular, that it provided no safeguard against the emergence of a minority president, and that state legislatures might be encouraged to gerrymander their congressional districts to maximize the advantage to one particular party.

There are, finally, those who advocate keeping the present electoral vote allocation but propose that those votes be distributed among the candidates according to the proportion of the popular vote received. If no candidate received at least 40 per cent of the electoral votes, then the members of the House and the Senate, in joint session, and each with one vote, would select from the leading two candidates. This proportional plan would abolish the now outdated office of elector, and provide a more accurate reflection of the strengths of the various candidates. It would also encourage greater two-party activity in one-party states, for any increase in support for a party could be reflected in an increase in the number of electoral votes it received (an argument which has less importance in these days when candidates are *party* candidates in little more than name, and when voters at the presidential level, at least, are displaying more volatility in their voting practices). The plan would not, however, rule out the possibility of a candidate being elected with a minority of the popular vote. Further, given the increased opportunities that would be offered to minority candidates to pick up electoral votes, there would be a strong possibility that most elections would be decided by Congress — for some, an argument in its favour.

In spite of the numerous attempts made to reform the

provisions for the election of the President, and Peirce recorded 513 up until 1966,[23] only one, the Twelfth Amendment which separated the voting for the Presidency and the Vice-Presidency, has been successful. Reform, when so many vested interests are at stake, is always difficult, and this has undoubtedly been a factor in the preservation of an institution which was outdated almost as soon as it was born. But there is probably more to it than just this defence of one's own interest. While little of what the Founding Fathers sought has been achieved by the College, it remains as the formal institution which elects the President, perhaps because it works. Until such time as it produces a patently unacceptable result, it is likely to remain, for many Americans subscribe to the sentiment expressed by Rossiter when he wrote that 'we should hesitate a long time before replacing a humpty-dumpty system that works with a neat one that may blow up in our faces'.[24]

The modern candidate-centred campaign has attracted much criticism from different quarters. There are many, among them Anthony King and Malcolm Jewell,[25] who are concerned that 'a disjunction seems to have developed ... between the qualities required to win the presidential nomination ... and the qualities required to be a good president' (King); that the 'selection procedures place a higher premium on the ability to campaign than on the ability to govern' (Jewell). Others are worried that the media circuses which characterize modern campaigns are now so prolonged that one election is barely over before would-be candidates are jostling in preparation for the next. Still others complain that the candidates, not the issues, are now the issue.

What is interesting about much of this criticism is the degree to which it echoes statements from the past. As Ceaser has written of the late nineteenth century, 'the power brokers who dominated the conventions were interested in selecting a successful candidate, not in choosing a good president'.[26] James Bryce had also pointed to this dichotomy when he wrote that 'the merits of a President are one thing and those of a candidate another. ... [T]o a party it is more important that its nominee should be a good candidate than that he should turn out to be a good President.'[27] Those who regard the lengthy campaigns of today as an undesirable modern phenomenon can turn to Martin Van

Buren's complaint in 1822 that campaigns were starting so early that they were 'a "premature" intrusion of electoral politics into the normal processes of governing'.[28] As Ceaser went on to point out, campaigns during the 1820s and the 1830s were never less than two years long, while that of 1828 began as soon as the campaign of 1824 had finished. As for the, at times unseemly, scramble for support by a multitude of contenders, Ceaser quotes the concern of the editor of the *Richmond Enquirer* in 1823 who disliked the idea of 'five or six candidates for the Presidency, traversing this continent and chaffering for votes'.[29]

It would appear then that, much as the continent has grown and technology has developed, selection techniques in the late twentieth century still evoke the same criticisms and worries as they did a century or even a century-and-a-half ago.

One of the most significant criticisms of present processes does, however, concern the effect they have on the political parties. The parties do provide, in Clinton Rossiter's words, the 'vast, gaudy ... umbrellas' under which the contest for the nomination takes place, and they do establish the ground rules for the primaries, the bases of state representation at the national conventions, and the procedures to be followed. But such functions do not amount to the control or direction one might expect from a national party. Like the earliest national conventions which, as we noted earlier, merely confirmed a frontrunner, these quadrennial meetings (of either major party) are no longer the occasion for bestowing the title 'presidential candidate'. They are, rather, gatherings which confirm a title already taken. And it has been taken in a contest among a number of candidates each of whom is more concerned with winning than with establishing a picture of party harmony. When Ostrogorski described the convention as a 'colossal travesty ...' (see p.30), he was writing of a time of party dominance, of a time when state party bosses accorded the accolade. Today, the term can still be applied, but it now relates to a situation in which party bosses play little or no role. Personal organizations, like Richard Nixon's notorious Committee to Re-elect the President (CREEP), have become the main focus of attention, with the candidates seeking the nomination, and then the election, as individuals with their own programmes rather than as keepers of a party conscience.

In 1958, V.O. Key could write that 'in a fairly real sense, the

National Convention is the national party. . . . Without it, or some equivalent institution, party government for the nation as a whole could scarcely exist.'[30] And yet, within a fairly short period the spread of the primaries had contributed towards rendering such an evaluation (and the national conventions themselves) largely obsolete.

It must be acknowledged, however, that not all students or observers of the political scene take such a bleak view of the situation. Thus, James W. Davis has written that:

> there is no better 'school for presidents' than the presidential primaries. They give the national convention delegates and the voting public the opportunity to assess first hand, over a period of several months, a presidential candidate's behaviour, reaction under pressure and statesman qualities — a comprehensive 'on the job' type of training.

Among other things, Davis considered that the primaries were an excellent test of candidates' physical stamina and were 'an invaluable measuring stick for comparing candidates' qualifications'.[31]

Few could quarrel with the suggestion that the primary trail demands physical stamina — indeed, as long ago as 1908 Woodrow Wilson was suggesting that 'we shall be obliged always to be picking our chief magistrates from among wise and prudent athletes'[32] — but does such an attribute rank high among the qualifications needed to be President? As for the rest of the statement, the nature of recent primary campaigns hardly appears to provide the electorate with any kind of yardstick for measuring how a candidate might handle delicate affairs of state of a national or of an international kind. And we might well ask how canvassing for votes in often bitter primary fights provides 'on the job' training for the tasks that will face the person who ultimately enters the White House.

The destruction of the power of the party oligarchies through the greater involvement of the mass of party members, which Key has suggested has been a persistent goal in the development of American nominating practices,[33] has occurred, it would seem, but at the expense of effectively destroying the power of the parties themselves. He wrote, approvingly, that the convention:

> does not limit access to the Pesidency to those who climb the ladder within the narrow confines of the inner circles of the representative

body: nor does it restrict competition to those who gain the
deference of their fellows within any narrowly defined group of
party notables'.[34]

And more recently, Gerald Pomper has written that 'there is
something admirable about a system that does make it possible
for an obscure governor from Georgia to become a presidential
candidate'.[35] But who is better geared to assess the merits of
candidates, their strengths and weaknesses — those who have
worked with them, or been acquainted with them, for a number
of years, or an electorate largely exposed to them only through
the media packaging which is so much a part of campaigning
today? Furthermore, it should also be borne in mind that 'the
mass of party members', to which Key refers and which makes
up the electorate in the primaries, does not comprise a fee-paying
membership in the European sense. Any who care to register as
Democrats or Republicans may participate in this candidate-
selection process, regardless of commitment to the party: indeed,
a few register as members of the party other than their own in
order that they may have some influence in selecting a weak
opposition candidate. Contenders, then, need not seek 'the
deference of their fellows' — of those who might adequately
review their qualities — but can instead concentrate on securing
the support of those less able to judge their capabilities. For
example, as Pomper has approvingly noted, in the 1970s Jimmy
Carter, an 'obscure' ex-governor of Georgia, with no national
reputation when he began his campaign — the question on
people's lips in 1975 was 'Jimmy Who?' — took the nomination
and subsequently the election owing nothing to the party leaders.

In a very real sense the 'party is no longer a collective institution
with a past and a future but merely a label temporarily owned
by a particular candidate'.[36] And Frenchman Alexis de
Tocqueville's comment in the early nineteenth century comes
close to capturing the reality of the late twentieth:

> Political parties in the United States are led to rally round an
> individual in order to acquire a more tangible shape in the eyes
> of the crowd, and the name of the candidate for the presidency
> is put forward as the symbol and personification of their
> theories'.[37]

In spite of the damage caused to the political parties by the
spread of primaries, there are those who advocate full-blown

national primaries as the means whereby presidential candidates should be nominated. This proposal, which can be dated back to the Progressive era, does have, if we can ignore the arguments above, a certain spurious appeal. It would, after all, simplify processes in the eyes of the average elector. Instead of a long series of campaigns spread out over many months, with their peaks and troughs, voting would take place across the nation on the one day. The undue influence which is at present accorded the early primaries would be eliminated as the 'bandwagon' effect would vanish. Suggestions have also been made that campaigns would thereby be shortened and costs diminished. There is little reason to believe, however, that the advantages attributed to a national primary would actually materialize. Candidates with little national status would still feel the need to pursue a lengthy campaign to establish name recognition and the attendant costs would still be great: indeed, they might be greater as the pressure to campaign in more, if not all, states increased. What does seem certain is that the introduction of national primaries would be accompanied by the final breakup of the national party system. The national conventions have largely lost any real role in the selection of presidential candidates, but they do still, at least, provide the forum in which the decision is registered. They remain as symbols of the parties as national entities within a federal system. National primaries would destroy the symbol, de-emphasize the federal aspect, and represent the triumph of media consultants over professional politicians.

Some two hundred years after the ratification of the Constitution the processes associated with the selection and election of Presidents still appear, then, to be in a state of flux. The early development of political parties had brought some order to an unstructured situation while the control exercized by the congressional caucus had provided a bridge between those institutions — President and Congress — which the Founding Fathers had wished to keep separated. 'King Caucus' was, however, dethroned and the right to select the presidential candidates was assumed by party bosses. Reaction to these wheeler-dealers in their smoke-filled rooms eventually produced the demand for more open, democratic methods which would open up the path to the White House. The primaries advocated by the Progressives appeared to do this, but ultimately, as it transpired, at the expense of the traditional and important links between candidates and party bosses. Today, in fact, many argue that the attempts to democratize the procedures have gone too far and have hastened the weakening of one of the principal agencies of democratic politics — the political party. Calls are made for reassertion of the party role, but they are probably too late. While individuals can attract the massive resources necessary to pursue the media campaigns to persuade the electorate of their suitability, the parties, no matter how much tinkering they undertake in an effort to restore their own role, will feel compelled to back the person they perceive to be a winner. The evils which were released when the Pandora's box of reform was opened are unlikely to be contained and Presidents, it would appear, will continue to emerge largely as a result of their own rather than of a party's efforts.

If this gloomy prognostication should prove accurate — gloomy, because I believe healthy political parties are invaluable in a representative democracy — Americans will be left with those lengthy campaigns of vituperation which have become the hallmark of recent elections. Significant issues will be avoided while stress is instead put on personality factors which may or may not be relevant to the task of choosing a well-qualified person for the office of President.

Notes

1. Thereby establishing a tradition (broken only by Franklin Roosevelt), subsequently converted by the 22nd Amendment into constitutional edict, that no President should serve more than two terms.
2. J.P. Roche, 'The Founding Fathers: A Reform Caucus in Action', *American Political Science Review*, December 1961, p.811.
3. Carl Becker, 'The Will of the People' *Yale Review*, March 1945, p.389.
4. James W. Ceaser, *Presidential Selection* (Princeton: PUP, 1979), p.66.
5. Alexander Hamilton in *The Federalist* (London: J.M. Dent, Everyman's Library), No. LVIII, p.347.
6. James W. Davis, *National Conventions in an Age of Party Reform* (Westport, Conn.: Greenwood Press, 1983), Chapter 2.
7. James Bryce, *The American Commonwealth*, 2nd edn (London: Macmillan, 1889), Chapter VIII 'Why Great Men Are Not Chosen Presidents'.
8. Quoted by Rita W. Cooley in Robert S. Hirschfield (ed.), *Selection/Election: A Forum on the American Presidency* (New York: Aldine, 1982), p.95.
9. M. Ostrogorski, *Democracy and the Organization of Political Parties*, vol.

2, edited and abridged by Seymour Martin Lipset (Garden City, NY: Doubleday, Anchor, 1984), p.143.

10. Ceaser, op. cit. p.219.
11. James W. Davis, *Presidential Primaries* (Westport, Conn.: Greenwood Press, 1980), p.42.
12. William J. Croty, *Political Reform and the American Experiment* (New York: Crowell, 1977). p.207.
13. Davis, *Presidential Primaries*, p.43.
14. V.O. Key, *Politics, Parties and Pressure Groups*, 4th edn (New York: Crowell, 1958), p.196.
15. Croty, op. cit. p.211.
16. Ceaser, op. cit. p.223.
17. William R. Keech and Donald R. Matthews, *The Party's Choice* (Washington, DC: Brookings Institute, 1976), p.194. Quoted by Ceaser, op. cit. p.240.
18. Davis, *Presidential Primaries*, p.40.
19. Croty, op. cit. p.241. We should note that a heated reaction to the Vietnam War was a major factor in the whole violent scenario.
20. See Cooley, op. cit. pp.98–9.
21. A state's electoral college vote is equal to the sum of its representatives in the two houses of Congress. Each state is guaranteed at least one representative in the House, regardless of population, and every state has two Senators. This, obviously, to an extent favours the smaller states.
22. Neil R. Peirce, *The People's President* (New York: Simon & Schuster. 1968). p.158.
23. Ibid. p.151.
24. Clinton Rossiter, *The American Presidency*, 2nd edn (Ithaca, NY: Harvest Books, 1960), p.199.
25. Anthony King in Austin Ranney (ed.), *The American Elections of 1980* (Washington, DC: AEI), p.323, and Malcolm Jewell in 'Presidential Selection', *Society*, July/August 1980, p.48. Quoted by James W. Ceaser *Reforming the Reforms* (Cambridge, Mass.: Ballinger, 1982), p.95.
26. Ceaser, *Presidential Selection*, p.209.
27. Bryce, op. cit. p.75.
28. Ceaser, *Presidential Selection*, p.133.
29. Ibid. p.137.
30. Key, op. cit. pp.471–2.
31. James W. Davis, *National Conventions*, p.65.
32. Woodrow Wilson, *Constitutional Government in the United States* (New York: Columbia University Press, 1908), pp.79–80.
33. Key, op. cit. p.407.
34. Key, op. cit. p.474.
35. Gerald M. Pomper, 'The Nominating Process: Primaries and Delegate Selection', in Hirschfield, op. cit. p.81.
36. Ceaser, *Presidential Selection*, p.257.
37. Alexis de Tocqueville, *Democracy in America* (as published in New York by Alfred A. Knopf, 1945), p.135

Candidates

The presidency of the United States is, in constitutional terms, open to all natural born citizens who have attained the age of thirty-five and who have lived in the country for fourteen years. Under the constitutional doctrine of the separation of powers, no one may simultaneously hold both legislative and executive office, and since the passage of the Twenty-second Amendment no person may be elected President more than twice. Such minor restrictions would appear to put the White House in reach of virtually all who have a mind to seek it. History, however, suggests otherwise, for a number of expectations (or prejudices) have arisen concerning the type of person who is considered eligible,[1] and these expectations do limit the potential field considerably.

During the lifetime of the Republic, no female, no black, no Jew, and no bachelor (apart from James Buchanan before the Civil War) has ever become President. The presidential stereotype has been a middle-aged, white, Anglo-Saxon, Protestant male, married, with children, and of solid middle-class background. Of course, we must recognize that these factors may change over time and that some who might have been considered unelectable a generation ago are now comfortably within the fold of the eligibles, or may be so within the next few years. For example, John Kennedy was elected President, despite falling foul of two of the criteria. He was a Catholic, and no Catholic had ever reached the White House before him: indeed, few Catholics had even run for the office — the previous Catholic to be a candidate was Al Smith who was resoundingly beaten in 1928 by Herbert Hoover. Kennedy was also young: the youngest person to be elected to the post (Theodore Roosevelt was younger when he took office, but he had succeeded upon the death by assassination of William McKinley). Similarly, the taboo against divorced men

48

seems to have been shattered by the election of Ronald Reagan who also overcame the age factor, being elected at a very ripe old age. A woman has been on the ticket as a vice-presidential candidate for the Democratic party, and there has been talk that General Colin Powell, Chairman of the Joint Chiefs of Staff, a black, might well be an acceptable candidate in the not-too-distant future.

Personal characteristics such as race, creed or sex are not the only limiting factors so far as candidacy is concerned. Some experience in public service has also been a *sine qua non* for becoming President this century, with, as we shall see, service in the Senate, or a governor's mansion, the two most common backgrounds. This apparent requirement has also helped to reinforce some of the other limiting factors. As women and blacks have been notoriously under-represented in elective office, at both national and state level, they have failed then to acquire that experience which might have rendered them more eligible for consideration for the highest post. In recent years, as both groups have gradually secured more self-awareness and more exposure through winning elective posts, they have slowly entered into calculations concerning their eligibility for the presidency. While these developments have had some effect upon the nature of the pool of those available for the presidential race, it is still largely to those in high public office, largely elective, that commentators turn when looking for the next possible President.

Some have suggested that changes in the processes of selection and in the funding of campaigns have contributed towards a shift in the background of presidential candidates in recent years. Governors, who had provided the Presidents for approximately half of the first 170 years of the Republic, were giving way, it was argued, to Senators. In 1960 John F. Kennedy was the first Senator to be nominated by the Democratic party since Douglas in 1860, and all the major challengers to Kennedy's nomination came from fellow Senators. For the next twelve years, indeed, the selection processes of both major parties were dominated by either serving or past Senators, or by Vice-Presidents who had served in the Senate. Such was this dominance, and such the apparent decline in the influence of governors, that explanations were sought and offered for what many considered to be a permanent shift in the power centres of the parties.

Governors, it was argued, had been the major source of candidates in the days when the parties were more disciplined and more subject to control by the governors who controlled the vast amount of patronage that was available in the states. Senators, on the other hand, had little patronage at their disposal and very little influence in the selection of delegates to the national conventions and, in those earlier days when federal government involvement in society and the economy was much less, those who served in the nation's legislature were not a primary focus of attention. However, the growth of primaries lessened the dominance of governors by breaking their hold over delegate selection, while the changes in the rules governing finance also weakened the parties in relation to those who sought the nomination. Furthermore, as the federal government had become more and more involved in all aspects of citizens' lives, so greater attention was paid to those who passed the laws and levied the taxes. When all of this was allied with the spread of the electronic media which tended to focus their political coverage on Washington rather than on the states, the situation seemed ripe for the replacement of parochial politicians by national statesmen. Senators with their six-year terms could easily establish a national image through careful manipulation of issues and media, while governors, concerned with the day-to-day running of their state, found it hard to project themselves beyond the borders of those states.

The explanations seem sound, the argument that a new era had arrived beyond challenge, but the rush to such a judgment, based on those four elections, was somewhat premature. Accordingly, if we consider the four elections since 1972, we find a quite different picture. Senators undoubtedly provided the bulk of the contenders in those years, but only one of the ultimate candidates of the major parties. In 1976 the incumbent Gerald Ford was defeated by an ex-governor, Jimmy Carter of Georgia. In 1980, Carter was himself defeated by Ronald Reagan, ex-governor of California. Four years later, Reagan retained the White House by defeating Walter Mondale who had been Carter's Vice-President and before that a Senator. Most recently, Reagan's Vice-President, George Bush, defeated another governor, Michael Dukakis of Massachusetts.[2] It might be tempting, then, to talk of another new era, of the resurgence of the governors, but this would, I feel, have as little validity as the previous analysis. All that we can say, given the relatively small time spans involved, is that the new conditions, by contributing to the weakening of the parties, have opened up the race to any who have the drive and the personality to establish themselves as presidential material in the eyes of the public. As recent years have demonstrated, service as a Senator or as a governor, or in the vice-presidency, may equally well provide the launching pad for such a presidential candidacy.

While Presidents during the twentieth century have come largely from the ranks of governors or Senators, they have also emerged from other backgrounds. Two members of the Cabinet, William Howard Taft, 1912, and Herbert Hoover, 1928, have reached the White House, as has one general, Dwight D. Eisenhower, in 1952. Two Vice-Presidents, Nixon and Bush, have sought and won the Presidency in their own right, while four became President on the death in office of the incumbent: Theodore Roosevelt, 1901, Calvin Coolidge, 1923, Harry Truman, 1945, and Lyndon Johnson, 1963. Another, Gerald Ford, succeeded to the presidency when the President, Richard Nixon, resigned in 1974 rather than face an impeachment trial.

An interesting point to note about the Vice-Presidents who succeeded on the death of their Presidents, and who went on to win an election in their own right, is that, probably, none of them would have been initially nominated for the highest post by their parties. They were selected as vice-presidential candidates for the balance they would bring to the ticket (or, in Theodore Roosevelt's case, to keep him quiet) rather than for their presidential potential. It was largely the power of incumbency that allowed them to retain the presidency.

When we consider the background of presidential candidates we should also give thought to the appropriateness of that background as a training ground or as an apprenticeship for the highest elective office in the nation, for the leadership of the most powerful nation in the Western world. In the United States, there is within the political parties, as we have noted, no hierarchical structure such as exists in the United Kingdom which provides a proving ground for future leaders. British political leaders move up through the ranks of the legislative party, from backbencher to member of Cabinet or shadow Cabinet, demonstrating ability to operate in a legislative as well as in an administrative capacity. They are at all times subject to the critical eyes of political colleagues who may also be rivals for the top post of party leader. The political parties, then, establish the parameters within which future leaders receive their training and achieve their goals. Such neatness is absent within the United States and no ordered progression exists for those who would be President. Different posts give different experiences — none gives all that are necessary — while party plays but a small role in assisting would-be Presidents to reach the White House.

The governorship of a state might be thought to offer the best kind of possible training for a President. The state, particularly a large one like California, and its institutions, might well be considered a microcosm of the nation as a whole. The chief executive has a legislature to deal with and a bureaucracy to control. He will have a legislative programme he wishes to have enacted and a budget to balance. The problems and demands of the citizens of his state, ranging from the rural to the suburban to the inner-city ghetto are the problems and demands of the nation, writ small. (Indeed, his state and its economy may be considerably larger than many of the independent nations of the world.) What better training, one might ask, for the task of chief executive of the whole nation? And yet there are limitations. First and foremost, perhaps, is the fact that virtually all of a governor's concerns are of a domestic variety, and when a man becomes President he is faced with a host of demands relating to America's position in the world, whether of a peaceful or of a military nature. No governor is ever exposed to such problems and while some, with an eye on a future campaign for the presidency, may seek to acquire some international exposure by travelling abroad and meeting heads of state, few have the opportunity to give serious consideration to such matters. Indeed, absences from the state may actually incur political and electoral liabilities, as governors who do travel abroad may be accused of putting their presidential aspirations before their gubernatorial responsibilities. Secondly, the federal government is now involved in so many aspects of American life that there are few domestic areas which are completely free of some federal input which, thereby, to a greater or lesser extent, inhibits a governor's freedom of action. In particular, of course, there are those limitations which spring from the federal government's first claim upon the tax dollars of the nation through the federal income tax. A governor's policies may well be circumscribed then by monetary and fiscal policy originating in Washington. In this sense, running a state may give a governor experience in handling legislators, may help him develop personnel skills useful for dealing with bureaucrats, may give him a feeling for what citizens want or need, and even for what may be possible, but over all hover the federal institutions with their financial clout.

Senators, on the other hand, serving in the national legislature, with six-year terms, are generally free from the parochial concerns that face a governor and are, rather, in a position to take a national or even an international view of events (although, of course, they do have to keep their political fences in the state mended if they wish to be re-elected). As members of a legislative body, involved in the policy-making processes, they are also exposed to the necessary give and take associated with legislative success — important training for a President when he faces a reluctant Congress, and notably lacking, for instance, in President Carter, an ex-Governor, when he became President. The role of the Senate in relation to treaties, and in the process of appropriations which may be essential to a President's foreign policy goals, does give interested Senators an opportunity to familiarize themselves with many of the international problems with which a President must deal. But membership of the Senate does not provide the experience in personnel management, in controlling a bureaucracy, which is such an integral part of presidential responsibilities.

Cabinet members undoubtedly acquire a useful experience with the bureaucracy, but the two who became President this century — William Howard Taft and Herbert Hoover — had little exposure to the realities of electoral contest. Apart from Taft's election to a Superior Court seat in Ohio, neither had any experience of even fighting an election, let alone of engaging in those activities central to political survival. Both did have considerable reputations as administrators — Taft as governor of the Philippines (an appointive not elective post as Hargrove and Nelson rather misleadingly fail to point out in their table on the career background of Presidents),[3] and Hoover as Chairman of the American Relief Commission — but their records in office do seem to suggest that such a background is insufficient for the tasks to be faced in the White House. Presidents need a range of political as well as administrative skills if they are to make the most of the potential of the office.

The one general to become President during the twentieth century, Dwight D. Eisenhower, brought to the office experiences quite different from his predecessors. His was a structured, hierarchical background which stood in sharp contrast to the practices of the political arena where persuasion or bargaining are the major means whereby goals are accomplished. Generals are accustomed to giving orders which are obeyed. Harry Truman captured that difference nicely when he said of newly elected Eisenhower: 'He'll sit there and he'll say, "Do this! Do that!" And nothing will happen. Poor Ike — it won't be a bit like the Army'.[4] The training that derives from military command is far removed from that which is associated with governing a state, or representing it in the Senate.

It might appear that the vice-presidency would provide the most suitable apprenticeship for the top job. The Vice-President has, after all, been elected on a national ticket, and prior to his emergence on the ticket he is likely to have had a political career of some importance, as a governor, member of Congress or as a member of the Cabinet. He is close to the centre of the action, well placed to observe the political game being played and, living only 'one heart-beat away' from the presidency, constantly aware of the responsibilities he might suddenly have to assume. The Founding Fathers had expected that the person who became Vice-President would be a worthy candidate for the presidency itself, but once political parties started to dominate the electoral scene the vice-presidential place on the ticket went, as we have seen, to candidates who provided balance, of a geographic or of an ideological kind, rarely to men of such stature in their own right that they might reasonably have hoped for the highest office for themselves. Throughout American history those who have held the second highest elective post have largely been of the second rank, often spending their four or eight years in a constitutional limbo, the forgotten men of politics who inspired the story of the two boys who ran away from home: one went to sea, the other became Vice-President. Neither was heard of again. (Perhaps the most telling comment on the status of Vice-Presidents can be found in Clinton Rossiter's much praised work *The American Presidency* where, tongue in cheek, he introduces a fictional Vice-President, from the musical *Of Thee I Sing*, into the pantheon of real-life Vice-Presidents, writing: 'somewhere along the line there was a Vice-President named Throttlebottom — and a good one too'.)[5]

As perhaps an additional comment on the quality of those who have held the second highest post, it is worth recording that after the very early years of the Republic, when two Vice-Presidents, John Adams and Thomas Jefferson went on to become Presidents in their own right (that is, without having first succeeded to the post), only one other managed this feat, Martin Van Buren in 1836, until Richard Nixon became President in 1968.

In relatively recent years some commentators have suggested that there has been a change in attitude concerning who should occupy the second place on the ticket, that there 'has been a greater emphasis in the selection of vice-presidential nominees on experience, ability, and ... ideological harmony'.[6] When, furthermore, one could point to the influence of Walter Mondale in the Carter presidency, 'broader and deeper ... than was the lot of any previous Vice-President' ranging 'across the entire face of the presidency',[7] or of Bush in the Reagan administration, it appeared that a new era for Vice-Presidents had dawned. And such men might well have the breadth of experience to qualify them for the higher post. However, while it may be possible to argue that the selection of one or two running-mates, or the increased involvement of one or two Vice-Presidents in affairs of state, betokens such a change, the selection of Dan Quayle to serve as Vice-President to George Bush has all the hallmarks of the bad old days. If a new era has dawned it has been subject to at least a temporary eclipse. It is more likely that the improved quality of a few vice-presidential candidates is simply a function of the presidential candidate's perception of what his ticket needs. Vice-Presidents are still likely to remain an uncertain source of qualified candidates for the presidency.

Of course, the quality of the Vice-President is of little consequence if the President serves out his term, for the formal functions and responsibilities associated with the post are slight

— so slight that Benjamin Franklin referred to *His Superfluous Excellency*. From the Constitution he is President of the Senate but may cast a vote only in the case of a tie. From laws and usage he may engage in a number of other activities. For instance, he may attend meetings of the Cabinet and of the National Security Council.[8] He may be used as a roaming ambassador abroad or as a co-ordinator at home. But in the final analysis most of what the Vice-President does is at the behest of the President and could well be done by others. The more than thirty-seven years when America has survived without a Vice-President bear testimony to the limited need for such an office, and suggestions have even been made that it should be abolished and the succession put into the hands of Congress. And yet, if perceptions of the value of the office changed, if Presidents chose their running mates according to quality and ability, rather than for mere balance, and if they then made consistent use of those qualities and abilities, Vice-Presidents, with their prior political experience, would quickly emerge as truly qualified candidates for the White House itself.

Many recognize the truth in MacGregor Burns' strictures concerning the methods by which candidates for high office emerge in the United States, but it seems unlikely that the call for improvement will occasion any significant change in the processes. Party leaders having largely abdicated, and having surrendered their function of selection to the populist primaries, the political parties now offer only the arena in which a wide variety of candidates and talents compete. So long as state politics as well as federal politics offer competing and independent launching pads for candidacies, little will be done to introduce some order or hierarchy into the proceedings. While all the candidates will have some conception of what they would do were they elected, personality rather than ideology is likely to continue to be the dominant theme in the selection and election contests, with the presidency appearing to be the goal rather than merely the means to a goal. The time is probably long past when one could reasonably hope for ideologically consistent, hierarchical parties which would choose the candidates, promote them in party terms, and then, if they were successful, offer them legislative support. Such an aspiration is, of course, Anglo-centric in nature, but it does derive from observing the void that the parties have left — a void in which money and the media have become the dominant factors in determining who the contenders will be. Despite all this, however, one is forced to concede that, although the system might appear to favour the emergence of the demagogue, America has generally been lucky (recalling Ostrogorski's comment) and most of those who have become President have been men of probity committed to upholding the constitutional norms of the society.

Notes

1. My discussion is concerned only with those who run as candidates of the two major parties which have dominated the electoral scene since the 1850s. Minor parties have often proposed candidates who fall into one of the classes ignored by the major parties.
2. Bush did have some legislative background, having served briefly in the House of Representatives, but his career prior to becoming Vice-President had been varied, ranging from Republican National Chairman, to Director of the CIA, to Ambassador to China. His period in the national legislature was hardly relevant to his securing the presidency.
3. Erwin C. Hargrove and Michael Nelson, *Presidents, Politics, and Policy* (New York: Knopf, 1984), Table 5.6, pp.144–5.
4. Quoted in Richard Neustadt, *Presidential Power* (New York: Wiley, 1960), p.90.
5. Clinton Rossiter, *The American Presidency*, 2nd edn (Ithaca, NY: Harvest Books, 1960), p.136.
6. Hargrove and Nelson, op. cit. p.31.
7. Louis W. Koenig, *The Chief Executive*, 5th edn (San Diego: Harcourt Brace Jovanovich, 1986), pp.183–4.
8. Thus making it unlikely that, should he succeed to the presidency, he would be as much in the dark about important matters as was Truman who, for example, knew nothing of the development of the atomic bomb until he became President on Roosevelt's death.

Money and the electoral process

American electoral campaigns have long been characterized by the money involved. While in Britain, with political parties as the sponsors of the mainstream candidates for the House of Commons, few have been deterred by the 'small change' costs likely to be incurred, in the United States, even in safe seats, incumbents may feel the need to spend millions of dollars to ensure re-election to Congress.[1] And if the costs for election to the legislature seem absurdly high to foreign eyes, the costs associated with getting someone into the White House appear almost beyond comprehension. But, of course, as we have already noted, the task faced by a presidential candidate is not faced by politicians elsewhere. The length of the campaigns, the size of the electorates, in the nomination process and then in the election proper, the vastness of the country across which the appeals must be made, all demand access to massive financial resources if a message and an image are to be put before the voters. In 1984, for instance, Democratic candidates spent $83.8 million in the nomination stages and $71.1 million in the general election proper, while the Republicans managed to spend $34.9 million in the pre-nomination period, even though there was no challenge to the incumbent Ronald Reagan, and $77.3 million in the general election. In 1988 presidential primary candidates who took public money (see p.62) were limited to $22.2 million, plus 20 per cent for fund-raising costs, while in the post-convention period the two candidates, Bush and Dukakis, were allowed to spend $46.75 million dollars each, and their respective parties could each spend another $8.3 million. In total, during the 1988 election approximately $400 million was spent on the campaign by the candidates and the political parties.

The overwhelming importance of money has, of course, raised questions concerning the ethics or the propriety of the methods whereby the money has been raised and the obligations which candidates may thereby incur. Money may corrupt, or at least appear to corrupt, the electoral system, making it seem that office is open to the highest bidder or to the candidate with the biggest campaign chest. Americans have for long spoken, with tongue only partly in cheek, of 'the best Senate that money can buy', and in recent years, as the costs of electioneering have soared, some have come to suggest that they now have 'the best President that money can buy'. In order to attempt to counter that suggestion, and to provide opportunities for the different candidates to compete on reasonably equal financial terms, a number of reforms have been instituted which have dealt with all of the various aspects of campaign finance: the sources of contributions; the amounts that may be donated; the expenditures which are permitted; and the disclosure of both sources and expenditure.

While regulations relating to campaign finance do in fact date back to 1867, to legislation which made it illegal to require payments as reward from the salaries of appointees to governmental posts, most early attempts at regulation were desultory. Early in the twentieth century, Presidents 'Teddy' Roosevelt and Woodrow Wilson both called for the federal funding of elections in order to eliminate the undue influence of money, while Roosevelt also proposed that limits should be placed on the amount individuals could contribute, and that there should be full disclosure of the source of campaign funding. Their calls were not very productive, although one or two steps in the direction of regulation were taken in this period. In 1907 legislation was passed making it unlawful for 'any corporation whatever to make a contribution to an election in which presidential or vice-presidential electors [were] ... to be voted for'. Three years later, Congress passed the first disclosure law when it required candidates for Congress and political committees to report their campaign receipts and expenditures. However, as primaries, still regarded as outside the ambit of federal regulation, were not included, the law was of limited value.

In 1925 the Federal Corrupt Practices Act required committees involved in presidential campaigns in two or more states to file financial reports, and prohibited contributions from corporations. While this was generally regarded as a weak law which, among other things, did not touch upon the contentious area of primary election gifts, in the early 1970s it did, as Asher has pointed out, help 'Common Cause force disclosure of the contributions to the Nixon campaign'.[2] It was ultimately replaced (see p.61) by the Federal Election Campaign Practices Act of 1971. In 1939, the Hatch Act imposed a limit of $5,000 on individual contributions to federal campaigns, and $3 million on contributions by political committees, but this was easily circumvented, not least through the creation of 'many theoretically separate national committees, each of which was allowed to spend $3 million',[3] and it did little to check the burgeoning costs of elections and the consequent need of politicians to raise the money to meet those costs. The following year, in an effort to block one of the means whereby the limitations on donations were circumvented, amendments to the Act made it illegal for anyone, or any corporation, 'to purchase or buy any goods, commodities, advertising, or articles of any kind or description where the proceeds' might directly or indirectly benefit candidates for any federal elective office.[4]

Shortly after the end of the Second World War, in June 1947, Congress passed the Taft–Hartley Act over President Truman's veto. Concerned to place limitations on the conduct of trade unions in labour–management disputes, the Act also forbade union contributions to political campaigns, thereby putting them in the same position as corporations. Section 313 of the Federal Corrupt Practices Act, which had incorporated the 1907 provisions quoted above, was amended to read: 'It is unlawful . . . for any corporation whatever, or any labor [*sic*] organisation to make a contribution or expenditure in connection with any election at which presidential or vice-presidential electors . . . are to be voted for, or in connection with any primary election or political convention or caucus held to select candidates' for the above offices.[5] While the prohibition appears totally restrictive, it has not, in fact, been a serious handicap. Direct contributions from union treasuries may be barred, but there is nothing to stop unions establishing associated committees to which union members may contribute. Indeed COPE, the Committee on

Political Education of the AFL–CIO (American Federation of Labour–Congress of Industrial Organizations), was one of the first of the Political Action Committees which are now so dominant in the funding of election campaigns.

The era of serious attempts to control both giving to, and spending by, political candidates came in the 1970s, initially in response to the sky-rocketing costs associated with the 1968 election when Richard Nixon spent about $25 million and Hubert Humphrey something in the region of $15 million. (Those figures seem incredibly small when put alongside those for 1988 which we cite above.) The first attempt at control came in 1970 when the Political Broadcast Act, which would have limited the amount candidates could spend in general elections on radio and television, was passed by Congress but vetoed by President Nixon. The next year, however, two pieces of legislation did become law — the Federal Election Campaign Act, and the Revenue Act. The first, which replaced the Corrupt Practices Act of 1925, did little to curb contributions, except those by candidates themselves and their families, who were limited to $50,000, but was much more concerned with throwing light on the source of the contributions and the direction of the expenditures. Every contribution or item of expenditure of $100 or more had to be reported, while any committee expecting to receive or expend $1,000 a year or more in support of a candidate for federal office was required to register and submit regular accounts. The Act was passed in 1971, but at President Nixon's insistence it did not take effect until 8 April 1972, thus enabling the President's fund raisers to mount a great fund-raising drive, free from the obligation to reveal the sources. As John McGarry, a member of the Federal Election Commission, has written:

> Nixon's finance chairman, Maurice Stans, was running around the country because the law was to take effect on April 8th and all you had to show on that date was your opening cash balance. So there was a mad scramble to get as much money in before they had to indicate where the money came from. In the two days before the law became effective, Richard Nixon raised $6 million and $1.5 million of it was in cash.[6]

The Revenue Act, on the other hand, by widening the source of contributions, did seek to reduce the influence of the wealthy and influential in campaign funding, of those who appeared to be in a position to buy influence or favours through the size of their donations to a politician's campaign chest. Under the Act, citizens were permitted to claim a tax credit or a tax deduction for their donations, and were also allowed to designate $1 of their taxes to be put into a fund which would be used to subsidize presidential campaigns. Candidates who decided to accept public funding of their campaigns were barred from seeking, or receiving, private funding.

Despite these laws, the investigations into the Watergate affair produced evidence of 'widespread corruption surrounding the Nixon administration. Not only were bribery and extortion practices common in the Nixon re-election effort ... but secret cash contributions were used to finance the Watergate burglary of the Democratic National Committee and then to pay hush money to the burglars'.[7]

In revulsion against these revelations, a new Federal Election Campaign Act was passed in 1974, amending that of 1971. Under this law, individual contributions to federal candidates were limited to $1,000 for the primary and to the same amount for the general election. Political action committees were limited to $5,000 contributions to each of the processes. Most significantly, perhaps, the Act provided for some public funding of presidential primaries: matching funds of up to $5.5 million were provided for any candidate who could raise $5,000 in individual contributions of $250 or less in at least 20 states. It also repealed the limits on media spending and replaced them with overall limits on spending in both the primary and general elections for candidates who received public funding. If a candidate declined to take public funds, and only John Connally, in 1980, has so far refused to take them, the limits did not apply. The disclosure requirements of the 1971 act were tightened up in 1974 and a bi-partisan Federal Election Commission (FEC), comprising six members, two each appointed by the President, the Speaker of the House of Representatives, and the President pro tempore of the Senate, was created to receive the details and to enforce the statutes. (In 1976 the Supreme Court ruled that as it stood the FEC was a violation of the separation of powers principle as its members were appointed both by the executive and the legislature. Congress had, then, to pass a new law under which the FEC became a six-member body wholly appointed by the President with the advice and consent of the Senate.)[8]

The 1974 Act, which has been described as the most comprehensive campaign finance Act ever passed, was soon under legal attack from an unusual coalition of both conservatives and liberals, and the Supreme Court was given yet another opportunity, which it did not refuse, to engage in an expansive interpretation of the Constitution which defeated, in part, the worthy intentions of Congress. James Buckley, Eugene McCarthy, the American Conservative Union and the New York Civil Liberties Union made strange bedfellows as they argued in Court that 'the disclosure requirements of the law violated their right to privacy and that the contribution ceilings limited their freedom of speech and association and their right to petition for redress of grievances'.[9] The Court, in its judgment, ruled against all the expenditure limits unless the candidates were in receipt of public funding, arguing that such limits were a denial of the First Amendment guarantee of freedom of speech, and it further asserted that the $1,000 limit 'would appear to exclude all citizens ... from any significant use of the most effective modes of communication'. While the Court thus recognized the high costs of modern communications techniques, it chose to ignore the fact that most Americans could not afford to spend even the limited amount decreed by Congress. The notion of equality which lay behind the requirements of the Act did not appeal to the majority of the Justices. Instead they suggested that 'the concept that government may restrict the speech of some elements of our society in order to enhance the relative voice of others is wholly foreign to the First Amendment'. The Court thus held, as Shockley suggests, that 'money was a form of speech, not merely speech-related conduct', an interpretation which 'echoes the nineteenth-century Court's conversion of the Fourteenth Amendment's concern for protecting the rights of newly-freed slaves into protection for the business corporation'.[10]

The Justices did, however, sustain the contribution limits, arguing that:

> by contrast with a limitation upon expenditures for political expression, a limitation upon the amount that any one person or group may contribute to a candidate or political committee entails only a marginal restriction upon the contributor's ability to engage in free communication.[11]

They also upheld the provision that denied presidential candidates the right to raise or receive private money if they accepted public funding of their campaigns. This part of the law has been fairly rigorously upheld, and there have at times been unwitting breaches of the regulations. Thus, as McGarry has recorded, shortly after Jimmy Carter was nominated as the Democratic candidate in 1976, he had lunch with two businessmen for the purpose of meeting members of the New York business community. They paid the bill and were subsequently found guilty of making a 'contribution' to the campaign of a candidate who had accepted public funding. They were fined, and Carter 'had to return the cost of the luncheon to the Federal Treasury in the form of a fine'.[12]

So far as the murky area of independent contributions was concerned, the Court ruled that if the candidate had not encouraged them, and indeed knew nothing of them, then such contributions could not be subject to limitation. This particular ruling provided the spur for an explosion in the number of committees created for the purpose of 'independent' expenditure on behalf of candidates. When, in 1985, in *FEC* v. *NCPAC*,[13] the Court declared that limits on spending by these Political Action Committees (PACs) violated the First Amendment, again on the grounds that the expenditure of money is apparently speech, the aim of the laws attempting to regulate campaign financing, in an effort to give candidates a roughly equal financial base in order that they might compete on roughly equal terms, was largely undermined. Since the 1974 Act, and the subsequent Supreme Court rulings, the number of PACs involved in the electoral processes has mushroomed and their expenditures have sky-rocketed — from \$21 million dollars in 1974 to \$265 million just ten years later, and they are still climbing. Furthermore, as the floodgates were opened for 'independent' spending in campaigns, a notable shift in the source of these funds occurred. While, in 1974, Labour PACs accounted for 52 per cent of the total, in 1984 that percentage was down to less than 18 per cent. Corporate and ideological groups had come to the fore.[14]

We should note that the Court was not unanimous in these 'creative' judgments. Justice Byron White was critical of both decisions, and in a dissenting opinion in 1985 argued that:

> The First Amendment protects the right to speak, not the right to spend, and limitations on the amount of money that can be spent are not the same as restrictions on speaking. I agree with the

majority that the expenditures in this case 'produce' core First Amendment speech. But that is precisely the point: they produce such speech; they are not speech itself. At least, in these circumstances, I cannot accept the identification of speech with its antecedents. Such a house-that-Jack-built approach could equally be used to find a First Amendment right to a job or to a minimum wage to 'produce' the money to 'produce' the speech.[15]

White's argument has much to commend it, but he failed, as we have seen, to persuade his fellow Justices.

While concern over the nature of campaign finance was understandable, the reforms which have been instituted have had certain unforeseen and, some would argue, undesirable consequences. Thus, although the Federal Election Campaign Act Amendments of 1979 eased restrictions on expenditures by state and local parties, with the objective of encouraging grass-roots activity by those organizations, the general effect of the laws regulating campaign finance has been to weaken the parties still further in relation to the candidates. The existence of public funds which are given directly to the candidates undermines one of the traditional functions of parties: that of raising money to support those who carry the party label. The candidate-oriented campaign is thereby given even greater emphasis. Further, if a candidate chooses to accept public finances, voters are barred from giving to him directly and are thereby denied the opportunity to demonstrate their support in a time-hallowed, if not time-honoured, tradition. Their support must now be channelled through committees which may make independent expenditures on behalf of the candidates. Such indirect activity appears to have little more to recommend it than the older methods, particularly when one must have doubts about the extent of that 'independent' element.

The attempts to broaden the base of support for candidates have meant that much more time and effort have had to be devoted to fund-raising, leading to the irony, as Orren sees it, 'that a law designed to reduce the importance of money in campaigns actually may have increased its importance'.[16] And this situation has been made more critical by two other 'democratizing' developments. The big increase in the number of primaries has greatly inflated costs, while the adoption of proportional representation for the allocation of delegates from the states to the national convention means that candidates must campaign in many more states. But, as Orren puts it, 'spending ceilings have not kept pace with these spiraling campaign costs' and 'spending limits designed for an earlier time of fewer primaries and different rules are simply inadequate'.[17] This in turn has led campaign managers to adopt creative accounting techniques in order to avoid some of the financial restrictions. Thus, when it appeared that the limit on spending in a particular state might be passed, expenditures were 'diverted' to another state. For example, cars might be rented in a neighbouring state, or television advertising bought on stations in one state which would be beamed into another. Staff might be required to commute across a state border, or not be paid until they had left the state in which they had performed the electoral work. These, and other practices, have become stock in trade of the professionals who seek to by-pass the law.

Decisions of the Supreme Court and developments in party practice have, then, combined to thwart, at least in part, the intentions of the Congress. While individual 'fat cat' contributions may have lost some of their significance and while, consequently, a President no longer appears beholden to just a few wealthy backers, the fact is that the amount of money needed to mount an effective campaign for the presidency rises year by year, and the time taken to raise an adequate sum lengthens. All but a handful of potential candidates are deterred by the difficulties associated with raising such amounts and by the possibility of incurring vast debts. In 1988, for instance, Gary Hart, (with his 'on again, 'off-again', candidacy, in which he challenged the media to discover any impropriety in his behaviour and then seemed to go out of his way to provide them with appropriate evidence) carried with him debts of several million dollars from the 1984 campaign.

The emphasis for candidates today, then, must be on moving early to attract financial support from a much wider base than previously. The realities of campaigning demand that candidates demonstrate strength and potential in those primaries which come early in election year, in order that they continue to attract backing. The pump of financial support has to be primed with so much expenditure in those early days that candidates who do not run well are likely to bankrupt themselves and end their challenge before the race has really got under way. Hence, the primary in a small state like New Hampshire acquires an importance out of all proportion to its population, as it is taken as a first litmus test for determining the relative popularity of the candidates. Contributors generally wish to give to winners not losers. Consequently, the significance of a good start can hardly be overexaggerated, for the momentum it gives to a campaign can be crucial.

In spite of all the concern that has been expressed over the years about the 'problem' of money in elections (although we should not overlook the fact that some do not see a 'problem'), we must recognize that legislation has not greatly improved the situation and may even have made it worse. Disclosure obviously throws light on what can be the murkier aspects of a campaign, while donation ceilings do appear to democratize the proceedings a little (although neither has much relevance to the less well off in society or to the vast numbers who remain outside the electoral processes). Public funding in a situation where the costs of campaigning are so great does appear to equalize opportunities, but when other 'independent' expenditures are permitted the equality factor is largely lost. Furthermore, as the public funds go directly to the candidates and are not channelled through the political parties the candidates ostensibly represent, another nail has been put in the coffin of those agencies which in other countries normally aggregate interests in order to put alternative programmes before the voters. Access to considerable amounts of money is still a vital factor in any presidential campaign. The biggest spender will not necessarily win, for diminishing returns will ultimately set in, but the minimum amounts needed to buy the media advertising, to employ the expensive political consultants, to engage in direct-mail targeting, which are central to modern campaigns, are sufficiently great to exclude most from the race. America, in Philip Green's term, is heading toward an 'elective oligarchy', while as Shockley argues, the Supreme Court, through its interpretation of the First Amendment has afforded 'both fundamental and exclusive protection to the wealthy in the political process'.[18]

Notes

1. In 1984, for instance, Jay Rockefeller spent more than $10,000,000 of his own money to win a seat from West Virginia.
2. See Herbert B. Asher, *Presidential Elections and American Politics* 4th edn (Chicago, Ill.: The Dorsey press, 1988), p.217.

3. Ibid.
4. See V.O. Key, *Politics, Parties and Pressure Groups* 4th edn (New York: Crowell, 1958), p.552.
5. Taft–Hartley Act, Public Law 101, 80th Congress Sec. 304.
6. John W. McGarry, in Robert S. Hirschfield (ed.), *Selection/Election: A Forum on the American Presidency* (New York: Aldine Publishing, 1982), pp.59–60.
7. John S. Shockley, 'All the Free Speech That Money Can Buy', in Michael W. McCann and Gerald L. Houseman (eds), *Judging the Constitution* (Glenview, Ill.: Scott, Foresman, 1989), p.380.
8. While most of the laws concerning campaign financing relate, quite naturally, to the position of the candidates of the two parties which have dominated the electoral scene since the middle of the nineteenth century, provision is also made for third-party candidates who receive at least 5 per cent of the popular vote to receive public support.
9. Asher, op. cit. p.221. The case was *Buckley* v. *Valeo* (424 US1 1976).
10. See Shockley, op. cit. pp.378–86 for the two quotations from the Court decision and for Schockley's comments.
11. *Buckley* v. *Valeo*.
12. McGarry, op. cit. p.60.
13. *Federal Election Commission* v. *National Conservative Political Action Committee* (470 US 480).
14. Shockley, op. cit. p.396.
15. Quoted by Shockley, op. cit. p.388.
16. Garry R. Orren, 'Presidential Campaign Finance: Its Impact and Future', *Commonsense*, vol. 4, no. 2, 1981, pp.50–66, reprinted in James I. Lengle and Byron E. Shafer (eds), *Presidential Politics* (New York: St Martin's Press, 1983), pp.17–30.
17. Orren, op. cit.
18. Shockley, op. cit. p.378. Green is quoted in the same work at p.399.

The media and the presidency

Political life in any developed country is closely tied up with the media, with the press, radio and television, which perform the vital tasks of disseminating information and opinion, as objective reporters or as biased propagandists. These tasks are central, for politicians seeking office, for office-holders looking for public support for their proposals, and for citizens wishing to stay informed. The modern, electronic media do now predominate and occupy much of the attention of politicians and their advisers, and of the average citizen, but the press, in newspaper and journal form, still has an important part to play — a role that it has played throughout American political history.

As in other countries, the printed word has long been a significant factor in the spread of political awareness in North America. During the eighteenth century 'the increased circulation of ... almanacs, broadsides and newspapers contributed to the development of revolutionary consciousness'. Pamphlets, of which 'more than 1500 had appeared by 1783',[1] were a major vehicle by which the arguments for revolution were spread. When the war was won and a new Constitution had been agreed in Philadelphia, but faced opposition in some of the states, it was, as we noted earlier in the chapter on the making of the Constitution, the Publius letters (Federalist Papers), in the pages of the press, that successfully advanced the defence of the new instrument of government.

However, while the press had been an important element in the transfer of power from the colonial system to the independent government of the United States, it was by no means a passive supporter of the new government. Indeed, it soon came to be resented because of its criticisms, many of which were seen as being politically motivated. George Washington complained about the attacks made upon his Federalist policies by Republican newspapers. Such was the antagonism aroused that when these attacks continued under the presidency of John Adams, the Federalists passed the 1798 Sedition Act, the wording of which was sufficiently broad that newspaper critics of the government might be imprisoned for criminal libel; and, indeed, some journalists were incarcerated for their criticisms. That it was not only Federalist Presidents who felt disenchanted with the press was evidenced during Thomas Jefferson's presidency. Jefferson had once written that 'were it left to decide whether we should have a government without newspapers or newspapers without a government, I should not hesitate to prefer the latter', but, while President, the blatant partisanship of the press led him to comment that 'newspapers, for the most part, present only the caricature of disaffected minds. Indeed, the abuses of freedom of the press have been carried to a length never before known or borne by any civilized nation'.[2]

For most of the first century of the Republic, newspapers were relatively small, largely associated with particular candidates, parties or policies, and made little attempt at objective reporting. Presidents were accustomed to use or abuse them according to the positions taken on issues or personalities. However, as this was a period in which the presidential role was at best co-equal with that of the Congress (the Civil War years aside), the relationship between President and press was not as significant as it was to become in the twentieth century. Nevertheless, the medium did perform the valuable functions of spreading information and assisting the recruitment of citizens into the political processes.

The press entered into a major new era in the latter part of the nineteenth century when the development of new technology made mass-circulation newspapers possible. A greatly increased readership followed, put at more than 24 million by 1909.[3] These newspapers began to operate free of specific ties to particular political parties or candidates, and Presidents were not slow to recognize the value of establishing relations with this independent, 'fourth estate', although their reactions, as with the early Presidents, did vary according to the treatment they received.

It was early in the twentieth century that the press entered into a somewhat more formal relationship with the White House. Theodore Roosevelt took the first tentative steps towards establishing presidential press conferences when he started to invite selected reporters to the White House for interviews and discussion. Woodrow Wilson, a believer in the value of 'pitiless publicity' went a stage further and inaugurated full-blown news conferences, to be held on a regular basis with all accredited news representatives. For a time, the relations between President and press were good, but Wilson objected to critical reports and ultimately ended the conferences when America entered the First World War.[4] Subsequent Presidents continued with the conferences, although they had different attitudes and responses. For example, Warren Harding, unable to control his tendency towards indiscretions, suffered at the hands of the press which printed them, and he inaugurated the requirement that questions should be put in writing and submitted in advance. Calvin Coolidge 'created' the 'White House spokesman', to whom all but the most trivial revelations had to be attributed. Under Herbert Hoover, relations between President and press reached a nadir. Journalists were once more required to submit their questions in writing and the President would, at times, reply in writing. Weighed down by the Great Depression, which he could not contain, he 'blamed reporters for his problems and for his diminished popularity, as if his hard times ... were their fault and the economic chaos was primarily a public relations problem'.[5] His news conferences dwindled in number, although he never ended them entirely, and he came to rely more and more upon press statements to get his messages to the public.

As Halberstam has written: 'Franklin Roosevelt changed all that. He was the greatest newsmaker that Washington had ever seen'.[6] He generally held two press conferences a week (337 in his first term, 374 in the second), abolished the requirement that questions should be submitted in writing, and did away with the mythical White House spokesman. He made himself the major source of news concerning government activities. Just as Washington, as opposed to the state capitals, had become the focal point of government activity as a result of the vast array of

New Deal programmes aimed at alleviating the effects of the great depression, so Roosevelt became the focal point of the government and, in Halberstam's words, 'this century's prime manipulator of the new and increasingly powerful modern media'.[7] The press conference was now fully institutionalized within the White House, a tool which Presidents could use to inform and perhaps to persuade the general public. None of Roosevelt's successors has used it to the extent that he did, although it has continued to grow in size, in terms of numbers attending, and it is now televised, but whereas FDR held about seven such meetings a month, President Reagan for instance held only seven in his first year.

If, through his regular news conferences, Franklin Roosevelt was the President who used the press to best effect to get his message across to the public, he was also the President who brought that relatively new medium of communication, the radio, firmly into the presidential armoury. With his famous 'fireside chats' he revolutionized the way in which Americans perceived their chief executive. Most had never seen their President and knew of him only through the pages of newspapers and magazines, but now they could hear him speaking to them directly in their own homes. The radio, later to be supplemented by television, was a medium which helped to transform the relations between President and people, and eventually, as we shall see, between politicians and people, and between politicians and their parties.

It has been suggested that the 'rise of the modern presidency has been closely linked with the rise of the modern media': indeed, that 'the modern media created the modern presidency'.[8] Certainly, if we look at the nature of campaigns for the presidency we become aware of the importance that candidates attach to radio and television, while if we consider Presidents themselves we note the attention paid by the media to the White House and, conversely, by the White House to the media.

The political significance of the media is perhaps most starkly evident during campaigns for the presidency. In a country of more than a quarter of a billion people,[9] spread across a continent and spilling over into two non-contiguous states, a major task facing a candidate is securing name recognition. Most candidates, the incumbent apart, will start a campaign little known to those whose support they will need if they are to secure the nomination. The candidate must, then, be sold to the electorate like any new product. Such selling is done largely through the media which are, as Paletz and Entman suggest, 'the main link between the presidential candidate and the overwhelming majority of the public',[10] and the balance of coverage they provide can determine the fate of many candidatures. An excellent example of media influence can be found in the early days of 1976. In January of that year Jimmy Carter, an ex-governor of Georgia, hardly well known outside of that state, emerged from the Iowa delegate selection caucuses in second place (behind 'uncommitted') and received thirteen of the forty-seven delegates to the national convention. The following month he came first in the New Hampshire primary but received a mere 28 per cent of the vote. These votes which were far from being overwhelming endorsements, and in two of the smaller states of the Union, were, nevertheless, seized upon by the media as though they were conclusive. And yet, 'were it not for the media, the ... results would be about as relevant to the presidential nomination as opening day baseball scores are to a pennant race'.[11] But the media do exist and do possess this power to translate the insignificant into the crucial. As a result of the attention given to Carter after these early results, his name recognition increased from 20 per cent to 83 per cent in just two months, while that of two of his rivals, Henry Jackson and Morris Udall, went up from 26 per cent to 42 per cent, and 23 per cent to 36 per cent respectively. *Time* and *Newsweek*, as Paletz and Entman report, decided that Carter 'was the man to beat' and gave him 2,630 lines of coverage, while Udall, who had finished in second place in New Hampshire, only four points behind Carter, was given only 96 lines.

Two major factors have contributed to the increased importance which is attached to the media in the nominating processes. The spread of primaries has meant, as we have noted elsewhere, that no serious candidate can afford to avoid the primary trail, and if such a candidate is to secure exposure to those who vote in the primaries he will need the media. And this point, of course, emphasizes the other key factor of the electoral scene — the decline of the political parties, associated not only with this abdication of the candidate-selection role, but also with the large increase in recent years of the numbers of uncommitted or only weakly committed voters, and with the changes in the campaign financing laws as discussed in the chapter on money and the electoral process. In place of party now stand the media. 'Party organisations are really quite irrelevant. The old precinct system, the old committeeman system, the ward system, the bosses, the clubs . . . all pale into insignificance beside the awesome power of radio and television'.[12] This point has also been made by Edward Costikyan who, in fact, went further, writing that 'the principal tools that a candidate has to reach the voters are television — and radio — not party workers, not the party, *not the press'*.[13] Such now is the role of party in the selection of candidates that it is almost reduced to being a spectator at a contest fought out largely in the media and orchestrated by media consultants who are the new kingmakers, having replaced the party professionals in their legendary smoke-filled rooms.

With the decline in voters' partisan loyalties, and with the readiness of so many to 'split their tickets', the political parties are also no longer the major source of information concerning candidates or policies. Instead, such information as is available comes either from the professional manipulators who fashion the candidates as marketable commodities, or from the journalists who determine which candidates are to be boosted or which policies are to be stressed. Some have argued that the predominance of the media consultants has involved a trivialization of politics as the emphasis in campaigns has moved from substance to ephemera, from the search for a good President to the search for a good candidate. But too much should not be made of this for, as we discussed in the chapter on selection and election, such charges have been around for some considerable time, having previously been levelled at the power brokers *within* the parties.

The ultimate triumph of the media over the parties came, in Dye and Zeigler's opinion, in 1980 when 'two media candidates faced each other. Both major contestants — Republican Ronald Reagan and Democrat Jimmy Carter — owed their career to the media, not to political parties'.[14] Jimmy Carter, the incumbent in 1980, had achieved national prominence as a result of early successes, relatively speaking, which brought him vastly disproportionate attention from the media (see pp.72–3). His consultants had advised concentration upon those early battles in order to establish a momentum which could be picked up by press and television, and they were correct. A politician from a southern state, with no particular claim to national prominence, was thereby propelled into the limelight, and ultimately into the presidency. Ronald Reagan, the ex-governor of California and former film actor was 'the best electronic media candidate in American history' according to Carter's own campaign advisers.[15] His career background was perfect training for the new style politics, and he was ideal material for his media consultant, Richard Wirthlin, to mould into the images he sought to create.

Costikyan's point above, that the principal tools at a candidate's disposal are television and radio, not the press, is in part borne out by William Adams who has written that 'since 1960 campaign advertising budgets have gone almost entirely to broadcasting and not to print media. The ratio is usually over ten to one'.[16] Robert Hirschfield, in similar tone, has asserted 'that ninety per cent of the money raised for a political campaign now goes on the electronic media'.[17] But while the direction of the campaign money may be indicative of the importance attached to television and radio, it would be naive to suppose that the printed word is no longer a significant element in campaign calculations, as indeed press coverage of the 1976 Carter campaign demonstrates. Campaign managers did not have to pay to secure the extensive attention which was given to their candidate. He received it because journalists considered him newsworthy, or decided to make him newsworthy. Much, indeed, of the exposure that a candidate receives, be it on radio, television, or in the press, is 'free', in the sense that no direct payments are made, although media consultants may well have spent much money in creating 'media events' which are reported as 'news'.

While, therefore, the press is still an important element in any campaign strategy which candidates can ill-afford to ignore, a change in the balance among the media has undoubtedly taken place. American voters have become accustomed to seeing aspirants for office on their television screens, whether as part of a 'managed' news item, or as the subject of a journalistic investigation, or in paid advertisements. And with this change, the perceived images of the candidates have acquired a significance which appears to be far greater than any message which may be conveyed. This was admirably demonstrated by the famous Kennedy—Nixon debates of 1960. Eight years earlier, Richard Nixon, as the Republican vice-presidential candidate, had successfully, even triumphantly, used television to counter charges that he had illegally diverted campaign contributions to his own personal use. His 'Checkers' speech (named after the puppy mentioned in the closing minutes) was a masterful use of the medium, and it might have been expected that this experience would have given him the edge in the confrontation with his young opponent in 1960. However, in the eyes of those who witnessed the Kennedy—Nixon confrontation, the image of the cleancut Kennedy clearly prevailed over the sallow, dark-eyed Nixon.[18] On the other hand, those who *heard*, rather than *saw* the debate, thought the outcome much closer. The win for Kennedy in the first of the debates, more attributable to image than to message, may just have provided him with the margin for his ultimate election victory, and Richard Nixon seemed to recognize how important this factor had been when he wrote in his book *Six Crises* 'that he did not pay enough attention to how he looked on television'.[19] Kennedy himself acknowledged the importance of the medium when he said 'we wouldn't have had a prayer without that gadget'.[20]

Since those inaugural debates of 1960, television and the demands of television timetables have been central to campaign strategies. Not every election year has seen a debate between rival candidates. Careful consideration enters into decisions to expose candidates in this way. While there may be much to be gained, there may also be much to be lost. They may be opportunities to demonstrate one's strength, but they may also turn into occasions when one's weaknesses are revealed. Furthermore, they do also provide a platform for the opposition. And yet, of course, to refuse a confrontation can itself be wounding, as it may be interpreted as political cowardice. Debates have, nevertheless, on occasion proven to be an admirable means of refuting arguments concerning a supposed weakness in the candiate's armoury. In 1960, for example, John Kennedy's youth (he was to become the youngest elected President) was a factor, but in the debates he came across as not significantly different in age or grasp of issues from Nixon, while at the same time he received much valuable additional exposure. In 1984, Ronald Reagan, the nation's oldest President, turned the age question around with a classic debating ploy when he promised not to make an issue of Walter Mondale's youth and inexperience. However, when incumbent Gerald Ford debated with Jimmy Carter in 1976 he appeared to lend credence to Lyndon Johnson's unkind quip that 'he was a man who couldn't walk and chew gum at the same time'. His comment that there was 'no Soviet domination of Eastern Europe' stunned most of the viewers, and many were led to question his competence or understanding.

However, the 'to debate or not to debate' question is but one small element in the calculations of campaign managers when considering television. Of much more significance is the ongoing news coverage that the medium can provide and which those managers hope they can tap. As Patterson, among others, has noted, the timetabling of certain programmes on television has become a major factor in the strategic planning of a campaign. Events must be so arranged that whenever possible they will be reported on the network evening news programmes.[21] This has been particularly the case since the early 1960s when the evening news was extended to half an hour. As a consequence, newscasters were given the opportunity to devote more attention to candidates for high office. And the 'free' coverage which the candidate may receive from such attention is, of course, backed up by extensive advertising campaigns (as extensive as campaign funds will permit) which will seek to project the image of a statesman while assiduously avoiding potentially harmful issues.

At times it appears that the candidates are merely the front men for the real professionals, the experts in the arts of presentation and selling, the 'hidden persuaders' as Vance Packard once described the profession. It is the consultants who tell the candidates what to do, what to say, and when. It is they, interpreting the polls which they take, who determine what they think the public will 'buy' and what should be avoided. In the cynical (but probably accurate) words of Robert Hirschfield, 'the media consultant is already more important than the candidate'.[22]

Of course, when an incumbent is running for re-election, other factors enter the picture. A President has a record for all to see which is difficult to disguise. Thus, even had Carter's campaign in 1980 matched that of Ronald Reagan in its professionalism it is doubtful that it would have erased public perceptions concerning Carter's lack of leadership, or worry over the economy or the fate of the American hostages seized in Iran.

It has been suggested that America today is in a state of 'permanent campaign': that 'once the selling of the President has been completed, selling *by* the President can begin'.[23] If one accepts President Truman's analysis of his position, that his principal power was the power to persuade, one can accept that a President must basically be a salesman. Having no loyal cadre, and often no nominal majority, in the legislature which will automatically respond in a positive manner to his requests, he must resort to tactics which will persuade Congressmen that their best interests lie in giving support to the President, tactics which will necessarily include resort to the media in all its forms.

We have already mentioned the development of the presidential press conferences from their beginnings during Theodore Roosevelt's presidency to their apogee with Franklin Roosevelt. Since those days, as we noted, they have been used less frequently — indeed, for a time during Watergate, Nixon avoided the press altogether, giving no interviews and holding no press conferences. When now held, they are usually covered by television, and this has changed their very nature. No longer are they small group, relatively informal, discussion meetings for the exchange of information. Now, open to the general public through the small screen, they are generally more formal. Presidents may take advantage of the opportunity to make an opening statement, and some have 'planted' questions among the journalists in an effort to ensure that the meetings should go along preferred lines. As George Reedy has written: 'a device universally hailed as a boon to communication has become a one-way street. It is the means by which a man can conduct a monologue *in* public and convince himself that he is conducting a dialogue *with* the public'.[24]

The introduction of the media of the modern age, of radio and television, has induced a major upheaval in the manner in which Presidents communicate with the public and, ironically, it was, as we have seen, the same President who revolutionized the press conference who paved the way for the use of techniques which would ultimately undermine it in terms of its original purpose.

Presidents today use other methods to communicate their thoughts and aims, to persuade their public, and to secure the support in the country which they hope to convert into political capital when dealing with Congressmen.

As 'the President is the most important continuing story the media deal with',[25] he has no difficulty getting publicity for any story, no matter how trivial. The significant factor, so far as he is concerned, is that it should get the right kind of publicity. To this end, Presidents have at their command a vast array of communications specialists in the White House. In addition to the formal Press Secretary, there are offices for Communication; Speechwriting and Research; Media Relations and Planning; Public Affairs; Communication Planning; Public Liaison; News Summary; and Audio Services. Denton and Hahn have estimated that more than fifty communications specialists were engaged in the White House in the mid-1980s whose jobs were 'to plan, coordinate, and orchestrate presidential public appearances and information'.[26] There is a constant outflow of material: daily handouts; background and 'off the record' briefings; transcripts of speeches. Media 'events' have to be planned, whether it be coverage of the President receiving a visiting head of state, or signing or, alternatively, vetoing a piece of legislation. Visits abroad, meetings with other leaders, summit conferences, if properly handled, and if events prove propitious, can be used to project an image of the President as a man of international stature, as a world leader who should be supported.

Denton and Hahn have suggested that 'the greatest source of presidential influence today is public approval',[27] and in the search for that approval a skilful President will make fullest use of the media, which turn naturally to the White House for the major stories of the day. And most of the advantages lie with him rather than with his political opponents. When he wishes to address the nation on a particular issue he will normally be accorded access to prime-time television, while his opponents have no automatic right of reply and can never be sure of more than indirect coverage of their case. Thus, for example, when Franklin Roosevelt gave his 1936 State of the Union address, an address so political in tone that it constituted, in Halberstam's words 'his campaign platform' for the forthcoming election, the chairman of the Republican National Committee asked for equal time to reply. The chairman of CBS denied the request, arguing that the State of the Union speech was an official message of the President.[28] Furthermore, the President and his advisers are in a position to attempt manipulation of the news. For instance, if at all possible, they will attempt to emphasize 'up-beat' at the expense of 'down-beat' stories through the careful timing of releases. A *positive* story can often be used to drive a *negative* report from the headlines. In addition, Presidents may well seek to suppress information which might reflect adversely upon them or upon their policies and give ammunition to their critics.

Interestingly, while so much attention is paid by the White House to the media, and while so much is done to project a desired presidential image, Denton and Hahn argue that 'historically, except in cases of foreign affairs, direct appeals to the nation usually do not succeed'.[29] Conversely, President Reagan's successful use of the media to gain support for his 1981 budget and tax-cutting proposals, which led to Congressmen being inundated by telephone calls from constituents, can be seen as a rare example of the public being stimulated by such appeals. Despite this, Presidents still appear to regard the media (television in particular) as a vital part of their armoury, and John Kennedy is recorded as saying 'we couldn't survive without T.V.'[30] As Denton and Hahn also point out, although the record is one of a general lack of success, Presidents continue to threaten that they will take particular matters to the public if they fail to receive congressional support.

We noted, early in this chapter, that while the medium of print had been an important factor in the spread of the ideas and arguments that helped to promote the revolution, it was not long before Presidents were complaining about the treatment they were receiving at its hands. Complaints continue to this day, with all Presidents ready at some time or another to blame the media for their difficulties. Some Presidents indeed have appeared to be quite paranoiac about the manner in which the media have reported or commented on their activities. Such feelings were perhaps best exemplified during Richard Nixon's presidency. Nixon had long distrusted most of the journalistic profession, as was demonstrated by his comment to newsmen after his loss of the 1962 race for the governorship of California — 'You won't have Nixon to kick around any more' — and while he was in the White House his attitudes hardened. Reporters who fell from favour were liable to be banned from White House press conferences, might have their phones tapped or their tax returns audited, and attempts were made to get them to turn over the rough notes upon which their unpopular stories were based. Anti-trust suits were brought against the large television networks. Spiro Agnew — Vice-President until he resigned and pleaded guilty to a corruption charge — was also used to fulminate against commentators who dared to criticize the administration. And yet, in fact, the media are not the bogeymen that they are made out to be. 'A striking feature emerging from 25 years of *Time* and *New York Times* articles and 10 years of *C.B.S.* news broadcasts is the consistent pattern of favourable coverage of the President.'[31] Content analysis suggests a general picture of stories running at about two to one in favour of the President. In light of these facts, it is difficult, at times, to understand the vitriolic attitude that some have had towards the media. That a Lyndon Johnson, beset by the disaster of Vietnam, or a Richard Nixon, desperately concerned to conceal the excesses and illegalities of his presidency, should feel so strongly is hardly to be wondered at. But for many of the other Presidents, reaction to negative stories seems to suggest a feeling that the press should not be neutral but a positive supporter of presidential initiatives; that any not *for* the President must be *against* him; that any criticism must spring from malice rather than from any honestly held alternative viewpoint.

For better or worse, the media are now central to the process by which people reach the White House and are a vital tool of those who attain the presidency. To paraphrase Costikyan, they have replaced the party as the selection agent,[32] while, in the words of Congresswoman Shirley Chisholm, they 'just control everything ... who is a bona fide candidate and who is not'.[33] Godfrey Hodgson may be guilty of some exaggeration when he writes that television 'has become the main forum in which American politics are conducted',[34] but he is not too far from the truth: for the media play an important part in helping both to fill the void created by the dismantling of the political parties and to bridge the gap, created by the Founding Fathers, between President and Congress.

Notes

1. Samuel P. Huntington, *American Politics: The Promise of Disharmony* (Cambridge, Mass.: Belknap Press, 1981), pp.99–100.
2. Both quotations cited by George Edwards III and Stephen J. Wayne, 'The President and the Press', in Harry A. Bailey Jr. and Jay M. Shafritz (eds), *The American Presidency* (Chicago, Ill.: The Dorsey Press, 1988), p.316.
3. See Huntington, op. cit. p.101.
4. See Bailey and Schafritz, op. cit. pp.306–13.
5. David Halberstam, *The Powers That Be* (London: Chatto & Windus, 1979), p.8.
6. Ibid.
7. Ibid. p.9.
8. Godfrey Hodgson, *All Things to All Men* (Harmondsworth: Penguin Books, 1984), p.171.
9. The American billion, i.e. 1,000,000,000.
10. David L. Paletz and Robert M. Entman, *Media, Power, Politics* (New York: The Free Press, 1981), p.32.
11. Ibid. p.36.
12. Douglas Ireland, in Robert S. Hirschfield (ed.), *Selection/Election* (New York: Aldine Publishing, 1982), p.142.
13. Ibid. p.48.
14. Thomas R. Dye and L. Harmon Zeigler, *American Politics in the Media Age* (Monterey, Cal.: Brooks/Cole Publishing, 1983), p.162.
15. Quoted by Dye and Zeigler, op. cit. p.220.
16. William Adams, 'Media Power in Presidential Elections', in Doris A. Graber (ed.), *The President and the Public* (Philadelphia: Institute for the Study of Human Issues, 1982), pp. 118–19.
17. Hirschfield, op. cit. p.187.
18. For an excellent description of the debate, and the preparations for it, see Theodore White, *The Making of the President, 1960* (New York: Atheneum, 1961).
19. See Adams, op. cit. p.122.
20. Quoted by Hodgson, op. cit. p.171.
21. See Thomas E. Patterson, *The Mass Media Election* (New York: Praeger, 1980), p.5.
22. Hirschfield, op. cit. p.183.
23. Donna Cross in *Media Speak* (New York: Mentor Books, 1983), p.188. Quoted in Robert E. Denton Jr. and Dan F. Hahn, *Presidential Communication* (New York: Praeger, 1986), p.49.
24. *The Twilight of the Presidency* (New York: World Publishing, 1970), pp. 164–6.
25. Martha Kumar and Michael Grossman, with the assistance of Leslie Lichter-Mason, in Graber, op. cit. p.102.
26. Denton and Hahn, op. cit. p.61.
27. Ibid. p.56.

28. Halberstam, op. cit. p.37.
29. Denton and Hahn, op. cit. p.57.
30. Hodgson, op. cit. p.171.
31. Martha Kumar et al., loc. cit. p.87.
32. See Hirschfield, op. cit. p.48.
33. In Hirschfield, op. cit. p.161.
34. Hodgson, op. cit. p.172.

The President and Congress

The Founding Fathers, as we have seen — some fearful of dominant legislatures, after the experiences of some of the states, others of an overbearing executive, on the model of the British monarch — made the separation of powers a central plank of their new Constitution. They created a system in which the legislature, the executive, and the judiciary were kept separate, and in which no one branch of government could assert itself at the expense of the others. However, while the personnel were separate, in that no person could serve in more than one branch at any one time, the separation was not total, for each institution was given certain functions which related to the others. It is, then, more appropriate to use the Neustadt term to describe the situation: 'separated institutions sharing power'.[1] For example, before a bill can become law it requires presidential approval, through signature, or refusal to veto, or a special majority of a two-thirds vote in each House of Congress to override a presidential veto. Furthermore, the President is required 'from time to time [to] give to the Congress Information of the State of the Union, and recommend to their Consideration such Measures as he shall judge necessary and expedient'.[2] This injunction, although not spelling it out explicitly, provides the constitutional basis for the modern presidential practice of sending a comprehensive legislative programme for congressional consideration. On the other side, the Congress, a body of 535 independently minded legislators, may reject the president's conceptions of the nation's needs, may deny him the legislation he seeks or the funds he requires. The House of Representatives may even vote for impeachment of the President, and if the Senate find him guilty he may be removed from office. The potential for conflict between these two institutions is great and the 'invitation to struggle', as one commentator described the work of the Founding Fathers, has rarely been declined.

The loose wording of the Constitution increased the likelihood that the struggle would occur, for while 'Article II of the Constitution emphasized the structural aspects of the Presidency ... [it] provided only the vaguest guidelines on the jurisdiction of the President'.[3] Was he restricted in the main to taking 'care that the laws be faithfully executed' or did he have wider powers and responsibilities that flowed from the implications of the Constitution? During the formative years of the Republic, the views of the early Presidents as to their appropriate roles in relation to Congress fluctuated considerably. George Washington, for instance, was apparently content with the division between legislature and executive and did not seek to control or lead the Congress. He only used his veto power twice, and then not for policy or political ends but because of objections on constitutional grounds. On the other hand, Thomas Jefferson, the first President to be something approaching a national leader of a political party, took advantage of that position and through careful intrigue played a significant part in directing Congress. Andrew Jackson, who had sought to democratize the office, saw the presidency as the appropriate institution for leadership of the nation and when Congress passed legislation of which he disapproved he would use his veto, for political rather than for mere constitutional ends. Abraham Lincoln, in prosecuting the Civil War, was ready to use every power of the presidency, explicit and implicit, to preserve the Union. When his actions were at times deemed illegal or unconstitutional, he ignored injunctions to desist, taking refuge in the implied powers he had as Commander-in-Chief. Subsequently, Congress gave *ex post facto* legal authority to the President's actions.

However, despite some of these examples which could be taken as heralds of the more aggressive presidencies of the twentieth century, the nineteenth century was largely a period of congressional dominance, with many of the Presidents of the era being little more than footnotes in the history books. It has been during the twentieth century — in part because of the

philosophies of those who have held the office, in part as a
response to increasing demands (both domestic and foreign)
made upon government — that Presidents have come to play a
more assertive role.

Early in the twentieth century, two advocates of strength and
vigour in the presidency, Presidents Theodore Roosevelt and
Woodrow Wilson, sought to assert themselves *vis-à-vis* Congress,
and developed something like presidential programmes.
Roosevelt believed it was the President's right and 'his duty to
do anything that the needs of the Nation demand unless such
action was forbidden by the Constitution or by the laws'.[4]
President Taft, chosen by Roosevelt to succeed him, defeated in
his bid for re-election by Roosevelt's intervention as the
Progressive, 'Bull-Moose' candidate, and largely overshadowed
by the Presidents who preceded and followed him, took what
appeared to be a diametrically opposed line, asserting that 'the
President can exercise no power which cannot be fairly and
reasonably traced to some specific grant of power or justly implied
and included within such express grant as proper and necessary
to its exercise'.[5] However, his comments were in large part an
attack upon Roosevelt rather than an outright condemnation of
an active presidency and his views on the powers of the office
were not much out of tune with those of his successor Wilson.
As he went on to write:

> The cry of Executive dominance is often entirely unjustified, as
> when the President's commanding influence only grows out of a
> proper cohesion of a party and its recognition of the necessity for
> political leadership. ... [P]eople ... should be willing to rely upon
> their judgment in selecting their Chief Agent, and having selected
> him, should entrust to him all the power needed to carry out their
> governmental purpose, great as it may be.[6]

It was Taft, indeed, challenging the domination of Congress in
the policy-making process, who was the first President of the
modern age to send a draft of a legislative proposal to the
Congress. Woodrow Wilson, who much admired the British
system of co-operation, through party, of the executive and the
legislature, harked back to the Jefferson model of party leadership
to control the Congress, and sought to use party to secure passage
of his legislative proposals. He fully recognized the importance
of maintaining close links between the White House and Capitol

Hill, and revived the practice, abandoned by President Jefferson, of delivering the State of the Union message to Congress in person. In Pfiffner's analysis, 'the Wilson Presidency and its New Freedom proposals marked one of the periods of greatest creativity and co-operation between the President and Congress in the years between the Reconstruction and the New Deal'.[7]

The bitterness which soured relations between the President and the Senate at the end of the First World War, when an ailing President Wilson ignored his own strictures that Presidents should always keep Congress informed of their plans, resulted in the failure of the Senate to ratify the Treaty of Versailles which established the League of Nations. Reaction to 'strong' Presidents and to international involvements set in, and as the 1920s were a period of prosperity, little was demanded of chief executives. Into the White House went conservative Republican Presidents whose political philosophy was based largely on a *laissez-faire* approach to government. As Roche and Levy put it: 'Warren Harding and Calvin Coolidge took their directions from the legislature and relaxed: Coolidge took a long nap every afternoon, avoided controversy, and saved much of his salary'.[8] Herbert Hoover, an engineer and administrator of international stature, a much more talented man than either of his two predecessors, unfortunately shared their basic political beliefs, which proved ill-suited to the demands which were to be made upon government by the onset in 1929 of the Great Depression.

The failure of the *laissez-faire* approach in face of the calamities of the depression brought Franklin Roosevelt to the White House and heralded the birth of the modern presidency. Roosevelt believed that leadership rested squarely with the President and proceeded immediately to demonstrate the role he expected a chief executive to play. His 'One Hundred Days' in 1933, when he bombarded Congress with his New Deal proposals for attacking the depression are a prime example of presidential, legislative leadership (or, in less friendly eyes, and there were many, of presidential usurpation). Yet even during this formative period of the 'modern presidency', Congress still retained considerable responsibility and, as Hodgson reminds us, 'a high proportion of the New Deal legislation originated on Capitol Hill, not in the White House'.[9] It was left to Roosevelt's successor, Harry Truman, to deliver a comprehensive programme to

Congress, and thereby establish a practice which has continued almost unbroken ever since. President Eisenhower at first demurred about following the Truman example, but he was quick to respond when Congress demanded such a programme. The situation today is that Presidents are expected to present Congress with a comprehensive statement of their goals, along with an annual budget message and an annual economic report. In fact, in 1947, 'congressional committees instituted the practice of requesting from BOB [Bureau of the Budget, now Office of Management and Budget] the President's position on all pending legislation, including items that had not originated with the executive'.[10] While ideas for legislation obviously originate in many areas, the presidency is now the chief source of most major legislative initiative: Presidents set the agenda, Congress responds.

It is, however, one thing for a President to present a programme for congressional consideration, quite another for him to receive the support necessary for that programme to be translated into law. As we have seen, in comparison with many other governmental systems in the Western world, America lacks the strong, disciplined political parties from which Presidents might draw strength and support. American political parties are weak, decentralized creatures owing allegiance to state or locality interests rather than to a national interest. As W.D. Burnham has suggested, they are 'not instruments of collective purpose but of electoral success'. They do not act in a co-ordinated, monolithic fashion in an attempt to secure a majority in the national legislature where a national programme might be pursued.

The absence of strong collectivities in Congress, ever ready to follow the line set by their national leaders, means that while 'the mainstay of presidential support in Congress occurs through the medium of party',[11] Presidents can never be assured of the automatic support of those who are nominally of their party. As most Congressmen are not usually deliberately perverse, there will generally be a natural tendency among them to back *their* President, other things being equal. Thus, as Hinckley demonstrates, for the years 1953–1978, 'House Democrats averaged 69 per cent support for Democratic Presidents and 46 per cent for Republican Presidents' while the figures for House Republicans were 64 per cent for Republican Presidents and 40 per cent for Democratic Presidents. [12] Similar figures obtained in the Senate. The interesting points to note for those accustomed to the quality of party loyalty in the British sytem are, first, the 30 per cent plus figure which did not support the party's President, and secondly, the 40 per cent plus support given to the other party's President.

As economists and Presidents are forced to recognize, other things are often not equal. Congressmen do have a number of demands made upon them. Constituents, interest groups, government agencies may all compete for their attention. And of course they may well have their own conceptions of the appropriate course to be followed. Presidential goals are then but one of the factors — and not necessarily the most significant — that legislators take into account. Furthermore, it must be recognized that, while party label *may* induce Congressmen to back a President of similar label, the parties encompass such a disparate range of opinions and attitudes that they contain within their nominal ranks some who have so little in common with the mainstream of the party that they offer little support either to party or to President. A good example of this almost anarchic situation is given by 'Tip' O'Neill, a former Speaker of the House of Representatives and leader of the Democrats in the House: 'We have ten fellows who haven't voted with us ten per cent of the time.'[13]

Such party links as have existed between the presidency and the legislature, tenuous though they may have been at times, have grown even weaker in recent decades. It is nearly thirty years since MacGregor Burns sub-titled his book *Deadlock of Democracy*, 'Four Party Politics in America',[14] to highlight the distinctions to be drawn between the presidential and congressional wings of the two parties. The distinctions are now much greater than at the time that Burns was writing. While John Kennedy had just reached the White House after a campaign which had placed great emphasis on personality, much of his activity toward the goal had been conducted within the mainstream of the party organization. Today, as we have seen, with the spread of the primaries, the much greater reliance on the electronic media, and the rise of the political action committees, a presidential nomination is achieved and a candidate becomes President largely as a result of personal efforts rather than as a creature of his party. The umbilical cord that joined the President and his party in Congress has been cut, if not completely severed, and its life-giving function severely impaired.

There is, then, in this highly unstructured party system, no party whip that a President can crack to bring his party members rallying around to pass his bills in the Houses of Congress. Furthermore, we must recognize that even if he could command that kind of loyalty and support, it might not be sufficient, for his party might not have the majority of the seats in Congress. During most of the history of the United States, there has generally been a congruence between the party in the White House and the party with the congressional majority. Mid-term elections, when all of the House and a third of the Senate are up for re-election, have on occasion altered the situation, but it has been usual for a President entering office to face a Congress with a majority of his own party. In the last forty years, however, things have changed. Voters have become more volatile, much more ready to split their ticket by voting for a President of one party and a Congressman or Senator of another. For example, in 1900, it has been estimated, a mere 4 per cent of the votes for the House and for the President were split, whereas by 1984 that figure had grown to 45 per cent. One concomitant of this altered pattern of behaviour has been that the Democrats now appear to be a firmly entrenched majority in Congress while the presidency has for most of the time gone to the Republicans. Thus, since the second half of President Eisenhower's first term, all Republican Presidents have had to face a House of Representatives dominated by the Democrats, and a Senate, apart from the early years of Reagan's presidency, also similarly controlled.

A President who looks across the Atlantic to the British system of government may well be envious of the British Prime Minister who can move from one piece of legislation to the next, secure in a relatively stable majority of party loyalists ready to convert proposals into law. The lives of the government and the legislature are inextricably linked: if the government fails to get its way, Parliament may well be dissolved. Congress, on the other hand, comprising its 435 delegates from the congressional districts and its 100 ambassadors from the fifty states, has its own life. The 535 legislators do not owe their continuance in session to the

President. Their term of office is set down by the Constitution and may not be altered by the President, while their political life span may be considerably longer than that of the chief executive. No matter the fate of the President's programme, the Congress remains unaffected.

In the absence of institutional means whereby he can ensure that his proposals receive favourable consideration by the legislature, and lacking overt coercive powers, any President seeking legislative success will need to engage in a number of different strategies to put together the majorities needed. Those strategies can range from friendly persuasion to hard political bargaining; from reasoned argument to partisan appeal; from direct approach to indirect threat. Circumstance will generally determine which tactic or tactics will be most suitable.

Most modern Presidents who wish to achieve their goals have long recognized the benefits to be derived from maintaining close and continuous liaison between the White House and Capitol Hill. It was Franklin Roosevelt who first started sending his personal representatives to Capitol Hill to press for the passage of his bills. His successor, President Truman, appointed two full-time persons for liaison work, while President Eisenhower, not, as we have already noted, overly keen on the aggressive legislative role for Presidents, became the first chief executive to establish an Office of Congressional Liaison, although in the first instance its primary function was to act 'as a buffer for demands for patronage and pork barrel'.[15] Similar offices have existed in succeeding presidencies, and have been recognized as a major part of the President's armoury in treating with Congress, although the use made of such offices has varied according to the character of the President and his aims. Larry O'Brien, appointed by President Kennedy to head his Office of Congressional Relations, soon organized the office into a highly efficient means of maintaining close links between White House personnel and Congressmen. Congressmen were divided into groups, usually along geographic lines, and one liaison officer would be assigned to each group, maintaining close and continous contact with its members. Such a procedure has been largely followed since, although President Carter moved from these across the policy-board links to a specifically policy-related organization — a move which, while it might have made sense, in policy terms, had the effect of sharply reducing the contacts between White House staff and Congressmen and, consequently, the usefulness of the office.

When a President first enters office he may well claim that his electoral victory has given him a mandate for his legislative programme. His campaign will almost certainly have been short on specifics, as the candidates will generally have sought to avoid making promises which, while pleasing some, might alienate others. The support accorded by the population at large (bearing in mind the turnouts of barely more than 50 per cent) may have been weak. Nevertheless, the fact that he has received the accolade does tend to create a readiness, short-lived though it may be, to look favourably upon presidential proposals, particularly if Congressmen believe support for such proposals may carry potential electoral advantage. Most Presidents are, then, accorded a 'honeymoon' period which may be the most fruitful time of their presidency. A study by Paul Light demonstrates the importance of those early days, and how quickly the advantage evaporates. He showed, for instance, that for the years 1960–1980, bills presented to Congress by the President had a success rate of 72 per cent if introduced in the January to March period of his first year; 39 per cent if introduced in the next three months, and a lowly 25 per cent if introduced between the July and September.[16] Presidents cannot, however, take such co-operation for granted, and they do need to take steps to ensure that they make the most of the inauguration euphoria, that they translate this initial resource into political clout.

An astute President will take advantage of his position in what Theodore Roosevelt described as 'the bully pulpit'. Through the use of the media, Presidents can reach out to people in their homes and try to persuade them of the value of t:.eir proposals, hoping that that those persuaded will then bring pressure to bear upon their Congressmen to persuade them to support the President. It was President Franklin Roosevelt, during the days of the Great Depression in the 1930s, who recognized the value of the radio for such purposes. His famous 'fireside chats' were the first significant use of this method of political communication. Today, with television sets in almost every home, and often in most rooms in the house, the message can be put across even more forcibly, and Presidents with a good television image, like a Ronald Reagan, may be able to reap a political harvest. Presidents cannot, however, resort to this tool too often as people will eventually turn off, figuratively and literally. But if they are discerning in the extent to which they appeal to the people in this manner, they may gain added weight for their bargaining with Congress.

Most of a President's efforts to persuade Congress to support his initiatives are, however, of a more direct nature and involve a number of techniques. Personal links between Presidents and Congressmen may well help to establish a rapport between the two branches, such that when the chief executive looks for help on a particular bill he may be able to tap an existing fund of goodwill. For instance, a President may well invite a number of crucial Congressmen to working breakfasts at the White House to discuss future policies or strategies. Few Congressmen can resist such an invitation, if only for the attendant publicity that they will ensure it will receive back in the home district. A summons by the President, a visit to the White House, is still something to which all but the most hardened of the legislators will respond in favourable fashion. The goodwill aspect of these occasions may often be as important to the President as any hard and fast commitments that may be worked out.

President Jimmy Carter, unversed in the ways of Washington — indeed, elected, in part, because of his innocence of the Washington scene — managed to squander such potential profit. For example, in his bid to economize, to keep White House expenses down, he sent Congressmen bills for these meals. Such a practice did little to secure for him the support or co-operation he was seeking. In similar fashion, the penny-pinching attitude which led him to dispose of the presidential yacht denied him an opportunity to keep Congressmen happy through harmless, and relatively cheap, invitations to cruise with him along the Potomac. The President seemed unable to recognize the political value of such gestures.

Lyndon Johnson, who had been a most powerful majority leader in the Senate, was very careful, as far as possible, to take Congress along with him. He would inform Congress in advance of his plans, would sometimes put Congressmen on to task forces concerned with designing policies, and would seek advice from them (including Republicans) on legislative and strategic matters. Nixon and Carter, on the other hand, were much more aloof and their efforts to secure congressional support suffered accordingly.

Presidents, in their efforts to secure congressional co-operation on a bill, may well appeal to Congressmen's patriotism and loyalty: loyalty to their President, to their party, to their country. And, at times, such appeals may work. However, more often than not, Presidents are forced to engage in that activity which is the life-blood of American politics — bargaining. Some Presidents have been much more adept at this than others, recognizing compromise as central to the world of politics. Such pragmatic Presidents have been ready to settle for less than they sought rather than lose everything. Franklin Roosevelt, Lyndon Johnson, even Ronald Reagan, might be counted among the ranks of such Presidents, while Richard Nixon and Jimmy Carter were of a different mind. As Carter himself said: 'horse trading and compromising and so forth have always been difficult for me to do'. 'I don't want to hear what the political implications are of this issue. I want to do what's right not what's political'.[17] Indeed, Carter seemed to go out of his way to make things more difficult for himself when, early on in his presidency, he cancelled a number of the pet, pork-barrel projects (often of dubious value, it must be admitted) that keep the voters happy with their Congressmen and now appear to be the price that has to be paid to secure authorization of worthwhile schemes. Such an attitude and such action might get a President into heaven, they do not help him to get his policies onto the statute books. The enmity thereby incurred represented a considerable loss of potential influence.

In its crudest terms, the bargaining may at times seem like a straightforward system of barter. In the past the patronage system, under which the President had a large number of jobs at his disposal, could be of some use in 'buying' support. The spread of the Civil Service merit system has considerably reduced the number of such posts and thereby the value of this particular resource. Some prestigious appointments are still within the gift of Presidents — ambassadors, judges, justices, members of the cabinet, for example, are all appointed by the chief executive — but few are now offered in return for support in Congress. Many will have been promised as rewards for support prior to the election, and may be subject to senatorial approval and, consequently, to senatorial courtesy.[18] Furthermore, there is a negative side to the appointing power, for, as President Taft astutely observed, when he made one appointment he created nine new enemies and one ingrate. (Taft was probably right about the ingratitude but also probably understated the number alienated.)

But if presidential patronage with regard to appointments has been severely circumscribed, the ever-increasing role of the federal government in most aspects of society has greatly increased the opportunities for economic patronage. The largesse which flows from Washington to the states and to the congressional districts in the form of grants, or loans, or contracts, may be important elements in a representative's relations with his constituents. While much of that largesse is closely linked to specific programmes or classes of beneficiary, with which the President cannot tamper, presidential action in some areas can undoubtedly be significant. For example, some grant or loan programmes may be phased out (or in), or delayed; contracts may be re-negotiated or re-directed; the credit for securing a programme for a particular area, and the patronage that may be associated with it, may be given to one person rather than another, thereby, perhaps, enhancing or diminishing a political career.

Promises of support for, or threats of opposition to, bills favoured by Congressmen may also be important factors in bringing a President support for his programmes, and in this area he has at his disposal what Woodrow Wilson described as his 'most formidable weapon', the veto power which enables him to act almost as a third branch of the legislature.[19] We noted, when talking of the early Presidents, that the wording of the Constitution left open the question of when the veto might appropriately be used, and debate over this point has continued into the twentieth century. Hamilton, in *The Federalist*, argued that the power was necessary in order that the President might 'defend himself against the depredations of the [legislature]', that it was chiefly designed to protect against 'an immediate attack upon the constitutional rights of the Executive'. But he added that it was also a 'security check against the enaction of improper laws. . . . a salutary check upon the legislative body, calculated to guard against the effects of faction . . . in a case in which the public good was evidently and palpably sacrificed'.[20] Washington, as we saw, took a very limited view of the power, using it to guard against what he considered unconstitutional activity, whereas Jackson was ready to use it for political ends, 'to guard against faction'.

While twentieth century Presidents have generally accepted the idea that the veto might be used for political purposes, there are still those who believe its application should be limited to protection of the Constitution. Edward Pessen, for one, in an article entitled 'This Arrogant Veto', argued that the veto should be used very sparingly, while Charles Black asserted that it should not be used 'as a means of systematic policy control over the legislative branch, on matters constitutionally indifferent and not menacing the President's independence'.[21] Both views were expressed during a period in which President Ford was establishing himself as 'the most important vetoer of the 1931–81 period',[22] and may have been coloured by that fact.

Regardless of these complaints concerning the unacceptibility of many vetoes, Presidents will undoubtedly use the power in their pursuit of political ends and will generally be ready to substitute their opinion for that of the Congress. As the only nationally elected officials, it does not seem inappropriate that they should veto bills which fail, in their judgement, to meet the public interest. Of course, that judgement will be politically coloured, but Presidents are, after all, elected carrying particular political labels, vague though they may be, and political judgements are consequently expected of them. However, in answer to those who fear presidential domination through the veto, it must be recognized that it is not an absolute but a partial power. When a President returns a bill to Congress with his message setting out his reasons for rejection, Congress, by a two-thirds vote of those present and voting in each House, may overturn that veto. Furthermore, the veto, in the formal sense, is a total veto. A President cannot accept those parts of a bill he likes and veto those parts he dislikes. Consequently, given the congressional habit of attaching riders (often the equivalent of new bills expected to attract presidential disapproval) to legislation that the President wants, the chief executive is placed in the invidious position of having to decide whether or not to pay the price that is being exacted.

There is, however, a circumstance in which the President's veto may be absolute, and that is when the so-called pocket-veto comes into play. If a bill is not returned to the Congress within ten days (Sundays excepted) it becomes law, 'unless the Congress by their adjournment prevent its return, in which case it shall not be a law'. This pocket-veto, which has been used regularly since the early nineteenth century, has the advantage from the President's point of view that it cannot be overridden. If a bill cannot be returned within the required period of time, it is dead and no subsequent action can revive it: to achieve the desired purposes, a new bill must be introduced.

Over the years, there has been some dispute about the nature of the adjournment and what constituted a situation in which the President was unable to return a bill, but the matter appears to have been resolved following an attempt by President Nixon to pocket-veto the Family Practice of Medicine Bill in 1970. The bill, which had received the unusually large majorities of 64−1 in the Senate and 346−2 in the House, was sent to the President on 14 December. Congress adjourned for Christmas on 22 December, and the Senate returned on 28 December, the House a day later. While neither House was away for more than five days, not counting the Sunday, and despite the fact that the Senate had appointed an officer to receive messages, the President announced that the bill was pocket-vetoed.[23] Senator Edward Kennedy challenged in the Courts this use of a brief intra-session adjournment to veto without opportunity of override. A District Court decision that the adjournment had not prevented a regular veto was upheld by an Appellate Court, and the bill was declared to have become law on 25 December 1970.[24] Subsequent presidential actions do suggest that such intra-session pocket-vetoes are now a thing of the past.

It was suggested above that the President's veto was a total veto, and in a formal sense this is true: a President must accept or reject *in toto*. The reality is, however, a little different, for once a bill has become law, Presidents may choose to ignore parts of it, to be selective in their enforcement or application, and, in some instances, to impound funds which have been appropriated for specific projects. Through such actions then, chief executives have acquired a limited-item veto over legislation.

The impoundment of funds, which became a hot political issue during the Nixon presidency, has a history which can be traced back to Washington's time, and 'it has long been the practice of the executive branch to regard appropriations as permissive rather than mandatory'.[25] Fisher suggests that there have been four different types of impoundment over the years: those related to efficient management; those that have statutory support; those that depend on constitutional argument, deriving particularly from the Commander-in-Chief clause; those that form part of the policy making and priority-setting of the Administration. The first two types have been largely uncontroversial, but the latter two have occasioned some considerable constitutional debate. President Truman, for instance, refused to spend Air Force funds voted by Congress in excess of his requests, justifying the action by pointing to his authority as Commander-in-Chief. In similar fashion, the Kennedy administration refused to release additional appropriations for the development of the B-70 bomber. While both of these instances provoked a degree of controversy, it was as nothing compared with the uproar associated with President Nixon's widespread use of 'impoundment to move toward his own priorities. . . . While the cutbacks were made in the name of fiscal integrity, in actual fact they were part of a redistribution of Federal funds from Democratic programs to those supported by the Nixon Administration'.[26] As Fisher went on to argue: 'Used with restraint and circumspection, impoundment had been used for decades without precipitating a major crisis. But during the Nixon years restraint was replaced by abandon, precedent stretched past the breaking point, and statutory authority pushed beyond legislative intent'.[27]

The Courts gradually found against this presidential usurpation. For instance, legal challenges were made to President Nixon's withholding of almost half of the funds voted for the first three years of operation of the Federal Water Pollution Control Act Amendments of 1972, and decisions were handed down which held that the Administration was required to allot the full sums, that 'nothing in the Act grants the Administrator the authority to substitute his sense of national priorities for that of the Congress'.[28] However, while these and similar verdicts established the constitutional duty of the President, they were of limited value because of the time involved in pursuing the legal challenges, and Congress itself sought to regularize the position in its 1974 Budget and Impoundment Control Act. For the purposes of applying the Act, presidential impoundments were split into two categories — those which merely sought to defer or postpone a particular expenditure, and those which involved the termination of programmes of which the President disapproved, or a permanent cut in the level of expenditure on particular programmes. In the former instances, the Act provided that if the President should announce his intention to defer expenditures, a resolution in either House of Congress could require the expenditure to be made. (Since the *Chadha* case in 1983, of which more later (see pp.103–4), a one-House veto on such a deferral is now unconstitutional.) In the latter cases, both Houses must agree a bill or a joint resolution within forty-five days of the President submitting his proposal to rescind funds. Without such congressional action, the programme must proceed. While the President now has legal authority to defer until such time as Congress acts, he can no longer terminate programmes, or parts of them, without the express approval of the legislature. Some balance has thereby been returned to the congressional– presidential relationship since the Nixon days. This was, perhaps, only a small victory for those concerned about the aggrandizement of the presidency, but the other part of the 1974 Act did offer greater opportunities to reclaim for Congress its constitutional power of the purse.

Over the years, particularly since the Budget and Accounting Act of 1921, which 'gave the President broad initiating powers in regard to the annual budget', presidential proposals 'have established the parameters within which Congress has exercised its most important prerogative — the power of the purse'.[29] Prior to 1921, practices were anarchic, with individual departments making their own bids to Congress for funds, and with no executive attempt to put together an ordered, federal budget. The Act, which created the Bureau of the Budget, provided the opportunity for order to be created out of the chaotic procedures — but only on the presidential side. It did not arm Congress with the appropriate machinery which would enable it to carry out its constitutional role. At no time before 1974 did Congress look at the budget as a whole or 'evaluate the relation between expenditures and total revenue'. Rather, a whole range of committees and sub-committees considered the authorizations and the necessary appropriations bills. 'Congress had no budget committees, skilled budget experts, or a comprehensive budget-making process to bring discipline to the process and to challenge the President's budget'.[30] The 1974 Act created separate budget committees in the House and the Senate, with the responsibility for establishing overall tax and spending levels. These budget

committees were given the 'power to direct other committees to
determine and recommend revenue and/or spending actions
deemed necessary to conform to the determinations made in the
budget resolution'.[31] A Congressional Budget Office was also
created by the Act to provide Congress with appropriate
information and analysis. Despite all this, however, Fisher argues
that 'the gap between promise and performance has been
awesome'.[32] The compartmentalism of Congress, its numerous
power centres (highlighted by the fact that the Health Services
Bill of 1979, for instance, was referred to nine standing committees
simultaneously), the absence of any strong leadership, the bi-
cameral system itself, all militate against the emergence of any
authority to rival the strength of the Office of Management and
Budget. In 1985, further steps were taken in the attempt to restore
the role of Congress. The Balanced Budget and Emergency Deficit
Control Act of that year (commonly known as the Gramm–
Rudman–Hollings Act after its sponsors), along with later
amendments, was aimed at requiring the President ultimately to
produce a balanced budget. Procedures were introduced which
were geared to progressive deficit reductions. Should the annual
maximum levels not be met, automatic spending cuts were to be
made by the Office of Management and Budget. Deficits can of
course be met by increased taxation, and as so much of the budget
(77.5 per cent in 1988) is made up of uncontrollables — among
them, payments to individuals, prior contracts and obligations
— which cannot easily be reduced, if only because of potential
for negative political spin-off, this may well be at least the short-
run answer to the Gramm–Rudman–Hollings requirements.
Indeed, in 1990 President Bush had to announce the
abandonment of his firm election pledge — 'Watch my lips: no
new taxes' — to comply with the law.

On the face of it, Gramm–Rudman–Hollings (GRH) had great
political merit, as it appeared to take hard choices over taxes and
spending out of the hands of the politicians, who have to answer
to electorates for their actions, and put them into the hands of
a semi-automatic mechanism to which little blame could be
attached. However, the law has been far from an unqualified
success. First, in 1986, in *Bowsher* v. *Synar* (478 US 714) the
Supreme Court declared that the role given to the Comptroller-
General — to review, reconcile as needed, and transmit to the

President the reductions proposed by the Office of Management and Budget (OMB) and the Congressional Budget Office (CBO) — was an intrusion by an officer of the Congress into the executive function. 'The Constitution', ruled Chief Justice Burger, 'does not permit such intrusion'. Then, the following year, a new law was passed which gave the OMB the responsibility of deciding if, and what, spending cuts might be needed, with the CBO merely playing an advisory role. More significantly, perhaps, for those who were concerned with attaining the balanced budget, the original targets were eased.

Since then, the exercise has attracted much criticism, even from one of its original sponsors. Thus, Senator Hollings in 1989 described its operations as a sham, while others have argued that it encourages bookkeeping chicanery to avoid cuts which might otherwise be required. According to Stephen Bell, former staff director of the Senate Budget Committee, 'it has taken most of the energy we should be devoting to important public policy issues and given it over to creating accounting gimmicks and highly technical silliness to get around the ... targets'.[33] The Budget Act and GRH have been described by Thurber as 'two of the most important structural and procedural budgetary reforms to be adopted by Congress in the last fifty years', although the *Congressional Quarterly* has suggested that the establishment of firm guidelines to which both institutions are required to adhere has led to a major erosion of both presidential and congressional authority over fiscal policy.[34] Thurber's further comments that 'the divisions over budget policy remain as entrenched as ever' and that 'Congress and the President will continue to muddle through (by bargaining and compromise over incremental funding changes',[35] were indicative of how little had been done prior to 1974 and of how little things had changed under the new arrangements.

The long-drawn-out negotiations between President and Congress in 1990 over the means whereby the deficit reduction targets might be met were a classic example of politicians seeking to avoid hard choices. Each side sought to evade the blame for necessary cuts in programmes or for increases in taxes just before the November elections. The goal appeared to be, in the words of Richard Darman, Director of OMB, a 'no fingerprints budget'. The autumn of that year saw an unedifying struggle in which a

Republican President sought to lay the blame for the impasse upon the Democratic House, even though the Democrats had been joined by Republicans disenchanted by the President's abandonment of campaign pledges, while from the other side, the Democratic leadership accused George Bush of acting like a party chairman and suggested it was time he started to act like a President. Political point-scoring rather than responsible policy making appeared to prevail at the expense of the country's urgent needs.

America, it must be recognized, still lacks a coherent process whereby major decisions regarding the economy can be reached by the country's representatives acting in a responsible manner. And until that sense of responsibility prevails, the introduction of other devices like Gramm–Rudman is likely to prove equally ineffective. If representative government is to work adequately, its representatives must also be prepared to accept a degree of responsibility, something which, on the recent evidence, members of Congress seem unwilling to do.

While as long ago as 1885 Woodrow Wilson was contending that 'quite as important as legislation is vigilant oversight of administration',[36] Congress, although possessed of the necessary apparatus, has generally failed to do an adequate job. The opportunities for oversight abound, arising from hearings, often protracted, on bills and authorizations, and from investigations by committees of one kind or another into specific problems or areas. A number of such investigations, famous or infamous, spring readily to mind: the work by the House Un-American Activities Committee, or by Senator Joseph McCarthy's Government Operations Permanent Investigations sub-committee, which both engaged in 'red-baiting' activity; Senator Harry Truman's investigations into the munitions industry during the Second World War; the Erwin Committee investigation of Watergate in 1973; the House Judiciary Committee work in relation to the possible impeachment of Richard Nixon in 1974; Select Committee investigations into abuses by the intelligence agencies in 1975–76; and, most recently, the congressional investigations into the Iran-Contra episode and the revelations of illegal activities. These all stand out as examples of what Congress is capable of, but they are not part of an on-going oversight. The general picture is one in which congressional activity has 'been sporadic and *ad hoc* rather than systematic and sustained. Congress succeeds in closing the door but only after the horse has gone'.

One power that did appear to give Congress a degree of control over presidential action was the legislative veto. While there are some instances of a legislative veto in nineteenth-century legislation, the device can really be dated from the 1930s and is a creature of the increased demands put upon government. As Mezey has put it, the legislative veto is 'a way to reconcile the need for executive discretion in administering the ever-increasing responsibilities of the federal government with the need to maintain some semblance of congressional control over the decisions'.[37] Basically, the legislative veto permitted Presidents, or the executive branch, to take specific decisions under a general grant of power, but with those decisions subject to possible congressional rejection in a number of ways: by an adverse vote in one or both of the Houses, or occasionally by action by a committee or by a committee chairman. Adoption of the practice was a tacit recognition that the legislative body was not in a position to deal with the vast range of detail associated with policy application. For those familiar with the British system of delegated legislation, where the executive branch, under the authority of an enabling Act, may issue subordinate legislation, subject to the approval (positive or passive) of the legislature, such an arrangement seems admirably suited to the demands of modern government. Many Presidents, and ultimately the Supreme Court, did not take that particular view. The attitude of the Presidents is a little hard to understand, unless one believes that they were concerned about the constitutional implications, for legislative veto clauses were only inserted into bills which extended the authority of the presidency. Congress was yielding up power while retaining the ultimate right to deny it, should it disagree with some executive decision, although the natural biases against action in the Congress meant that it was unlikely that executive action would be checked too often.

On one occasion when the House did overrule a decision by the Immigration and Naturalization Service, the device was challenged by the affected party and the Supreme Court ruled it unconstitutional.[38] In its decision, the Court declared that a one-House veto was unconstitutional because it violated the principle of bi-cameralism. It also stated that a two-House veto would be unconstitutional because that would violate the presentation clause of the constitution, which requires that legislation be presented to the President for his signature or veto. An interesting but puzzling aspect of the decision arises from the fact that the Justices struck down the veto aspect of the appropriate law, but left intact the allocation of authority to the President. As the legislation had intended a careful balance between legislative and executive interests, the judgement disturbed that balance. The legislative veto could be seen as a *quid pro quo* for the cession of authority, and Justice (now Chief Justice) Rehnquist argued that the whole section should be struck down, but his view did not prevail.

Such had been the spread of the legislative veto that Justice Byron White, dissenting from the majority decision, suggested that the *Chadha* case 'strikes down in one fell swoop provisions in more laws enacted by Congress than the Court has cumulatively invalidated in its entire history'. While some have argued that the denial of the right of the legislative veto has struck at one of the important weapons of congressional oversight, this interpretation does seem to ignore the basic context within which the veto developed. It grew as part of a congressional allocation (if not abdication) of power to the President, and was not an extension of congressional control over existing presidential authority. Consequently, the outlawing of the legislative veto was in reality a blow to the President rather than to Congress. However, Louis Fisher, with percipience, wrote that 'we should not be too surprised ... if, after the Court has closed the door to the legislative veto, we hear a number of windows being raised and perhaps new doors constructed, making the executive— legislative structure as accommodating as before for shared power',[39] and it does appear that since *Chadha* a number of quasi-legal devices have been developed which have had the same effect, and it may be, as Mezey writes, 'that *Chadha* may prove to be as effective in limiting legislative vetoes as the Eighteenth Amendment was in limiting the consumption of alcohol'.[40]

Burns has argued that the Washington power system 'is rooted in a structure of divided and competitive voting and interest-group constituencies that keep White House and Congress separated',[41] and our survey of relations between the two arms of government would seem to confirm this view. A President is usually accorded a brief honeymoon period in which his proposals to Congress may be received with some degree of favour, but, generally speaking, relations between the executive and the legislature are likely to be characterized by struggle, and the further into the presidency, and the closer to the next election, the more determined the Congress becomes. As the President enters office with only a modicum of experience for the roles he will have to play, but will acquire certain skills 'on the job', the 'irony is', to paraphrase Pfiffner, that 'the cycle of increasing competence is mirrored by a cycle of decreasing influence'.[42] It is more than a century since Woodrow Wilson complained that 'the federal government lacks strength because its powers are divided; lacks promptness because its authorities are multiplied; lacks wieldiness because its processes are roundabout; lacks efficiency because its responsibility is indistinct and its action without competent direction'.[43] Were he writing today, it is doubtful that his judgements would be modified to any significant degree, unless perhaps to suggest that matters are worse than in the nineteenth century.

Notes

1. Richard E. Neustadt, *Presidential Power* (New York: Wiley, 1980 edn), p.26.
2. *Constitution of the United States*, Article II, Section 3.
3. John P. Roche and Leonard Levy (eds), *The Presidency* (New York: Harcourt Brace & World, 1964), p.2.
4. Theodore Roosevelt, *An Autobiography* (New York: Macmillan, 1913), p.372.
5. William Howard Taft, *Our Chief Magistrate and His Powers*, (New York: Columbia University Press, 1916), p.138.
6. Ibid. p.157.
7. James P. Pfiffner, 'The President's Legislative Agenda', (Sage Publications, The Annals, American Academy of Political and Social Science (AAPSS), vol. 499, September, 1988), p.31.
8. Roche and Levy, op. cit. p.28.
9. Godfrey Hodgson, *All Things to All Men* (Harmondsworth: Penguin Books, 1984), p.116.
10. Michael Mezey, *Congress, The President and Public Policy* (Boulder, Colo.: Westview Press, 1989), p.90.
11. Barbara Hinckley, *Problems of the Presidency* (Glenview, Ill.: Scott, Foresman, 1985), p.156.

12. Ibid. pp.156–7.
13. Quoted in *How Congress Works* (Washington, DC: Congressional Quarterly Press, 1983), p.16.
14. James MacGregor Burns, *Deadlock of Democracy: Four Party Politics in America* (Englewood Cliffs, NJ: Prentice Hall, 1963).
15. Pfiffner, op. cit. p.23.
16. Paul Light, *The President's Agenda* (Baltimore: Johns Hopkins University Press, 1982). Quoted by Pfiffner, op. cit. pp.26–7.
17. Quoted by Mezey, op. cit. p.100.
18. Under the convention of senatorial courtesy, the Senate will not ratify presidential nominations if they are not acceptable to the Senators from the states in which the appointments are to be held. This undoubtedly puts considerable power over appointmemnts into the hands of the Senate.
19. Woodrow Wilson, *Congressional Government* (Boston: Houghton Mifflin, 1885), p.52.
20. *The Federalist* (London: Dent, Everyman's Library), no. LXXIII, pp. 373–8.
21. Both quoted in Louis Fisher, *Constitutional Conflicts Between Congress and the President* (Princeton: PUP, 1985), p.142.
22. Richard A. Watson, 'The President's Veto Power' (Sage Publications, The Annals, AAPSS, vol. 499, September 1988), p.42.
23. For a discussion of the case, see Fisher, op. cit. pp.151–2.
24. *Kennedy v. Sampson*, F. Supp. 1075, 1087 (DDC 1973) and *Kennedy v. Sampson* 511 F. 2d. 430, 437 (DC Circ.1974).
25. Louis Fisher, *Presidential Spending Power*, (Princeton: PUP, 1975), p.148.
26. Ibid. p.169.
27. Ibid. p.201. For the full discussion see Chapters 7 and 8, pp. 147–201.
28. Ibid. p.190.
29. Mezey, op. cit. p.64.
30. James A. Thurber, 'Consequences of Budget Reform for Congressional–Presidential Relations' (Sage Publications, Annals, AAPSS, vol. 499, September 1988), p.102.
31. Ibid. p.103.
32. Fisher, *Constitutional Conflicts*, op. cit. p.239.
33. Quoted in the *Congressional Quarterly*, 14 October 1989, p.2684.
34. *Congressional Quarterly* 7 January 1989, pp.3–15.
35. Thurber, op. cit. p.113.
36. Thurber, op. cit. p.290.
37. Mezey, op. cit. p.169.
38. *Immigration and Naturalization Service v. Chadha* (462 US 919, 1983).
39. *Constitutional Conflicts*, op. cit. p.183.
40. Mezey, op. cit. p.170.
41. James MacGregor Burns, *The Power to Lead* (New York: Simon & Schuster, 1984), p.193.
42. Pfiffner, op. cit. p.27.
43. *Congressional Government*. Quoted by Burns, *Power to Lead*, p.190.

The President and foreign affairs

The particular goals which a President is pursuing are often an important factor in determining his relations and success with the Congress. Thus, while the Founding Fathers did not spell out any special distinction between the domestic and the diplomatic fields, it has long been recognized that diplomacy, treaty making, defence matters, generally require a degree of speed and secrecy not commonly associated with large legislative bodies. Consequently, the practice has developed, in light of the responsibilities accorded by the Constitution or arrogated by the presidency, of usually according the President a freer hand in matters relating to diplomatic or foreign policy, or to the military, than in matters domestic. Such freedom has two major sources. In addition to the recognition that he is America's chief negotiator with the rest of the world and is Commander-in-Chief of the military establishment, there is the fact that foreign affairs do not usually loom large in electoral terms and that Congressmen are therefore more often concerned to concentrate their efforts on matters closer to home.

This apparent divergence between attitudes towards domestic and foreign policy led Aaron Wildavsky to declare, in a thought-provoking article in December 1966,[1] that 'the United States has one President, but it has two presidencies; one presidency is for domestic affairs, and the other is concerned with defence and foreign policy'. To buttress his argument, Wildavsky pointed to the fact that after 1938, Franklin Roosevelt failed to secure congressional approval for a single piece of significant domestic legislation; that, apart from his housing policy, Harry Truman lost most of his domestic programme; as Dwight Eisenhower did not attempt much his record does not add to the general picture, but John Kennedy, who had a far-reaching programme, had considerable problems with Congress. Nevertheless, all the Presidents were both very active and successful in getting support for their policies in the foreign field. This was the period when America joined the United Nations; when the North Atlantic Treaty Organisation was established; the Truman Doctrine, of advancing aid to nations that resisted communist aggression, was declared; the Marshall plan, to speed the recovery of Western European countries after the ravages of the war, was put into effect; the Vietnamese conflict began, and much more. Between 1948–1964 Congress approved 73.3 per cent of defence policy bills, 70.8 per cent of treaties, general foreign relations, State Department and foreign aid bills, and only 40.2 per cent of presidential domestic policy proposals. Wildavsky went on to assert that 'in the realm of foreign policy there has not been a single major issue on which Presidents, when they were serious and determined, have failed. . . . Serious setbacks to the President in controlling foreign policy are extraordinary and unusual.'

A decade after the Wildavsky thesis was first propounded, it no longer appeared quite as self-evident as it had in the 1960s. Reaction to the Vietnam War had led to much more questioning of presidential policies and objectives with regard to defence and foreign policy. The relative success rates of presidential initiatives in the domestic and foreign and defence fields were no longer so great. Barbara Hinckley cites figures for the 1965–1975 period which suggest a domestic policy success rate of 46 per cent (up from 40 per cent), and a defence policy success rate of only 61 per cent (down from 73 per cent).[2] Lee Sigelman's more sophisticated analysis of congressional voting patterns, also cited by Hinckley, which looked only at key votes, suggested that the divergence pointed to by Wildavsky did not really exist at all, and that consequently the two-presidencies thesis could not be sustained.

Reliance upon mere voting patterns in Congress to bolster or refute the argument is not, of course, sufficient. Many Presidents will act in ways that either do not need or that avoid congressional sanction. Others, bolstered by a Supreme Court decision, will acquire a *new* constitutional authority which increases their power to act. Others, through their actions, may leave Congress with little alternative but to support the chief executive. A mere examination of votes in the Congress perforce ignores all of these factors.

The Constitution certainly does not give the President untrammelled freedom in the field of foreign relations, for treaties with other countries require the approval of two-thirds of the Senate, while only the Congress may declare war or vote the funds which may be necessary to pursue a certain policy. Indeed, as Adler has written, in constitutional terms 'the President is vested with only modest authority in this realm and is clearly only of secondary importance'.[3] Throughout American history, however, these restrictions have not significantly deterred Presidents from pursuing their chosen goals. Indeed, from the very earliest days, they have sought to assert their powers *vis-à-vis* Congress.

George Washington, for example, refusing to send to the House of Representatives documents relating to the Jay Treaty, made the first claim of what has come to be known as 'executive privilege' (a term first used in 1958). There is 'not a single utterance in the Constitution nor in the Federalist which remotely suggests that the executive was or should be empowered to withhold information from Congress',[4] and yet it quickly became accepted that the President should be entitled so to do. This apparent right was spelt out by Deputy Attorney-General William Rogers in 1971 when he claimed that the President had 'uncontrolled discretion' to withhold information. Assistant Attorney-General (now Chief Justice) William Rehnquist argued that the power was not unbridled, but then went on to indicate that he believed any restrictions on its use came from the exercise of the President's own judgement — hardly a check in which Berger, among others, placed much confidence.[5]

Washington further extended presidential authority in foreign affairs when, in 1793 while Congress was in recess, he issued a Proclamation (commonly known as the Proclamation of Neutrality) which kept the United States from allying with France in the war against Great Britain. While his cabinet gave him unanimous support in this matter, there were those, the principal spokesman of whom was James Madison, who opposed this unilateral exercise of power. In another 'pamphlet controversy', of which eighteenth-century Americans appeared fond, Madison, as Helvidius, now opposing his fellow Federalist Hamilton from the Publius days, argued that the President was but a partner with the Congress in foreign affairs and that in matters of diplomacy and the use of the military the chief executive could not act alone. The President's view prevailed.

Early in his presidency, Washington did appear to accept the notion that treaty making was a function of both Senate and President working together and 'believed oral communications with the Senate indispensable'. Consequently, he met with the Senate 'to advise with them the terms of a treaty to be negotiated with the Southern Indians'. However, the meetings did not go well and it was reported that the President was 'in a violent fret' at the manner in which the Senate proceeded and 'he never again personally consulted with the Senate about tactics',[6] thereby 'restricting it to consent and very little advice'.[7] The pattern and the precedents were set for future Presidents to follow, although as American history demonstrates, presidential self-aggrandizement has not been accompanied by an automatic congressional abdication.

The fact that most Presidents have been successful in having their treaties ratified does not mean that the Senate has not taken its responsibilities seriously in this area. It has often subjected treaties to lengthy investigation, and while many Presidents may not involve the Senate directly in the negotiating processes they may often, in fact, maintain close links with influential Senators and members of the Senate Foreign Relations Committee in an effort to forestall possible opposition when the time for ratification arrives. A classic example of the dangers involved in ignoring the Senate can be found after the end of the First World War when President Wilson failed to secure ratification of the Treaty of Versailles which would have taken America into the League of Nations. Having negotiated the treaty without reference to Senate leaders, and having refused to compromise on its terms, the President was defeated. With regard to this last point about compromise, it must be recognized that the presidential success rate is also kept high by the fact that many Presidents will accept amendments to their treaties in order to meet Senate objections, as did President Carter with the two treaties under which the

United States agreed to return the Panama Canal to Panama. The President may be compelled to accept such amendments or lose the treaty. Finally, even if a President gets a treaty ratified in the form he prefers, the ratification may only come after a debate in the Senate that may be couched in chauvinistic or even xenophobic terms — which can do much to undermine the gentle diplomacy that may have gone into the treaty making in the first place.

With all these possibilities, it is hardly surprising that Presidents have on many occasions sought to avoid the need for senatorial concurrence in their diplomatic efforts through the use of what are known as 'executive agreements'. Such agreements can be traced back to the early nineteenth century. While many were concerned with mere technical details, Schlesinger suggests that 'as early as 1817, the executive agreement became an instrument of major foreign policy when Monroe arranged with Great Britain for the limitation of naval forces on the Great Lakes'.[8] Gradually the number of such agreements came to exceed the number of formal treaties sent to the Senate for ratification — in 1976 the United States made 402 executive agreements and only 13 treaties — and the importance of their subject matter also increased. For instance, before America entered the Second World War, the British Prime Minister, Winston Churchill, had sought assistance from the United States in the form of ships. President Roosevelt, recognizing that he would probably not get congressional approval for such a move from a basically isolationist Congress, simply made an agreement with Britain. A few years later he made agreements with the Russians and the British at Yalta which were to have long-term consequences for the future of Europe. All this without recourse to the cumbersome treaty-making provisions.

Interestingly, bearing in mind that the use of the agreements was an obvious ploy to avoid the constitutional restrictions and to place the President firmly in centre stage with regard to foreign affairs, the Supreme Court did not give such action its imprimatur until the 1930s. The importance of the case does, I believe, warrant the fairly lengthy extract which follows. In the case of *US* v. *Curtiss-Wright Corporation et al.*,[9] Justice Sutherland, speaking for the whole Court, apart from Justice McReynolds, declared that:

the federal power over external affairs [is] in origin and essential character different from that over internal affairs, but participation in the exercise of the power is significantly limited. ... [T]he President alone has the power to speak or listen as a representative of the nation. ... [He] alone negotiates.

Sutherland went on to assert that:

we are here dealing not alone with an authority vested in the President by an exertion of legislative power, but with such an authority plus the very delicate, plenary and exclusive power of the President as the sole organ of the federal government in the field of international relations — *a power which does not require as a basis for its exercise an act of Congress.* ... It is quite apparent that if, in the maintenance of our international relations, embarrassment — perhaps serious embarrassment — is to be avoided ... congressional legislation ... must often accord to the President a degree of discretion and freedom from statutory restriction which would not be admissible were domestic affairs alone involved.[10]

The following year, in *United States* v. *Belmont*,[11] Sutherland again speaking for the Court argued that international compacts did not always have to be treaties which required senatorial concurrence: 'There are many such compacts, of which a protocol, a *modus vivendi*, a postal convention, and agreements like that now under consideration are illustrations'. Presidential discretion in this area then appears unfettered, if unspecified; for, as Professor Henkin put it: 'There are agreements which the President can make on his sole authority and others which he can make only with the consent of the Senate, but neither Justice Sutherland nor any one else has told us which are which'.[12] The Court, it would seem from these, and later judgments, had become, as we suggest in the chapter on the judiciary, 'an arm of the executive branch'.

While many executive agreements have actually been made under the authority of congressional statute, others, some of considerable significance, have not had such congressional authority, a matter of concern to some Congressmen. Stephens and Rathjen captured that worry nicely when they quoted Senator Fulbright to the effect that:

while the Senate was being convened to approve by a two-thirds vote a treaty to preserve cultural artifacts in a friendly neighbouring country, the President was moving American men and material 'around the globe like so many pawns in a chess game and doing so without express congressional authorization'.[13]

Congress has sought at times to impose some limitations upon presidential discretion in the whole field of making treaties and agreements. The most publicized attempt came in 1954 in the form of the 'Bricker' amendment to the Constitution. This proposal, made by a group of neo-isolationists, was aimed at restricting the power of the President to make treaties and agreements which might limit American sovereignty. The proposal failed to get the necessary two-thirds vote in the Senate, while a watered-down version, having received the necessary votes when first put to the Senate, failed by one vote to get the necessary support for it to be sent to the states for their consideration. Then, in 1972 the Case Act was passed which required the publication of 'all international agreements other than treaties to which the United States is a party' and 'transmittal of all executive agreements to Congress'.[14] The requirement of such publication has done little to curb determined chief executives for Congress has no power to veto such agreements. Presidents may, rather, be checked if the agreements into which they enter require subsequent congressional action, for in such cases the legislative body may refuse to support presidential objectives, or may only support them in return for concessions on other matters. Once again, then, the bartering principle which enters into so much of the American political process may be in evidence.

While the Constitution is quite explicit about the processes involved in the making of formal treaties, it makes no mention of the processes whereby treaties may be terminated: is this a function of those who adopted the treaty — the President and two-thirds of the Senate — or is it a power resting with the President alone? In 1979 President Carter asserted the right of the President alone to wield the power when, after giving full recognition to the People's Republic of China, he announced that he was terminating America's Mutual Defence Treaty with the Republic of China (Taiwan). Senator Goldwater and others challenged this action in the courts, and the case eventually reached the Supreme Court. Four of the Justices ruled that the case was 'political' and 'non-justiciable' because it involved 'the authority of the President in the conduct of our country's foreign relations and the extent to which the Senate or Congress is authorized to negate the action of the President'. Justice Powell concurred with the rejection of the case but did not accept the ground of 'political' question. He argued, rather, that:

> if the Congress, by appropriate formal action, had challenged the President's authority to terminate the treaty with Taiwan, the resulting uncertainty could have serious consequences for our country. In that situation, it would be the duty of this Court to resolve the issue.

Justice Brennan argued that 'our cases firmly establish that the Constitution commits to the President alone the power to recognize, and withdraw recognition from foreign regimes'.[15] The case probably establishes for the future that Presidents have a free hand in this area, even though it was basically decided on the shaky grounds that the Courts had no authority to act. But in David Adler's opinion, the Court, by adopting this approach, had abdicated its duty, ignoring a Court pronouncement of ten years earlier 'that its principal duty was to decide "whether the action of [another] branch exceeds whatever authority has been committed"'.[16] As he went on to point out, Justice Powell had reminded the other Justices that in the past the Court had been willing to determine 'whether one branch of our government has impinged upon the power of another'. And yet Powell was himself ready to avoid the issue, for as he also stated: 'if the Congress chooses not to confront the President, it is not our task to do so'.[17] Such an attitude is, of course, quite frightening in its implications for, were it to secure widespread acceptance, it conjures up the possibility of a dominant President, faced by a supine Congress, able to ride roughshod over the Constitution, with the Supreme Court unwilling to pronounce upon his actions; surely not what most envision as the appropriate role for the Court.

The development of presidential power and authority in the field of treaty making and relations with other countries is a prime example of how a constitution can change, and how limitations upon the exercise of power can be circumvented without formal constitutional amendment or even congressional cession of power. And yet, for some, this growth in the diplomatic field is overshadowed by what they see as a far more undesirable development — the aggrandizement of presidential power in relation to the use of military force.

The Constitution ordained that: 'The President shall be

Commander in Chief of the Army and Navy of the United States, and of the Militia of the several States, when called into the actual service of the United States'. It left unspecified the manner in which the President was to command but, rather, in giving to the Congress the power to declare war or to call the States' militia into the service of the nation, appeared to be limiting severely his ability to engage the country in hostilities or to establish a dictatorship based on control of the military. In practice, the constitutional limitations have not proven to be a significant check upon presidential policy, and since the very earliest days of the Republic, Presidents have been ready to engage in what was effectively war with other countries without benefit of any formal declaration of war.

A few examples, from the more than one hundred instances that have been recorded, will serve to demonstrate presidential freedom to act in this area. In 1793 there were naval hostilities with France, while in 1804 there was an expedition against the Barbary pirates. In 1846 Polk sent troops into Mexico, thereby inviting war, and occasioning action by Congress. Theodore Roosevelt intervened in Panama in 1903 and in Santo Domingo in 1904. Nicaragua has been the object of such attention on numerous occasions — 1895, 1910, 1912, 1926, the 1980s. After the Russian Revolution, there was the 1919 involvement in Archangel and Siberia. More recently, the war in Korea did not follow a declaration by Congress, neither did the protracted conflict in Vietnam. President Eisenhower sent troops into the Lebanon in 1958 in order, he claimed, to protect American lives. His successor, President Kennedy, authorized the Bay of Pigs attack on Cuba in 1961, and the following year engaged in a blockade of Cuba, in a confrontation with the USSR which might have resulted in a nuclear conflict. Apart from his escalation of American involvement in Vietnam, President Johnson sent troops into the Dominican Republic in 1965 to avert a feared communist takeover. President Nixon, while winding down the American commitment in Vietnam, invaded Cambodia. President Reagan, as we discuss later, gave support to the anti-government forces in Nicaragua. Congress has, in fact, declared war on only five occasions — the War of 1812, the War with Mexico in 1846, the Spanish–American War in 1898, and the two World Wars of the twentieth century. Of particular interest perhaps is the fact, as

Louis Fisher reminds us, that 'in only one [instance] (the War of 1812) did members of Congress actually debate the merits of entering into hostilities. In all the other cases members simply acknowledged that a state of war did in fact exist'.[18]

While the executive does appear to have pre-empted the constitutional authority of Congress in this particular area, Presidents have from time to time called for a statement of congressional support for their actions which fell short of the formal declaration of war. Thus, in 1955, President Eisenhower sought congressional authorization for action to defend the Pescadores Islands and Formosa on the grounds that a 'congressional resolution would clearly and publicly establish the authority of the President as Commander in Chief to employ the Armed Forces of this Nation promptly and effectively for the purposes indicated if in his judgment it became necessary'.[19] Such a resolution was necessary in Eisenhower's eyes not for authority (which he believed he already had) but for political and public support. It was more in the way of a public relations exercise than a constitutional requirement. The Middle East Resolution of 1957 was of much the same order.

The most famous, or infamous, of these congressional statements of support for the President, and worthy therefore of a more detailed consideration, came in the Gulf of Tonkin Resolution of 1964 which Under-Secretary of State Katzenbach was to describe as the 'functional equivalent' of a declaration of war.[20] America's involvement in Vietnam dated back to the 1950s when, having failed to support the old-style colonial power, France, it poured money and arms into South Vietnam, bolstering a corrupt and ruthless regime supposedly aginst commmunist insurgents within the South and a potentially predatory regime in the North. President Kennedy increased the aid, and the number of American 'advisers' in the country grew, but the situation, so far as American policy was concerned (an unthinking anti-communism), deteriorated. Advisers stopped being 'advisers' and became troops, and yet still the South Vietnamese government and army proved incapable of handling the situation. Hard-line anti-communists within the United States started to call for tougher action in South-East Asia and President Johnson, seeking to avoid the politically damaging description of being 'soft' on communism, took the steps which would launch America into a full-blown conflict, which would last nearly another decade, involve half a million American troops (many thousands of them killed or injured), and end in ignominious withdrawal.

The Gulf of Tonkin Resolution was sent to Congress following the claim by President Johnson that two American destroyers had twice been attacked in international waters by North Vietnamese gunboats. The President wanted from Congress an assertion that it was determined 'to take all necessary measures in support of freedom and in defense of peace in Southeast Asia'. The Resolution, which passed unanimously in the House and with only two dissentients in the Senate,[21] had the stated intention 'to promote the maintenance of international peace and security in Southeast Asia'. Repeating the allegation that 'naval units of the Communist regime in Vietnam ... have deliberately and repeatedly attacked United States naval vessels lawfully present in international waters' as 'part of a deliberate and systematic campaign of aggression', the Resolution went on to state that 'the Congress approves and supports the determination of the President, as Commander in Chief, to take all necessary measures to repel any armed attack against the forces of the United States and to prevent further aggression'.

The Resolution thus gave congressional support to a presidential war. As Katzenbach has said: 'What could a declaration of war have done that would have given the President more authority and a clearer voice of the Congress of the United States?'[22] Perhaps, in the modern era, that is as much as can be expected. But the whole Gulf of Tonkin incident and the war itself do demonstrate the power in the hands of the executive to do as it wishes. This is particularly highlighted by the subsequent revelations that the claims made by President Johnson concerning the attacks on the two destroyers were far from accurate: the ships were probably spying in Vietnamese waters, suffered no damage or loss of personnel, and the captains of the vessels could not confirm that a second attack even took place. When placed alongside the fact that the Resolution had been prepared some months before the alleged incidents, it does appear that the President was determined that the United States would be involved militarily in Southeast Asia and that Congress was duped into supporting what was to be America's most bloody and costly war.

However, the disastrous course of the war and the divisions

which appeared in Congress and throughout the United States, with draftees burning their draft cards, fleeing the country or facing imprisonment, gradually had their effects upon the presidency. In 1968, after repeated attacks on his Vietnam policy, and after a disappointing performance in the New Hampshire primary, President Johnson felt compelled to withdraw from the re-election campaign. Then, in 1971 Congress demonstrated its growing concern over the situation by twice adding riders to larger bills in which they stated that American fighting should end 'at the earliest practicable date', that a date should be set for withdrawal, and asserted that this was the 'policy of the United States'. President Nixon, for his part, indicated that he did not accept this limitation upon his prerogatives. At the signing ceremony he declared:

> I wish to emphasize that [the rider] ... does not represent the policies of this administration. ... It is without binding force or effect and it does not reflect my judgment about the way in which the war should be brought to a conclusion. My signing of the bill that contains this section, therefore, will not change the policies I have pursued and that I shall continue to pursue towards this end.[23]

The same year Congress did go on to repeal the Gulf of Tonkin Resolution, although this did not seriously impede President Nixon who was content to use his authority as Commander in Chief.

In 1973, with the war finally over, Congress took action to try to put some curbs upon a President's war-making powers with the passage of the War Powers Resolution which survived a presidential veto:

> The constitutional powers of the President as Commander in Chief to introduce United States Armed Forces into hostilities, or into situations where imminent involvement in hostilities is clearly indicated ... are exercised only pursuant to (1) a declaration of war, (2) specific statutory authorization, or (3) a national emergency created by attack upon the United States, its territories or possessions, or its armed forces.
> The President in every possible instance shall consult with Congress before introducing United States Armed Forces into hostilities [etc] ... and after every such introduction shall consult regularly with the Congress of the United States until United States Forces are no longer engaged in hostilities or have been removed.
> ...

The President shall submit within 48 hours ... a report [to Congress]. ...

Within sixty calendar days ... the President shall terminate any use of United States Armed Forces ... unless the Congress (1) has declared war or has enacted a specific authorization for such use of United States Armed Forces, (2) has extended by law such sixty-day period, or (3) is physically unable to meet as a result of armed attack upon the United States. Such sixty-day period shall be extended for not more than an additional thirty days if the President determines and certifies to the Congress in writing that unavoidable military necessity respecting the safety of the United States Armed Forces requires the continued use of such armed forces in the course of bringing about a removal of such forces. At any time that United States Armed Forces are engaged in hostilities outside the territory of the United States, its possessions and territories without a declaration of war or specific statutory authorization, such forces shall be removed by the President if the Congress so directs by concurrent resolution. ...

Nothing in this joint resolution (1) is intended to alter the constitutional authority of the Congress or the President ... or (2) shall be construed as granting any authority to the President ... which ... he would not have had in the absence of this joint resolution.[24]

President Nixon argued in his veto message that the Resolution would 'undermine the nation's ability to act decisively and convincingly in time of international crisis ... [and] would give every future Congress the ability to handcuff every future President' but some critics have disagreed with this sentiment. Indeed, they have argued that, far from limiting a President, the Joint Resolution broadens presidential power by putting a 'sixty-to ninety-day congressional "stamp of approval" on presidential actions',[25] and in effect gives the President ninety days for unilateral war making. Furthermore, it may be noted, an astute President, determined to get his own way, could so embroil his troops within that period that Congress would be compelled to accept the situation and accede to the President's wishes. Even the requirements for Presidents to consult with, and report to, Congress are, as Fisher points out, ambiguous, leaving considerable discretion to the President.

Since the passage of the Joint Resolution, Presidents have engaged in a number of actions apparently unencumbered by its provisions. The first of these occurred in 1975 and concerned the *Mayaguez*, an American merchant ship which was seized in (possibly) international waters by the Cambodians. President Ford immediately involved military forces in an attack to recover the ship. The Marines were sent in, air strikes were launched against Cambodia, and Cambodian ships were sunk. All of this without any advance consultation with Congress. It was only sometime later that full report was made to Congress — hardly in keeping with the letter of the Resolution — and yet congressional response was largely one of support for a President who had acted in such a resolute fashion. (Some attitudes changed later as detailed reports of the action became available: the deaths, the over-reaction to what was essentially a very minor incident, took the gloss from the President's determination to 'wave the big stick' in the shadow of the Vietnam defeat.)

In 1980, President Carter authorized a military operation in an endeavour to rescue the American hostages in Iran who had been seized by militant Iranians in November 1979. A long period of diplomatic effort preceded the military action, but when the decision was reached to send in troops, Congress was not consulted. The rescue mission failed, and in its aftermath many prominent Congressmen complained about the President's failure to consult them, some arguing that the attempt violated the War Powers Resolution. But here the ambiguity of the Resolution was again demonstrated, for Senator Alan Cranston argued that it 'applied to military actions, and that "this was viewed as a rescue mission, not a military action"'.[26] And yet, of course, it could be argued that putting troops into such a situation could well have precipitated the hostilities with which Congress was concerned when it passed the Resolution.

In 1982, President Reagan sent troops into Lebanon as part of an international peacekeeping force, without informing Congress. While there, the Marines suffered casualties which led to Congress in 1983 passing a Joint Resolution invoking the War Powers Resolution and authorizing their stay for another eighteen months. Some have seen President Reagan's signing of the Resolution as implicit acceptance of the War Powers Resolution, but he himself indicated that if he felt it necessary the troops would stay longer than the eighteen months. Certainly, other actions during his presidency seemed to suggest that he did not feel bound by Congress. Thus in 1983 he authorized the invasion of Grenada when a Marxist regime took over the government of that small Caribbean island, again without reporting to Congress.

The action, which proved popular with the electorate at large, upset some Congressmen who argued that the President had usurped the right of Congress to declare war, and eleven of them brought a case against President Reagan. The court took the stand, as it has generally done with regard to the field of foreign relations, that this was a 'political' rather than a 'judicial' matter and therefore beyond the competence of the courts.[27] Other examples of presidential circumvention of the spirit and the letter of the War Powers Resolution could be cited, but these will suffice to capture the flavour of the relations between the two branches of government in this area. Senator Eagleton expressed the mood of many of his colleagues when he proclaimed that 'the War Powers Act is like what John Garner [Franklin Roosevelt's first Vice-President] said of the Vice-Presidency: "It ain't worth a pitcher of warm spit"'.[28]

Of course, Congress is not limited in its attempts to curb 'imperial' Presidents to Resolutions which a President may choose to ignore. It does have to hand a weapon which can play a decisive part in determining the boundaries of presidential discretion — the power of the purse. Presidents may command the armed forces, may have the treaty-making power, may enter into executive agreements, but to the extent that the forces, the treaties and the agreements require appropriations, they are, in part at least, at the mercy of the Congress with its power to approve or deny the necessary finances. Co-operation with Congress is, then, an essential ingredient in much of a President's manouevres in pursuit of his foreign goals.

On occasions, Presidents may present Congress with a *fait accompli*. There is, for example, the instance of Theodore Roosevelt wishing to send the Navy on a goodwill tour around the world and being denied the necessary funds by Congress. His response was that he had enough money to send it to the Pacific: 'if Congress did not choose to appropriate enough money to get the fleet back ... it could stay in the Pacific'.[29] The money was found. In more serious vein, presidential deployment of troops may often produce appropriations by a Congress not willing to withdraw support from forces in a combat situation. For this reason, American involvement in Vietnam was sustained for some time after the wisdom and morality of the conflict had come under serious scrutiny. In 1973, however, Congress did flex its financial muscles when it forbade the use of funds to support President Nixon's combat activities in Laos and Cambodia. Nixon vetoed the bill and Congress failed to override the veto. Ultimately a compromise was reached which, while giving the President another forty-five days in which to bomb Cambodia, did in effect signal success for Congress in ending American military involvement in Southeast Asia through the power of appropriations.[30]

While such a success should not necessarily be taken as a sign of Congress resurgent, the long conflict in Vietnam, in which America had become involved with no apparent grand design in mind, had created the circumstances in which Congressmen were not prepared to accept the possibility of continued drift into further fighting in another country in the region. Accordingly, in the 1980s Congress did react against presidential policy in Central America. It sought, for instance, to make appropriations for continued aid to El Salvador conditional upon the government of that country making progress in the field of human rights. It was, however, Nicaragua that occasioned most concern. The Sandinista government, Marxist in orientation, attracted the anathema of the President who was intent upon supplying aid, both civil and military, to the Contra rebels who were fighting the government forces. Many in Congress, and among the public at large, feared that the situation could escalate into another Vietnam-style conflict. Congress therefore cut off military funding for the Contras and forbade the President to continue such aid.

The congressional injunction against supplying aid to the Contras was, in part at least, circumvented by the Reagan White House in what has been called the Iran–Contra (or Irangate) affair. President Reagan, while exhorting America's allies not to trade with Iran, authorized the secret sale of arms to that country in the hope of securing the release of American hostages. It was revealed, however, that some of the proceeds from that sale were diverted to assist the Contras. When Congress began its investigations into the matter, two of the President's National Security staff excused their actions on the grounds of the Curtiss–Wright decision that the President is the 'sole organ' in foreign affairs. Admiral Poindexter, National Security Adviser and Colonel North, a National Security Council aide, claimed that they could ignore laws passed by Congress, and that the President and his aides could operate abroad without answering to the Congress. Poindexter even argued that congressional power over appropriations should not extend to restricting what the President could do in the field of foreign affairs. Such an extreme interpretation of presidential authority was not acceptable to most Congressmen.

The President himself, rather than taking refuge in such claims, chose instead to deny any knowledge of this diversion and, indeed, when called upon to give evidence in the trial of Admiral Poindexter, on charges of destroying documents and lying to Congress, demonstrated a considerable (and convenient?) degree of amnesia. The President could not, apparently, remember, among others, the name of his former Chairman of the Joint Chiefs of Staff. Blame, instead, was left to fall on some of his National Security staff: Oliver North, Robert McFarlane, Poindexter's predecessor as National Security Adviser, and Admiral Poindexter himself, were all found guilty of various illegal activities concerning the affair.[31]

Apart from the fact that a number of the President's closest advisers were found guilty of criminal acts (verdicts which may in fact be overturned on appeal), and the President's reputation was put under a cloud, Irangate did occasion a slight, and perhaps temporary, shift in the congressional/presidential balance in foreign affairs. When the 1987 Central American peace talks were held, one of the principal players was the Speaker of the House of Representatives — certainly a change from the days when Congress was simply presented with a *fait accompli* worked out by the President and his aides, with little or no input from the legislature.

Investigations into the conflict in Vietnam, and the more recent Iran–Contra revelations, demonstrated the relative ease with which Presidents or their agents are able to pursue policy abroad which may not have congressional approval or which may even run counter to congressional injunction. Quite obviously there will at times be a need for some secrecy or dispatch in the dealings that Presidents have with foreign powers. The negotiations associated with treaties or executive agreements, for instance, are often best conducted out of the political limelight, while the speed which Presidents may feel is necessary in some military matters is likely to militate against any serious consultation with Congress before action is taken. Thus, when President Bush (albeit in conjunction with a United Nations' resolution) ordered the massive build up of American forces in the Middle East in the summer of 1990 in response to Iraq's invasion of Kuwait, he did so without recourse to Congress which had adjourned for the summer, and was not recalled for its opinion to be given. Nevertheless, this action once more raised that important constitutional question: who may commit American troops to what is in fact a war? The Secretary of Defense, Dick Cheney, argued that, as Commander-in-Chief, the President had all the authority he needed and did not require any additional authorization. Congressional Democrats on the other hand, supported by a number of eminent constitutional lawyers, asserted the President could not initiate any offensive without congressional approval unless American lives were in danger. After considerable lobbying by the White House, the Congress did ultimately adopt resolutions which authorized military action by the President against Iraq, if he first reported to Congress that the United Nations sanctions, aimed at persuading Iraq to withdraw from Kuwait, were not working.

While the President was in the event given support by Congress, many remain worried that the general picture is still one of arrogance on the part of the White House and its staff. Indeed, they are left pondering what steps the President would have taken in face of a negative vote by Congress. In light of the claims to an unfettered presidency, as made, for instance, by Poindexter, or of the assertion by Cheney, it would appear that while congressional approval may be seen as a message to the world that the government is united, it is not seen by the presidency as a *sine qua non* of action. Certainly, it now seems likely that if there is any future declaration of war by Congress it will be inspired by an already-existing state of hostilities rather than as a precursor to such events. Congress may ultimately rebel and force a President to withdraw the armed forces or to sign a treaty, but the initiative and responsibility for military action are even more firmly in the hands of the President than they were when President Polk in the 1840s managed to create the situation which forced the hand of Congress into declaring war upon Mexico.

The aggrandizement of presidential power in the field of foreign relations over the last two hundred years has been a natural, and some would argue necessary, development. The balanced system that the Founding Fathers instituted was probably doomed from the start, for the initiatives which a President possessed gave him the ability to establish the parameters for both debate and action, either through the treaties or agreements he negotiated, or through the situations into which he sent the troops he commanded. The development has not been smooth, but in spite of the hiccoughs of occasional congressional reassertiveness it would appear to be irreversible. Many are indeed prepared to argue that the more recent attempts to curb presidential activity in foreign matters are undesirable, if not unconstitutional. Others, however, have suggested that the stakes involved in military confrontation — even one which does not involve thermonuclear weapons — are so great that the *de jure* constitutional separation of the Commander-in-Chief from the power to declare war should be augmented to prevent the *de facto* waging of war. This, of course, the War Powers Resolution sought to achieve, but, as we have seen, it would appear to be a weak reed in curbing determined Presidents.

Presidents may often be constrained by political considerations, by the need to have funds appropriated or treaties ratified, but ultimately they alone stand as the nation's symbol abroad, its spokesman and its defender. In such a role, astute Presidents may make appeals for support which transcend partisan politics and which encourage politicians, who are generally more concerned with matters domestic rather than foreign, to rally around the flag. While Congress may from time to time rebel and deny a President what he seeks, the more common picture will be one in which he continues to set the agenda which will establish the nature and scope of American foreign and military policy. The President may not be an emperor: he is surely more than a constitutional monarch.

Notes

1. *Transaction* 4, no. 2.
2. Barbara Hinckley, *Problems of the Presidency* (Glenview, Ill.: Scott, Foresman, 1985), pp.159–60.
3. David Gray Adler, 'Foreign Policy and the Separation of Powers',

in Michael W. McCann and Gerald L. Houseman (eds), *Judging the Constitution* (Glenview, Ill.: Scott, Foresman, 1989), p.154.

4. Raoul Berger, *Executive Privilege: A Constitutional Myth* (Cambridge, Mass.: Harvard University Press, 1974), p.13.

5. Berger, op. cit. pp.2 and 8. In concluding his very thorough study of the history of executive privilege, his views on which are captured in the title of his work, Berger asks the question, 'are the occasional excesses of congressional investigations ... as damaging to the nation as the evils which have flowed from unrestricted secrecy?' (p.346). He quite obviously thinks not.

6. Ralston Hayden, *The Senate and Treaties: 1789–1817* (New York: Macmillan, 1920), pp.21–6.

7. Harry A. Bailey Jr and Jay M. Shafritz (eds), *The American Presidency* (Chicago, Ill.: The Dorsey Press, 1988), p.229.

8. Arthur M. Schlesinger Jr, *The Imperial Presidency* (New York: Popular Library Edition, 1974), p.93.

9. 299 US 304 (1936).

10. My emphasis.

11. 301 US 324 (1937). Concerned with agreements following America's recognition of the USSR in 1933.

12. Quoted by Schlesinger, *The Imperial Presidency*, p.111.

13. O.Stephens and G.J.Rathjen, *The Supreme Court and the Allocation of Constitutional Power* (San Francisco: Freeman, 1980), p.315.

14. See Louis Koenig, *The Chief Executive*, 5th edn (San Diego: Harcourt Brace Jovanovich, 1986), p.206.

15. See *Goldwater et al v. Carter*, 444 US 996 (1979).

16. David Gray Adler, 'Foreign Policy and the Separation of Powers' in *Judging the Constitution*, edited by Michael W. McCann and Gerald L. Houseman (Glenview, Ill.: Scott, Foresman, 1989), p.171.

17. Ibid. p.174.

18. Louis Fisher, *Constitutional Conflicts Between Congress and the President* (Princeton: Princeton University Press, 1985), p.287.

19. Quoted in Committee on Foreign Relations, US Senate Report, 'National Commitments Report', 90th Congress, 1st Session (Washington: US Government Printing Office, 20 November 1967). Quoted by Duane Lockard, *The Perverted Priorities of American Politics*, (New York: Macmillan, 1971), p.263.

20. Lockard, *Perverted Priorities*, p.264.

21. Senators Morse and Gruening, to their credit. Both were defeated in the 1968 election. We should note that only 416 of the 435 membership voted in the House and only 90 of the 100 Senators in the Senate.

22. Quoted in Lockard, op. cit.

23. See Robert J. Sickels, *The Presidency* (Englewood Cliffs, NJ: Prentice Hall, 1980), p.126.

24. 87 Stat. 555 (1973).

25. Louis Fisher, *Constitutional Conflicts between Congress and the President* (Princeton: PUP, 1985), p.312.
26. Quoted by Koenig, op. cit. p.382.
27. *Conyers v. Reagan*, 578 F.Supp.324 (DDC 1984). See Fisher, op. cit. pp.318–23.
28. Senator Thomas Eagleton, *The Virginia Papers on the Presidency*, edited by Kenneth Thompson (Lanham, Md: University Press of America, 1986–7), vol.XXIII, p.47. It should be recorded that for the sake of propriety reporters made a slight change in the spelling of the substance to which Garner was referring.
29. *Theodore Roosevelt: An Autobiograhy* (New York, 1913), pp.552–3. Quoted by Schlesinger, op. cit. p.296.
30. See Fisher, op. cit. p.322.
31. During the course of the investigations into this rather sordid tale, one interesting similarity with a subsequent development in the United Kingdom can be found. At one stage, in the early revelations, the CIA, which had been involved in the transport of the arms to Iran, claimed that it had not realized it was shipping arms, that it had thought it was shipping oil drilling parts. Four years later, when British Customs officers seized what they claimed was the barrel of a huge gun destined for Iraq, the manufacturers asserted it was not a gun but merely a pipe for the Iraqi oil industry.

The President and Cabinet

When a man becomes President he becomes responsible for a vast bureaucratic empire of nearly three million persons employed in the thirteen executive departments of state, in bureaux established in the executive office of the President, and in more than fifty independent agencies, all with 'their own agendas set by laws that long predate the President's arrival in office'.[1] Something like 2,000 federal agencies, it has been estimated, have the power to make rules for the nation. The Federal Register, with its 60,000 plus pages listing all the regulations issued in a year, bears testimony to the considerable activity of those agencies. The President can hope to get to know but little of this empire during his term(s) in office, and yet he will need its co-operation if many of his plans are to reach fruition. It is an organization (if that is not too strong a word) of great complexity, with many overlapping jurisdictions and inter-agency rivalries, and within which there is 'a massive undertow ... that pulls ... toward continuity'.[2] The nature of the difficulties that these can occasion is nicely captured in a quotation used by Harold Seidman. He cites a memorandum from President Franklin Roosevelt:

> I agree with the Secretary of the Interior. Please have it carried out so that fur-bearing animals remain in the Department of the Interior. You might find out if any Alaska bears are still supervised by (a) War Department (b) Department of Agriculture (c) Department of Commerce. They have all had jurisdiction over Alaska bears in the past and many embarrassing situations have been created by the mating of a bear belonging to one Department with a bear belonging to another Department. F.D.R.
> P.S. I don't think the Navy is involved but it may be. Check the Coast Guard. You never can tell.'[3]

128

While reflecting FDR's sense of humour, this note does in fact highlight the consideration Presidents must give to the different components of the sprawling edifice which is the federal bureaucracy.

We have so far been talking of the President doing this, or seeking that, as though he were a monolith. This is quite obviously far from the truth. No President could possibly operate without aid and a modern-day President is surrounded by a veritable army of advisers and assistants, councils and agencies, that can provide him with the back-up services which *may* enable him to get his way with Congress or help him to secure the co-operation of a reluctant bureaucracy. Foremost among those agencies, in stature if not in influence, is the Cabinet. Comprising the heads of the great departments of state, plus any others to whom the President may accord Cabinet rank, the United States Cabinet might well appear a familiar institution to those acquainted with the British system of government. But, as we shall see, in saying so little, we have said almost all there is to say about the similarities between the two systems.

While the origins of the United States Cabinet can be traced to the earliest days of the Republic it is, in fact, unknown to the Constitution and, as Richard Fenno records in his excellent little book on the institution, its name did not even reach the statute books until 1907, although it had been used by Madison as early as 1793.[4] That it emerged when it did (George Washington called the first Cabinet meeting in 1791) is hardly to be wondered at when one bears in mind the circumstances of the time. Americans were accustomed to the old colonial governors having advisory councils, and at the constitutional convention many had sought to provide such a body to advise and perhaps to check the President. While that particular move failed, the Constitution did provide that the President might 'require the Opinion ... of the principal Officer in each of the executive Departments' and in Washington's eyes:

> the impossibility that one man should be able to perform all the great business of the state I take to have been the reason for instituting the great departments, and appointing officers therein to assist the supreme magistrate in discharging the duties of his trust.[5]

The terms of the Constitution did not require that presidential consultation with departmental heads should take place in collective fashion, but Washington's precedent soon established the practice as a recognized part of executive office processes.

This development does not alter the fact that 'the American Cabinet ... is ... an extralegal creation, functioning in the interstices of the law, surviving in accordance with tradition, and institutionalised by usage alone'.[6] Such extra-constitutional status has undoubtedly contributed to the very different methods of operating that may be perceived in the Cabinet over the years and in the range of influence that different members of the Cabinet have been able to wield.

Washington's first Cabinet met frequently, almost daily at times, and the President was at pains to take votes, a practice continued by Jefferson who wrote that in such votes 'the President counts himself but as one. So that in all important cases the executive is in fact a directory'.[7] This depreciation of the presidential role to that of merely a *primus inter pares*, a first among equals, did not last however, and indeed there would have been little justification for its continuance, for it is the President who holds the elective post, the members of the Cabinet are but his appointees. The oft-repeated and (probably) apocryphal story concerning President Lincoln captures the change in attitude and reflects the constitutional situation: after a vote in Cabinet which went against the President, 7 noes to 1 aye, the President's response was, 'the ayes have it'.

That first Cabinet also contained men of sharply different political persuasion — Alexander Hamilton as Secretary of the Treasury and Thomas Jefferson as Secretary of State (Foreign Secretary in British terms). The presence of these two men with such divergent views did not prove to be a happy experience. They had numerous confrontations in which Jefferson usually found himself a lone figure confronting the rest of the Cabinet, and before long he resigned. The experience of a Cabinet containing such divisions was enough to demonstrate to President Washington that he should be looking for Cabinet members whose views were in harmony with his own. The general tradition since those days has been for Presidents to appoint to their Cabinets members of their own political party: they have, on occasions, appointed members of the other party, but only when they have held congenial views so far as presidential goals were concerned.

In contrast with the British Cabinet, those who are invited to join an American Cabinet may not be active politicians, or even have had a political career at all. In Britain, membership of the Cabinet is seen as the pinnacle of a political career (apart from those few who deem themselves prime ministerial material) whereas in the United States such membership may be an interval in a career pursued elsewhere. There is no natural route or progression to a Cabinet post in the United States, no background or political activity which leads to an automatic consideration for such an appointment. Thus, Presidents have turned to presidents of large corporations, to lawyers, to academics, and sometimes to politicians to fill the Cabinet posts. Most Cabinets will have some 'politicians' within them but President Nixon's first Cabinet was unusual in that a majority had been governors of states in the past. Such is the field from which a President may draw his candidates that many may not even be personally known to him before he interviews them for the post. He may know them by reputation, from their writings, or from their place in the business community, or they may simply have been recommended by his close advisers. And if the appointees may not be well known to the President before appointment, they are even more likely to be unknown to the public at large. Whereas in the United Kingdom there is some conception of who might be appointed to a government post, few in the United States would presume to forecast the make-up of the American Cabinet. (On the other side of that coin, while the resignation or dismissal of a Cabinet member in Britain creates headlines in the media and may lead to speculation about the strength of the government, it is a rare occurrence for such an event in the United States to attract significant comment.)

The world, or at least the nation, would appear, then, to be the President's oyster when it comes to choosing Cabinet officers, but he is, in fact, subject to a number of constraints that limit his freedom of manoeuvre. Apart from the party or ideological compatibility mentioned above, certain other general expectations have developed. The Cabinet must now, in some sense, offer representation to the wide range of interests and sections in society, with particular posts going to people in some way connected with or familiar with the interests and concerns of the departments: thus, a westerner with farming interests to Agriculture; someone acceptable to the labour movement to

Labor. Sex and race are also factors which now enter into presidential calculations, with few Presidents ready to risk the wrath which would be heaped upon them if they failed to appoint a woman or a black. Furthermore, thought has to be given to some kind of geographic representation. Presidents cannot easily overlook the claims of any significant sector of the nation for a post. All seek some part of the Cabinet pie. A few examples from President Reagan's first Cabinet demonstrate the application of these principles. Thus, John Block, a farmer, was appointed to Agriculture; Terrell Bell, an education administrator to Education; Jeane Kirkpatrick (a right-wing Democrat) as Ambassador to the United Nations (a Cabinet post); Samuel Pierce, a black lawyer, to Housing and Urban Development.

Constraints upon Presidents in their Cabinet-forming role are not limited to the factors we have just mentioned. Appropriate names to fill the posts may emerge, but those approached may decline to serve. Some may be reluctant to abandon lucrative private occupations for the relatively small financial rewards associated with government service. Others may prefer the power associated with running a large corporation to living in the shadow of a President who may not be readily accessible and who may or may not accept their advice. Others, serving in Congress for example, may not wish to abandon a secure political base to move into a bureaucratic quagmire of indefinite term which will do little to advance any future political ambitions that they might have. The Cabinet has not been the source of many presidential candidatures. While, for those coming to the Cabinet from outside the public sphere, the move may be but temporary, with the private career still available once the Cabinet service is at an end, those abandoning an elective office may effectively be ending their life in politics. Again, unlike the situation in Britain, service in the Cabinet is not the pinnacle towards which aspiring politicians strive. Having said this, the offer of a Cabinet post is undoubtedly seen by many as an honour which cannot be lightly rejected, even though acceptance may demand sacrifice. Many have left highly paid posts in industry, while Congressmen have been induced to give up safe seats on Capitol Hill to serve in far from secure positions in the Cabinet.

Finally, although it has been but a limited check upon Presidents, there is the constitutional requirement that all Cabinet nominees must be approved by the Senate. The general approach of the Senate has, in fact, been that, while presidential nominees to other posts will be subject to considerable scrutiny, the President is entitled to have his own people in the Cabinet, that the Cabinet is, in some sense, the President's official family. Consequently, very few nominees to the Cabinet have been rejected during the life of the Republic: indeed, up until 1991 only nine had failed to secure approval. The most recent example came in 1989 when the Senate rejected President Bush's nomination of John Tower to the post of Secretary of Defense. Tower's record of alcohol abuse and, perhaps more significantly, the consulting contracts he had with a number of weapons builders, were central to the arguments raised against his confirmation, particularly as the Pentagon (Department of Defense) had been racked by scandal concerning its procurement practices. However, Republicans protested that these arguments were only a smokescreen for a partisan attack upon the nominee, and through him upon the President. Certainly the final vote did demonstrate a remarkable degree of party unity, with only one Republican voting against Tower and only three Democrats voting for him. Whatever the reasons for the rejection, it was unique in that it represented the first time that the Senate had denied a President a Cabinet nominee at the start of his first term.

The paucity of these examples does seem to suggest that, at least so far as the Cabinet has been concerned, the Senate has taken to heart Hamilton's words in *The Federalist* LXXVI where he wrote that rejection of a candidate 'might have the appearance of a reflection upon the judgment of the chief magistrate'.[8] However, while this may be the case, this does not mean that Congress merely rubber-stamps the names sent down by the President. Hearings are held and votes, sometimes displaying considerable dissension, are taken. Furthermore, we should not overlook the probability of some kind of antenatal check felt by Presidents who may well be at pains to discover whether or not certain candidates would be acceptable to the Senate. It is highly likely that the requirement of senatorial approval does at times induce discretion in the White House, with some potential nominees being quietly dropped before their names enter the public debate. After all, if, as Hamilton suggested, the Senate will not often seek to reflect adversely upon the judgement of the

President, Presidents, on the other hand, will shy away from presenting the Senate with occasions for that judgement to be challenged.

Coming from such diffuse backgrounds, and probably knowing little of each other before they meet as 'The Cabinet', there is little prior sense among Cabinet members that they are part of a collectivity or that they have a common purpose. Conversely, while many Presidents come into office with a pledge that they will seek to work closely with their Cabinets, in practice they tend to rely on other agencies or persons. During some presidencies, meetings of the Cabinet have been regular and publicized, and some Presidents, as I discuss further below, have put together interdepartmental task forces of Cabinet and non-Cabinet advisers, but the more common situation has been one in which Cabinet meetings have been irregular and occasions for the presentation of presidential views rather than opportunities for discussions from which collective decisions might develop. As Abe Fortas put it:

> With regard to the cabinet *as an institution*, as differentiated from the individuals who compose it, it is a joke. As a collegium, it doesn't exist. Its members, serving as a cabinet, neither advise the President nor engage in any meaningful consideration of serious problems or issues.[9]

It is, in Heclo's words, 'a communication — not a decision-making device'.[10]

Clinton Rossiter agreed with George Graham's assertion that the Cabinet has been, for at least a generation, 'a bleeding and anemic patient', supporting this judgement on the grounds that the institution 'is at best a relic of a simpler past',[11] of a time when it was staffed by the President's most important and intimate associates. Today such associates are to be found elsewhere in the presidential entourage. Some writers now appear, in fact, to accept the statement by Charles Dawes, the first director of the Bureau of the Budget, that 'Cabinet members are ... the natural enemies of the President' as they tend to fight for departmental interests against, perhaps, the wider interests of the nation as embodied in presidential aims. Certainly, many suggest that Cabinet members often 'go native', become captured by the ethos of the departments they head, and by the attendant interests, whether they be congressional committees, government agencies or private groups. In such situations, 'they often appear to the President ... not as counsellors but as special pleaders'.[12]

One writer who does not accept this rather simplistic assessment of the situation is Harold Seidman, and he disagrees with the Dawes judgement. Giving an extended version of the Dawes quotation — 'Cabinet members are Vice-Presidents in charge of spending, and as such they are the natural enemies of the President' — Seidman suggests that while Cabinet members may be the natural enemies of the Budget Director or White House staff, they are, by contrast, the President's natural allies. As he continues, 'a President may not like his Cabinet members; he may disagree with them and suspect their loyalty, but he cannot destroy their power without seriously undermining his own'.[13] And yet even this judgement is misleading if taken out of the context of the further arguments developed in the book.

Seidman recognizes that while an alliance is a joining together in pursuit of common goals, an 'individual member will find it necessary at times to act contrary to the interests of the alliance when compelled to do so to protect his own vital interests'.[14] Herein lies an interesting comment on a fundamental distinction between, say, the British and the American Cabinets. A British Cabinet member is not perceived to be in a position to pursue goals which are contrary to the goals of the government. He is a part of a collectivity, continued membership of which is dependent, in the final analysis, on acceptance of the collective approach. If he is unable to accept the Cabinet line, he is expected to leave the Cabinet. He has little in the way of a power base outside the Cabinet. In America, on the other hand, there exist a number of power centres to which a Cabinet member may turn or, perhaps more frequently, to which he must answer. A primary allegiance to the President who has appointed him may well be balanced or offset by the need to work with Congress, particularly congressional committees, with bureaucrats in the agencies and with the myriad of groups which surround those committees and agencies. The departmental head may then find himself in a cleft stick, caught by presidential needs on one side and demands from these competing centres on the other.

Furthermore, occasions may arise when disagreements over appropriate goals to be pursued spill over into the public domain. There was, for example, the occasion in January 1957 when, on the day that President Eisenhower sent his budget to Congress, the Secretary of the Treasury, George M. Humphrey, came out with a swingeing attack on the President's plans. Arguing that the tax burden on the country was far too high, he said that if this were not reduced 'I will predict that you will have a depression that will curl your hair. . . . There are a lot of places in this budget that can be cut'.[15] Such an attack by so high-ranking a Cabinet member was unprecedented, and occasioned considerable embarrassment within the White House and anger within the Budget Office. However, Humphrey stayed as Secretary of the Treasury and Eisenhower made a number of statements that seemed to suggest that he accepted the burden of his Secretary's complaints. More recently, the rivalry and conflicting aims of two of President Reagan's Cabinet members, Secretary of Defence Caspar Weinberger and Secretary of State George Shultz, were highly publicized. Weinberger was seen as a hard-liner with regard to the Russians while Shultz was inclined to be more conciliatory. On the other hand, while Shultz advised that Libya should be bombed, Weinberger was more cautious.

When dealing with his Cabinet members the tools that are available to a President pursuing certain goals are strictly limited. He may, at times, order his Cabinet secretaries to do certain things but he can never be certain that those orders will be carried out. One of the most public of confrontations between a President and a Cabinet member occurred in 1973 when President Nixon sought to have his Attorney-General, Elliot Richardson, sack the Special Prosecutor, Archibald Cox, who had become too diligent, in Nixon's eyes, in pursuing his investigations into the Watergate affair. Richardson made it clear to the President that he would resign rather than fire Cox, but Nixon was adamant that Cox should go. Richardson resigned and his deputy, William Ruckleshaus, was fired when he too refused to carry out the President's wishes. It eventually fell to the Solicitor General, Robert Bork, to dismiss Cox. Generally, of course, matters do not reach such a confrontational stage, but in this instance the President was fighting desperately (and ultimately unsuccessfully) for his political life.

In more normal circumstances, a President will turn to persuasion, but with no assurance that his persuasive tactics will be successful, for others will also be seeking to persuade.

Ultimately, perhaps, he will have recourse to that technique which, as we noted in the chapter on Congress, is central to American politics and government — bargaining or 'horse-trading' — but even here the chances of success are limited. As Godfrey Hodgson has put it:

> All too often he finds that when it comes to swapping wampum and glass beads, even within his 'own' executive branch, others have more desirable trade goods than he has. . . . [T]he President finds he has too few sticks and others have more enticing carrots.[16]

The links that Cabinet members develop with the other agencies, both public and private, would appear to give them the necessary knowledge and expertise both to be valuable advisers to the President and efficient executors of his policies. But while Congress controls the legislative programme (even if it does not initiate much of it), and appropriates the money vital to that programme, and while career bureaucrats, with their own ties to Congress and to interest groups, can so effectively 'defend their own turf', members of the Cabinet may be more concerned to fight their own, rather than presidential, battles.

There exist, of course, exceptions to this general picture of the Cabinet and its members painted above. There have been those who were neither faceless nor bound to their agencies' clientele — members who acquired a stature, national and international, as important advisers to Presidents, almost as statesmen in their own right. While few have attained such standing as a John Foster Dulles, who has an airport named after him, or a Henry Kissinger, who was awarded the Nobel Peace Prize, many have formed an inner circle 'to whom the President looks for expert advice'.[17] Such members, Seidman suggests, may be those without strong constituency ties, for instance the Secretaries of State, Defense, and the Treasury, plus the Attorney-General, who from time to time may 'tend to function more as staff advisers to the President than as administrators of complex institutions' with 'their effectiveness and influence . . . only coincidentally related to their access to institutional resources'.[18] However, while these most prestigious of cabinet offices may indeed represent an inner coterie, it can hardly be because of the absence of constituency ties, particularly in the case of the Secretary of Defense. The Department of Defense is the 'primary employer, contractor, purchaser, owner and spender in the nation'[19] and, as such, has a clientele of considerable size and influence. Their importance derives rather, it would seem, from their areas of concern. With Presidents so involved in the international field, State and Defense are quite obviously central to presidential goals. The Treasury one might expect to play a crucial role in all governmental programmes, but the Office of Management and Budget, in the Executive Office of the President, often supersedes the more venerable institution, and the Director of the Office, holding status as a Cabinet member (in some eyes its most important member), may well be found within the group. The office of Attorney-General is often given to a person who has been particularly helpful to the President in securing election and who is likely, consequently, to have a special relationship with the chief executive.

However much a President uses his Cabinet, or parts of it, the institution still remains in a constitutional limbo, subject to the whims and desires of the President. Presidents are not bound by the actions of their predecessors, and the manner in which one President uses his Cabinet is no guide to the future use which may be made of it. Individual members may demonstrate expertise in handling the bureaucrats, placating Congressmen, fighting off predatory interests, and their advice may from time to time be sought in the policy-making processes, but their ultimate stature will be dependent upon presidential readiness to listen to them rather than to the numerous other advisers who surround the White House. As actors on the political stage, the roles of Cabinet members are constantly changing as Presidents keep rewriting the script and introducing new parts.

Woodrow Wilson, a professor of political science, before he became governor of New Jersey and ultimately President, was particularly concerned about the place of the Cabinet within the governmental structure. As an admirer of the ordered system of government in the United Kingdom, he proposed that the Cabinet should be a link between the President and his party in Congress. He suggested that the Cabinet should comprise the leading members of the President's party in Congress, that, while members of the Cabinet, they should be permitted to sit in Congress, and that, should a proposal they had supported be defeated, they should resign. Furthermore, he argued that a sense of collectivity should be encouraged by having the Cabinet stand or fall together. Such a plan, of course, struck at the very heart of the doctrine of the separation of powers. Wilson was seeking, through the medium of party, to break down the barriers that the Founding Fathers had erected. By having Cabinet members sitting in the Congress and acting collectively, in response to presidential and party desires, he was advocating in effect a parliamentary style of government which would have been radically different from the presidential system then existent.[20] Indeed, such a root-and-branch approach to the problem as Wilson perceived it would probably have led to a serious weakening of the President and to a shift of power into other hands. It proved to be a non-starter.

Concern over co-ordination within the executive branch is well justified. The competing pressures upon government, the numerous power centres and the apparent inability of one man adequately to oversee or to co-ordinate all the different strands, have evoked many calls for reform of the formal structures through which the country is administered and in which many of the demands upon government originate. The frustrations that Presidents may feel are well recorded but are perhaps encapsulated in President Franklin Roosevelt's despairing comment about the Department of the Navy which he likened to a featherbed: 'you punch it with your right and you punch it with your left until you are finally exhausted, and then you find the damn bed just as it was before you started punching'.[21]

Leaving aside proposals such as those above of Woodrow Wilson, which seemed little geared to the practicalities of the existing political system, one of the most significant attempts to change the nature of the Cabinet came from President Nixon in 1971. In his State of the Union message of that year he proposed keeping the inner circle of the Departments of State, Treasury, Defense and Justice, but consolidating all the remaining departments into four: Human Resources, Community Development, Natural Resources, and Economic Development. Such a reorganization had the appeal that it would probably have permitted the development of more coherent policies, as the multitude of seemingly independent agencies and bureaux were made more accountable within a rationalized structure. But such a development would, naturally, have disturbed much hallowed turf and this, allied with the President's political troubles which followed upon Watergate, led to its rejection by Congress. Later in the decade, President Carter tried to secure the creation of super-Cabinet departments — Natural Resources; Community and Economic Development; Trade, Technology and Industry — but opposition from within the executive branch itself, and from the interest groups which had a vested interest in leaving things the way they were, led to the plan being abandoned.

However, while these formal plans for reconstruction of the Cabinet failed, other steps have been taken in an effort to secure the co-ordination that they sought. Thus, shortly after President Reagan entered the White House, the creation of five Cabinet councils was announced — for economic affairs; natural resources and the environment; commerce and trade; human resources; and food and agriculture. Two others were added in 1982, for legal policy, and for management and administration. Cabinet members had primary assignments to these councils as a consequence of the departments they headed, but any member of the Cabinet could attend the meetings of any of the groups. While these councils might have been of great use to the President and he did meet with them regularly — of importance in itself for bringing Cabinet members regularly into the White House orbit, their value was severely limited by the fact that they were largely precluded from any significant consideration of budgetary matters by the pre-emptive actions of the Director of the Office of Management and Budget, David Stockman. They were then 'effectively relegated to policy issues and proposals of essentially secondary importance',[22] and in 1984, following Ronald Reagan's re-election, they were reduced in number to three.

While the Cabinet Secretary, as departmental head, is the obvious focal point of the department, we cannot overlook the fact that he is by no means the only appointive person therein. The President does have the responsibility for filling something like 2,500 other posts within the bureaucratic machine: under-secretaries, deputy secretaries, commissioners, and most bureau directors. Of these, approximately 600 are in policy-making positions. Generally speaking, this appointive power has been treated as a last vestige of the old 'spoils' system which began to be eroded with the passage of the Pendleton Act in 1883. Under this system, Presidents would make appointments as rewards for past services or as incentives for future support: sometimes because of the political stance or attitude of the appointee. When Ronald Reagan became President, he used the power to fill these posts with those he knew would support his policies. 'The primary qualification for appointment — overshadowing managerial competence and experience or familiarity with issues — appeared to be the extent to which an appointee shared the President's values'.[23] Lynn's assessment of Reagan's policy in this regard was that the President had 'helped his cause' but that had he 'and his recruiters . . . had a more explicit understanding of how lasting change in governmental activity is achieved, they might have used the power of appointment to even greater effect'.[24]

Most Presidents, as we have noted, enter office with a promise to make better use of the Cabinet than their predecessors. Such a pledge may indeed derive from a belief that the Cabinet should be restored to centre stage, that 'Cabinet government' is a desirable goal. But in light of the history of the Cabinet it would appear that such a belief represents the triumph of optimism over experience. Presidential tinkerings with the Cabinet have rarely had lasting impact upon its operations, for its members have still to achieve a balance among a variety of claims which will be made upon them — claims which derive on the one hand from the President who appointed them and on the other from the various interests which lie within and around their departments. The potential for conflict is, consequently, considerable, and Presidents who wish to achieve their policy goals soon discover that all too often neither the Cabinet, nor its individual members, can provide the necessary assistance. Presidents are not, however, limited to their Cabinet and sub-Cabinet appointees for aid with their programmes. They do have others to whom they can turn. Indeed, in many respects the Cabinet takes second place to the Executive Office of the President which now represents, as it were, the powerhouse of the modern presidency.

Notes

1. Francis E. Rourke, 'Grappling with the Bureaucracy', in Arnold J. Meltsner (ed.), *Politics and the Oval Office* (San Francisco, Calif.: Institute for Contemporary Studies, 1981), p.125.

2. Ibid.
3. Harold Seidman, *Politics, Position and Power*, 3rd edn (New York:, OUP, 1980), p.101.
4. Richard E. Fenno Jr, *The President's Cabinet* (New York: Vintage Books, 1959), p.17.
5. Ibid, p.14.
6. Ibid. p.19.
7. Ibid. p.18.
8. Quoted by Louis Fisher, *Constitutional Conflicts Between Congress and the President* (Princeton: PUP, 1985), p.41.
9. Quoted by Graham Allinson in 'The Advantages of a Presidential Executive Cabinet', in Vincent Davis (ed.), *The Post-Imperial Presidency* (New Brunswick, NJ: Transaction Books, 1980), p.117. My emphasis.
10. Hugh Heclo, 'The Changing Presidential Office', in Arnold J. Meltsner (ed.), *Politics and the Oval Office* (San Francisco: Institution for Contemporary Studies, 1981), p.181.
11. Clinton Rossiter, *The American Presidency*, 2nd edn (London: Harvest Books, 1960), pp.244–5.
12. Allinon, op. cit. p.117.
13. Seidman, op. cit. pp.84–5.
14. Ibid. p.86.
15. Quoted by Richard Neustadt, *Presidential Power*, 2nd edn (New York: Wiley, 1980), p.50.
16. Godfrey Hodgson, *All Things To All Men* (Harmondsworth: Penguin Books, 1980), p.82.
17. Seidman, op. cit. pp.247–8.
18. Ibid. p.136.
19. D.V. Edwards, *The American Political Experience*, (Englewood Cliffs, NJ: Prentice Hall, 1979). Quoting James Clotfelter at p.36.
20. For a fuller discussion of the Wilson proposals see Fenno, op. cit. Chapter 7.
21. Quoted in Neustadt, op. cit. p.33.
22. Michael Turner, 'The Reagan White House, the Cabinet and the Bureaucracy', in John D. Lees and Michael Turner (eds), *Reagan's First Four Years* (Manchester: MUP, 1988), p.52.
23. Laurence E. Lynn Jr, 'The Reagan Administration and the Renitent Bureaucracy', in Harry A. Bailey Jr and Jay M. Schafritz (eds), *The American Presidency* (Chicago, Ill.: The Dorsey Press, 1988), p.127.
24. Ibid. p.151.

The Executive Office of the President

A distinction that might fairly be drawn between the Cabinet and the Executive Office of the President is neatly expressed by Harold Seidman when he writes:

> So far as the President is concerned, a Cabinet member's primary responsibility is to mobilize support both within and outside the Congress for presidential measures and to act as a legislative tactician. Major questions of policy and legislative strategy are reserved, however, for decision by the White House staff.[1]

That there should exist two such presidential institutions as the Cabinet and the Executive Office may seem odd to constitutional purists brought up in the British tradition where the Prime Minister and Cabinet coordinate all of these activities. However, as we have seen, the members of the American Cabinet are not free to be just the President's agents. They do also have to live and operate within the environment of those networks of alliances which link together private interest groups, congressional committees and bureaucrats — alliances which, if they do not completely establish the parameters within which the Cabinet members work, do nevertheless impose considerable constraints that ensure that the President seems always to be in a state of conflict with the bureaucracy. Indeed, Rourke suggests that 'historically, the cleavage between the White House and the executive bureaucracy has held Presidents back from their policy goals as much as has poor relations with the co-equal branch of government on Capitol Hill'.[2] Such a conflict is not conducive to the swift or unambiguous action which modern government demands.

The modern presidency, in the sense of an institution fully committed to using the powers of government to tackle the range of problems facing society, might, with some justification, be dated back to Franklin Roosevelt and his New Deal efforts to cope with the worst effects of the depression of the 1930s. The introduction of that vast array of programmes involved the unprecedented assumption by the federal government of responsibility for problems hitherto left to state and local governments or to the private sector. The increased responsibility brought additional burdens to the White House, but not an administrative structure capable of dealing with them effectively. Roosevelt was by no means the first to complain about the pressures on the presidential office and the inadequacies of the existing arrangements. As he wrote, in a message to Congress: 'it has been common knowledge for twenty years, that the President cannot adequately handle his responsibilities; that he is overworked'.[3] Roosevelt's reaction to the problem was to appoint, in 1936, a Committee on Administrative Management under the chairmanship of Louis Brownlow. The Committee reported the following year and asserted that 'strong executive leadership is essential to democratic government today. Our choice is not between power and no power, but between responsible and capable popular government and irresponsible bureaucracy'. A terse four word sentence set out their basic conclusion: 'The President needs help'. They then went on to recommend that the President be given 'a small number of executive assistants who would be his direct aides in dealing with the managerial agencies and administrative departments of the Government'. More controversially, and guaranteed to incur the wrath and opposition of those who would be adversely affected, the Committee recommended that 'the whole Executive Branch of the Government should be overhauled and the present 100 agencies reorganized under a few large departments'.[4] More or less coinciding with the President's battle over the court-packing plan, the report seemed to give weight to the arguments of those who suggested that Roosevelt was seeking the aggrandizement of the presidential office. Consequently it was another two years before Congress passed the Reorganization Act which provided that the President should have the assistants that the committee had called for, but, while permitting him some authority to reorganize the executive branch, the Act denied him the power of widespread consolidation of agencies. In September 1939, under the terms of the Act, Roosevelt issued an Executive Order (8248) which brought into being the White House Office and the Executive Office of the President. Six presidential assistants were appointed to the White House Office to be the President's personal advisers. More significantly, perhaps, the Bureau of the Budget was taken from the Department of the Treasury and put into the new Executive Office of the President. This meant that for the first time the President had a potent weapon in his struggle to establish his authority over the departments.

There had always, of course, been people to whom Presidents would turn and from whom they would seek advice and support, those dubbed by Patrick Anderson 'distinguished outsiders'[5] (or by others, at times, *eminences grises*). But these were people who stood, as Anderson's phrase implies, outside any formal relationship with the President. The creation of the White House Office and the Executive Office of the President, and their subsequent growth, provided opportunities for such persons to be given a recognizable place and status within a presidential entourage.

While acceptance of the principal recommendation of the Brownlow Committee marked the birth of what has come to be described as the institutionalized presidency, two Acts of Congress passed shortly after the end of the Second World War were responsible for giving this new development a considerable boost. In 1946, the Employment Act, which required the President to seek to maintain full employment, also provided him with a Council of Economic Advisers to advise him, among other matters, on how best to achieve that goal. Comprising three members — generally, but by no means always, taken from the ranks of academe — appointed by the President, but subject to senatorial confirmation, the Council 'has no direct operational responsibilities but serves entirely in a consulting capacity'.[6] The following year the National Security Act, which brought the armed forces together under the Secretary of Defense and created the Central Intelligence Agency, also created the National Security Council (NSC) comprising the Secretaries of State and Defense and the Secretaries of the three arms of the military. The remit of the NSC was to advise the President:

with respect to the integration of domestic, foreign and military policies relating to the national security so as to enable the military services and the other departments and agencies of the government to cooperate more effectively in matters involving the national security.

An executive secretary to the Council was appointed and made an assistant to the President. As we shall see later, developments did not follow the paths expected by those who created the Council, and the National Security Adviser came, at times, to rival or even supersede the Secretary of State.

From the almost grudging creation of the 1930s, this institutionalized presidency has developed to the point where it now contains ten major units and something like two thousand staff. This has not, however, been an ordered growth, but one which has been subject to inputs from a number of sources and to presidential tinkering on a fairly considerable scale. Over the years, units have been created and discarded in response to a variety of initiatives which have been associated with presidential or congressional goals, or which have originated in particular political situations, or which have derived from the burgeoning involvement of the government in the economy. John Helmer lists forty-four units which at one time or another were to be found in the Executive Office of the President between the years 1939 and 1981.[7] These range from the long-lived Bureau of the Budget which, as we noted above, went into the Executive Office in 1939 (and had a name change in 1970 — to the Office of Management and Budget), the Council of Economic Advisers, and the National Security Council, to the short-lived President's Committee on Consumer Interests (1964–66), the Council for Urban Affairs (1969–70) and the Energy Policy Office (1973–74). Approximately half were created by public law, half by executive order, with President Nixon creating more units (fourteen) than any other President during that period.

The White House Office (WHO), which since 1976 has had an Intelligence Oversight Board attached to it, has a staff of about five hundred in some two dozen or so sub-divisions, and contains personal assistants and counsel to the President; a congressional liaison office; advisers on consumer, Hispanic, and ethnic affairs, and on ageing; speech writers; and appointments secretaries. Many, although by no means all, of the President's closest advisers will be found in this group which has been described as 'the lengthened shadow of the President' or as an 'unrecognized fourth branch of government'.[8] In addition to the WHO, the Office of Management and Budget, the Council of Economic Advisers and the National Security Council, the Executive Office, at the time of writing, contains the Office of Policy Development (formerly the Domestic Policy Staff, and before that the Domestic Council established by President Nixon in 1970); the Office of Science and Technology Policy (1959); the Council on Environmental Quality (1969); the Office of Administration (1978); the Council on Wages and Price Stability (1974); the Office of the Special Representative for Trade Negotiation (1974).

While the Brownlow Committee were quite right to suggest that the President needed help, in part at least to deal with the growing bureaucracy, they can hardly have foreseen the full consequences of their proposals. A new bureaucracy, it would seem, has been heaped upon the old, thereby creating new tensions. Controlling the new can be nearly as difficult as directing the old, and in order to deal with both of these bureaucracies, Presidents have come to rely more and more heavily upon those close friends from the campaign trail who generally hold appointments in the White House Office. Certainly, since Franklin Roosevelt's time at least, campaign teams have been the source of a large proportion of those whom Presidents have taken into the White House with them, but the demands of recent years have increased to the point where, to paraphrase Hodgson, these persons have moved from being the Presidents' eyes and ears to being their 'strong right arm'.[9]

This expansion of the role of the White House staff has come in for some considerable criticism. The power which has been wielded by men personally appointed by the President and loyal to his conception of the nation's needs, is worrying to many, particularly as the qualification for appointment seems to be based less upon ability than upon that loyalty. Months, or years, upon the campaign trail, building an image of a candidate that can be sold to an electorate, do not necessarily ensure a sensitivity of touch or understanding when it comes to dealing with holders of elective office or with appointees who have been required to receive senatorial confirmation. Of course, men of ability, tact and probity have been appointed by Presidents, but so have others who have lacked these qualities. As Patrick Andersen has put it: 'A wonderful variety of men has made its way to the White House staff in recent years. There have been men of extraordinary ability, clowns, scoundrels, ruthless sons-of-bitches, men of rare sensitivity, even a hero or two'.[10] This range would not be so important were it not for the fact that in the expanded presidency those close to the President have come to assume a formal stature that few before them had attained.

Sherman Adams, President Eisenhower's Chief of Staff, is, perhaps, a role model for certain later developments. He controlled the gateway to the Oval Office, largely determining who saw the President, and kept at bay Senators and Cabinet members alike. Even messages reached the President only after he approved them. His were the briefings and the advice upon which Eisenhower largely relied. Adams was a most powerful and much hated assistant and few mourned when he fell from grace.[11]

As the use that Presidents make of their White House staff is dependent upon their own personalities and their own perceptions of how tasks should be approached, one should not expect a neat pattern of development from one presidency to the next. Indeed, the Kennedy and Johnson White Houses were quite different from the Eisenhower. But with the election of Richard Nixon there was a reassertion of an Adams style in which 'the White House/EXOP bureaucracy exercised "vise-like" control over the rest of the Executive establishment'.[12] This time, however, a degree of lawlessness entered the picture that brought shame and disgrace to the presidency and occasioned further debate about the appropriateness of the institutional arrangements in the White House. Bob Haldeman and John Ehrlichman played the part that Adams had played and, as they were supported by others with Germanic-sounding names, they came to be known, among other soubriquets, as the 'Prussian Guard'. Haldeman, an advertising executive who had helped promote Walt Disney Productions, soft drinks and insecticides, and then Richard Nixon, was made Chief of Staff and became, in some opinions, the second most powerful man in Washington, able, like Adams, to keep Senators and Cabinet Secretaries from the President, and the chief dispenser of the powers and privileges within the White

House.[13] Ehrlichman, a lawyer and college friend of Haldeman, was the assistant for domestic affairs and chief executive officer of the Domestic Council. His arrogance matched that of Haldeman. Both men ultimately resigned from the White House staff, prior to their convictions for involvement in the Watergate cover-up, but that did not stop President Nixon from describing them as 'two of the finest public servants it has been my privilege to know', a testament, perhaps, to his own sense of values.

The fact that Nixon and his close aides should have attracted such adverse criticism and aroused such hostility has not stopped subsequent Presidents from relying upon close advisers, or those advisers from acquiring power which rivalled or even exceeded that wielded by Haldeman. After the 1988 election, the governor of New Hampshire, John Sununu, who was an important factor in the Bush victory, sought a post of influence within the administration, while making it clear he would not accept a mere Cabinet post (yet another reflection on the place of Cabinet members in the pecking order of power). He was made Chief of Staff in the White House and has become one of the most powerful men in Washington, leading Supreme Court Justice Thurgood Marshall to pronounce that the President was 'dead' and that Sununu was 'calling the shots'.[14] To his critics, according to Stothard, 'he is like a malevolent eunuch at an oriental court'. Certainly during the protracted budget talks between the executive and Congress he managed to alienate both Democrats and Republicans with his arrogant behaviour, and he is widely credited with forcing the resignation of Bill Bennett as Chairman of the Republican National Committee after only two weeks in the job. Sununu has even, on occasion, overstepped the mark in his position *vis-à-vis* the President, as when in 1990 he seemed to contradict the President's statement which signalled new thinking on the tax question. He was subsequently disavowed by the White House spokesman, but he still remains the loyal and trusted ally of the President and foe of those who would divert the chief executive from his espousal of conservative policies. However, many Republicans are calling for his resignation, claiming that his tactics and unbridled rudeness may split the party and adversely affect the President's chances of re-election in 1992.

Apart from worry over the power that has accrued to these

activists (often young and arrogant, although Sununu is not young) with whom Presidents have tended to surround themselves, considerable concern has been expressed in recent decades over the developments related to the National Security Council (NSC) and in particular to the National Security Adviser.

The 1947 Act which provided for the establishment of the Council specifies that it shall be composed of the President; the Secretary of State; the Secretary of Defense; the Secretaries of the Army, Navy, and Air Force, and the Chairman of the National Security Resources Board (also established by the Act). Other named officers might be designated by the President to be members, but their membership would be subject to senatorial advice and consent. No mention was made in the Act of the position of Assistant to the President for National Security Affairs, a post which was created by President Eisenhower in 1953. Originally, the Assistant was to act merely as the principal executive officer of the Council, keeping the President briefed on Council matters and supervising staff. The picture changed, however, when John Kennedy became President. His Assistant, McGeorge Bundy, became a personal adviser on national security matters, and acquired a degree of importance that bore comparison with that of the Council members.

I.M. Destler has suggested that the National Security Advisers could be roughly allocated to one of two categories.[15] The first, more concerned with management-centred activity, have concentrated on policy analysis, communication and the building of consensus between the often sparring-partners of State and Defense, and have played an important, but dependent, part in the foreign policy processes. The second, more directly concerned with policy, have made policy, conducted negotiations, and become strongly associated, personally, with the policies and the negotiations, and thereby rivalled if not replaced the Secretaries of State and/or Defense. Through this latter category, Presidents have been able to maximize their personal roles in foreign affairs.

While the use made of the National Security personnel has varied considerably from President to President, there has been a gradual shift in emphasis in the direction of more personal involvement by the President, either directly or through his personal advisers. Thus, the staffing which was formally attached to the NSC, and originally served the Council, has come much more to serve the President, and 'the power and influence of the National Security Assistant now tends', in Destler's words, 'to more than equal that of the Cabinet members'.[16] Henry Kissinger, who ultimately became Secretary of State, was a 'most notable and dramatic example' of a presidential appointee, not subject to senatorial confirmation (until he became Secretary of State), dominating the field 'in a way that no other foreign policy official has ... since the Second World War, with the possible exception of Dean Acheson'.[17] He took an active part in negotiations with foreign powers, and when President Nixon met with Chou En-lai, and with Brezhnev, it was Kissinger, not the Secretary of State, who accompanied him. Indeed, such was Kissinger's personal association with policy that, as we noted in the chapter on the Cabinet, he was awarded, controversially, the Nobel Peace Prize, while Senator Stuart Symington was led to comment that 'the national security assistant had become "Secretary of State in everything but title"'.[18] Thus, when he was ultimately made Secretary of State in 1973, little was added to his stature. Similarly, during the Carter presidency, Zbigniew Brzezinski, the National Security Adviser, who saw the President every morning, often played a more dominant role than Secretary of State Cyrus Vance. 'Usually, Secretary Vance was in the air somewhere, going to conferences or to funerals and those sort of things'.[19]

In contrast to the Nixon–Kissinger, Carter–Brzezinski relationship, when Ronald Reagan became President he determined to restore 'Cabinet government' and, in the process, he initially downgraded the role played by the assistant for national security. His first appointee to the post, Richard Allen, was required to report to Edwin Meese, a presidential adviser, and was denied direct access to the President himself. However, later incumbents, William 'Judge' Clark, Robert McFarlane and Admiral John Poindexter, did have that access restored, although none of them attained the standing or the influence of a Kissinger, either nationally or internationally. Nevertheless, during the later years of the Reagan presidency, two National Security Advisers and one of their staff acquired an unsought prominence when they were convicted on charges related to the Iran–Contra affair.

While contradictory statements by those involved, along with an apparently weak presidential memory, make it difficult to determine exactly where responsibility lies in the Iran–Contra matter, it is possible to point to a number of apparently illegal activities by the President's advisers, if not by the President himself. The heart of the affair concerned the sale of arms to Iran in 1985/1986 and the transfer of the profits from those sales to assist the Contra rebels in Nicaragua. The sale appeared to violate the United States embargo on exporting American-made arms to Iran or Iraq, while the diversion of military assistance to the Contras ran counter to a congressional vote banning such aid. The whole matter was conducted, according to George Shultz, the Secretary of State, without reference to the State Department, and was the responsibility of the National Security Advisers and their staff. Robert McFarlane, who was the Adviser at the inception of the policy, stated, before a congressional hearing, that the shipment of arms to Iran had been specifically authorized by the President, thereby contradicting White House insistence that the President knew of the shipments only after the event. Accusation and denial abounded, while Lieutenant Colonel Oliver North, a National Security Council aide, avoided self-incrimination about forty times by claiming the protection of the Fifth Amendment when testifying before a Senate committee.[20] As such claims have more traditionally been made by the more lurid members of the criminal fraternity, their use by an NSC aide merely increased the suspicion of wrongdoing in the White House.

Memories of Nixon's comments about Haldeman and Ehrlichman during the Watergate crisis were evoked when President Reagan described North as a 'national hero'. But just as Nixon's encomium failed to save his advisers from the application of the law, so Reagan's tribute proved of little value to North who was found guilty of two felonies associated with the investigation into the Irangate affair — obstructing Congress, and destroying documents — and of another, a spin-off from his position, of receiving an illegal gratuity. North was, however, in the words of the judge who sentenced him, 'a low-ranking subordinate', following the orders of his superiors. Of those superiors, Robert McFarlane pleaded guilty to four misdemeanour charges of withholding information from Congress, while, eventually, in 1990, Admiral Poindexter, McFarlane's successor as National Security Adviser, was found guilty on five charges of destroying documents and of lying to Congress. President Reagan, the ultimate superior, continued to prevaricate and, while his statements and denials convinced few, insufficient evidence was forthcoming to make a case against him.

The whole Iran–Contra affair did provide much ammunition for those who see the expanding White House staff, adequately directed by the President or not, as a threat to proper governmental processes. And yet, for others, the case is not at all clearcut. Central to most of the accusations and investigations, and yet not addressed in the court cases, was the question of the right of Congress to limit the President in his conduct of foreign policy. If one accepts the Supreme Court interpretation of the President's powers and responsibilities as set forth in the Curtiss-Wright case, which we have discussed elsewhere (see p.000), then a reasonable case can be made for the President pursuing particular goals which may run counter to expressed congressional positions, and pursuing them through the agency of the National Security Adviser and the NSC staff rather than through, say, the State Department. After all, if secrecy is seen as essential to the success of the operation it is more likely to be achieved by a small dedicated group of personnel within the White House than by those in the formal ranks of the bureaucracy who may not share the President's aims. But even accepting the President's constitutional prerogatives in this area, the Iran– Contra affair did still occasion concern, for although the evidence is far from complete (and how could it be complete when some of those involved destroyed so much of it), it did appear that the President, while he may have been aware of, and have approved, the sale of arms from the very beginning, may only have been informed of the assistance to the Contras some time after the diversion. If this were in fact the case, then Americans would have every right to be concerned that congressional desires were ignored, not by a President who might have a constitutional right so to do, but by appointed aides acting in the President's name but perhaps without his knowledge or authority.

Accusations of unconstitutional or even criminal activity levelled against certain of the President's closest advisers should not, of course, be used as a general condemnation of the Executive Office and of those who serve in various capacities therein. The President does still need the help recognizably absent in the 1930s, and the agencies which have been created to provide that assistance do form a vital part of the President's armoury in his attempts, as Helmer has put it, 'to give strength to the symbol [of the presidency] and substance to the illusion [of presidential government]'.[21]

Foremost among the agencies which exist to help the President attain his domestic goals is the Office of Management and Budget which was created in 1970 from the Bureau of the Budget and given additional management responsibilities and political staff. The Budget Bureau was originally created in 1921 by the Budget and Accounting Act which required the President to submit the annual budget estimates for the departments and the agencies. (Hitherto, they had made their own uncoordinated approaches to Congress.) The Budget Bureau was 'to act as the President's surrogate in those matters'.[22] Charles Dawes, the first Budget Director required that any piece of legislation which would involve the expenditure of funds had to receive approval before its submission to Congress. This practice was extended in the 1930s to include all executive branch requests for legislation, whether or not they were likely to involve expenditure. This time the officials were concerned to determine whether or not the proposal was in accord with the President's legislative programme.[23] In the 1940s, the practice developed of congressional committees contacting the Bureau to discover the President's position with regard to legislation they were considering. When the 1970 reorganisation took place, a shift in emphasis also occurred with authority passing from the career civil servants to the political appointees within the OMB. As Wayne has written, the Office became more politically responsive to the President on policy matters and less amenable to negotiations and compromises sent up by the Civil Service. 'Instead of ideas welling up, initiatives were sent down', and the OMB became a 'major coordinating and policing agency' with regard to the legislative process.[24] Furthermore, as Mezey notes, 'after Congress acts, OMB develops recommendations for the President about whether he should sign or veto a bill'.[25]

The politicization of the Office of Management and Budget has attracted criticism from many quarters and has evoked some accusations of presidential imperialism. James Sundquist and Hugh Heclo, among others, have pointed to the destructive effects of such politicization upon the career civil service in general and upon the management elite in the OMB in particular, while Harold Seidman has bemoaned the fact that the 'important distinction between agencies in the Executive Office of the President such as the Bureau of the Budget, serving the presidency as an institution, and those serving the President in a personal, political capacity has been lost'. He went on to cite President Nixon's acknowledgement of the fact that the 'tendency to enlarge the White House staff . . . has blurred the distinction between personal staff and management institutions'.[26]

The centripetal forces at work did receive a slight setback in 1974 when Congress passed a law requiring senatorial confirmation of all future nominees to the posts of Director and Deputy-Director of OMB, thereby giving the Senate a veto power over appointment to two of the key posts in the presidential entourage. As the Director of OMB is more powerful than most Cabinet members, and almost all other appointive posts which require senatorial concurrence, such a law did not seem unreasonable — particularly in the immediate post-Watergate years, with the Nixon excesses fresh in the mind. However, the requirement of senatorial approval does not appear to have been significant, in the sense of denying to the President the persons he wishes to fill the posts. As with other Cabinet appointments it would seem that the President is still entitled to select the members of his official 'family'. It is probably desirable that this should continue to be the case. Nevertheless, the situation does still remain that 'there is hardly any Cabinet post now that does not have a parallel over in the bowels of the White House somewhere, some person who has never been confirmed [by the Senate] and whose name might not even be known to the public'.[27] That this should be so is, to many, an unacceptable bypassing of the advice and consent clause of the constitution.

It may be regretted that the growth of the WHO/EOP has had an adverse effect upon the morale of career civil servants throughout the bureaucracy, but it is surely necessary that a chief executive should be served by those who support his policy stands, by persons who have not been sucked into those issue networks which have often worked to frustrate rather than to promote presidential goals. Furthermore, of course, while much of the Civil Service (around 85 per cent) is now under the merit system as originally established by the Pendleton Act 1883, there has long existed the tradition of political involvement in the Service. The worst of the excesses of the political spoils system may have been assuaged by the Act, but there have continued to be many opportunities for political appointments at a senior level which contrast starkly with the basically apolitical system in the United Kingdom.

The haphazard and piecemeal development of a semi-official bureaucracy which now contends with the formal bureaucratic structure of the state is the very imperfect answer to the problems that flow from the dispersal of power and authority, which is the hallmark of the American system. Presidents who have interpreted their roles in a positive, rather than in a passive, way have been forced by the competing pressures to create their own machinery, or to modify the existing apparatus, in order to achieve their goals. The study of the White House Office/ Executive Office of the President is then, apart from the fairly general observations of a chapter such as this, a study of different presidential styles and goals.

Notes

1. Harold Seidman, *Politics, Position and Power*, 3rd edn (New York: OUP, 1980), p.91.
2. Francis E. Rourke, 'Grappling With the Bureaucracy', in Arnold J. Meltsner (ed.), *Politics and the Oval Office* (San Francisco: Institute for Contemporary Studies, 1981), p.124.
3. Quoted by Robert Sickels, *The Presidency*, (Englewood Cliffs, NJ: Prentice Hall, 1980), p.173.
4. Quoted by Clinton Rossiter, *The American Presidency* 2nd edn (London: Harvest Books, 1960), pp.128–9.
5. Patrick Anderson, *The President's Men* (Garden City, NY: Anchor Books, 1969), p.2.
6. Barbara Hinckley, *Problems of the Presidency* (Glenview, Ill.: Scott, Foresman, 1985), p.221.
7. John Helmer, 'The Presidential Office: Velvet Fist in an Iron Glove', in Hugh Heclo and Lester M. Salamon (eds), *The Illusion of Presidential Government* (Boulder, Colo.: Westview Press, 1981), pp.58–9.
8. Theodore White, *Breach of Faith* (New York: Dell Publishing, 1975), p.145.
9. Godfrey Hodgson, *All Things to all Men* (Harmondsworth: Penguin Books, 1980), p.97.
10. Anderson, op. cit. p.3.

11. Eisenhower had the mistrusted Richard Nixon as his Vice-President and many raised the spectre, 'What if Eisenhower should die and Nixon should become President?' Others, hinting at Adams' influence, asked, 'What if Adams should die and Eisenhower should become President?'
12. Graham Allison, 'The Advantages of a Presidential Executive Cabinet', in Vincent Davis (ed.), *The Post-Imperial Presidency* (New Brunswick, NJ: Transaction Books, 1980), p.118.
13. See White, op. cit. p.147.
14. Peter Stothard, 'The Loudest Whisper in Washington', in *The Times*, 31 August 1990, p.14.
15. I.M. Destler, 'National Security Advice to Presidents', *World Politics*, 29 January 1977, pp.150–8.
16. I.M. Destler, 'Staffing the White House for Foreign Policy', in K. Thompson (ed.), *The Virginia Papers on the Presidency* (Lanham, Md.: University Press of America, 1986), vol. XXI, p.40.
17. Ibid. p.41.
18. Quoted by Louis Koenig, *The Chief Executive*, 5th edn (San Diego: Harcourt Brace Jovanovich, 1986), p.216.
19. Former Attorney-General Griffin Bell, in K. Thompson (ed.), *The Virginia Papers on the Presidency*, vol. XVIII, 1984, p.42.
20. Amendment V: 'No person . . . shall be compelled in any criminal case to be a witness against himself'.
21. Helmer, op. cit. p.49.
22. Stephen J. Wayne, *The Legislative Process* (New York: Harper & Row, 1978), p.71.
23. Ibid. pp.71–2.
24. Ibid. pp.89 and 91.
25. Mezey, *Congress, the President and Public Policy* (Boulder, Colo.: Westview Press, 1989), p.90.
26. Seidman, op. cit. p.227.
27. Bell, op. cit. p.42.

The President and the Supreme Court

Among the more important of the powers given to the President by the Constitution is that of appointing judges to the Federal courts and in particular to the United States Supreme Court, although that importance is not even hinted at by the words of the Constitution. The bland statement of Article III in no way suggests the fundamental role that the Court would ultimately come to play, not just as a part of the legal system but also as an actor on the political stage. Nowhere is there suggestion that the Court might one day curb the Congress; limit Presidents; buttress slavery; legitimize (and ultimately de-legitimize) segregation; expand federal power; create new rights and much more. Apart, perhaps, from its very earliest days at the end of the eighteenth century, the Court has never been the 'least dangerous' branch of government, that Hamilton described in the Federalist papers.[1]

It was the second President, John Adams, who was apparently the first to recognize the potential in the Court and in the presidential appointing power. During his 'lame duck' period (the period between losing the election to Thomas Jefferson in November and the end of his term of office in March) he nominated John Marshall to be Chief Justice to ensure that while Jeffersonian-Republicans (his political enemies) might hold the Presidency, Federalist principles would still prevail in the country.

Marshall amply justified the trust that President Adams had shown in him. The thirty-five years of his Chief Justiceship were a period in which the Supreme Court emerged from the relative obscurity of its first dozen years — when membership was little

158

prized — to a place firmly in the spotlight of national politics, and a period in which Federalist notions of expanding central powers at the expense of the states became dominant.

During this time, Marshall also arrogated to the Court the right to declare Acts of Congress unconstitutional. This he did in the case of *Marbury* v. *Madison* in 1803. Marbury, a Federalist, through a writ of mandamus, sued Madison, Republican Secretary of State, for delivery of his commission as Justice of the Peace, an appointment, like Marshall's, made in the lame-duck days of the Adams' presidency but not finalized by the handing over of the commission by Madison's predecessor, John Marshall himself. Marshall found himself in a cleft stick. His natural desire was to find for his fellow Federalist, but he was political realist enough to recognize that, given the still tenuous position of the Court in the governmental process, to find against Madison would be to invite the government to ignore the judgement and thereby to demonstrate the impotency of the Court — a demonstration which might well have jeopardized its future development. On the other hand, Marshall had little desire to give aid and comfort to his political enemies by sustaining the Madison position. In an apparent cleft stick, the Chief Justice played a masterly stroke. He ruled that he thought Marbury should be given his commission but also declared that the Supreme Court was not the appropriate body to pass judgement in the case as it did not have jurisdiction.

Marbury had brought his case to the Supreme Court because the Judiciary Act of 1789 had apparently given the Court original jurisdiction in cases of mandamus. Marshall argued, however, that in the wording of the Constitution the founding fathers had explicitly set out the areas of original jurisdiction for the Court and must, thereby, have intended to exclude all other areas. There was, thus, an apparent conflict between the 1789 Act and the Constitution, and in Marshall's reasoning 'the Constitution controls any legislative act repugnant to it' for 'those who have framed written constitutions contemplate them as forming the fundamental and paramount law of the nation, and, consequently, the theory of every such government must be that an Act of the Legislature repugnant to the Constitution is void'.[2]

In one fell swoop, in a case of no apparent intrinsic constitutional importance, John Marshall thereby established a precedent that would help to keep the Supreme Court at the centre of many political controversies. That his motives were political cannot be doubted: the Constitution was hardly under threat from an extension of the Court's original jurisdiction. That his reasoning was at times strained is apparent: for instance, he adverted to the oath that Justices take to discharge their duties according to the Constitution while ignoring the oath that Congressmen similarly take. That his legacy has had profound implications for American political and constitutional development is a matter of record.

Adams' appointment of Marshall thus set a precedent which Presidents have followed to this day. They have sought to appoint to the Court those who have shared their political and socio-economic preferences, people who, they have hoped, would hand down decisions which reflected the presidential viewpoint. The history of the Court, so far as its membership is concerned, has been, then, in the words of G. Edward White, a history 'of minor court-packing plans'; although one should perhaps modify that judgement to 'attempted court-packing plans', for, as we shall see, not all Presidents have been successful with their nominees, in the sense that, once on the Court, some have demonstrated unsuspected attitudes and have delivered judgements of which the appointing Presidents did not approve.

While Presidents have a fairly free hand when they make nominations to the Supreme Court and while the vast majority of their recommendations have been accepted by the Senate, they do face certain constraints upon that freedom. While there is no constitutional requirement that the Justices should have a law degree, all who have served on the Court have been so qualified and one cannot imagine a President having the temerity to suggest a candidate without such a degree. In addition, there are expectations that those nominated should have attained a degree of eminence in the practice of law or some other public office: as judges, advocates or academic jurists; or as holders of political posts. Examples from the past include an eminent professor of law, Oliver Wendell Holmes Jr; a former President of the United States, William Howard Taft; a former candidate for the Presidency, Charles Evan Hughes; a former governor, Earl Warren; a former counsel for the NAACP, Thurgood Marshall. Furthermore, over the years, it has come to be expected that some kind of rough and ready regional balance will be maintained on the Court, while people also now talk about seats which relate to religious or ethnic groups; and it may well be, now that a woman, appointed by President Reagan, has breached the hitherto all-male institution, that in future there will be talk of the female seat.

When a vacancy occurs on the Court, Presidents will often have a candidate in mind — an old friend or political colleague, or perhaps someone unknown to them personally but with a reputation. However, they will not usually make their nominations without taking advice and without having the backgrounds of the potential candidates checked, although this last may be done with varying degrees of thoroughness. Attorneys-General have often, although by no means invariably, been persons to whom Presidents would turn for consultation and from whom they might receive reports on the suitability of their proposals. At times, the American Bar Association has been asked for its views.

In spite of the prior presidential knowledge of the candidates and in spite of these checks, people have been nominated who have not proven suitable, or acceptable, and have been rejected by the Senate, or have reached the Court and disappointed the President who nominated them. In the recent past, examples of the first group include two judges from the federal courts in the South, Clement Haynsworth and G. Harold Carswell, nominees of Richard Nixon. Although they were Democrats, while the President was a Republican, Nixon expected that they would display a solid conservatism which would accord with his own views. Furthermore, they were to form part of his 'southern strategy' of building a bridge between the Republican party and the fairly solid Democratic South. Unfortunately, for presidential aims, the initial investigations of the two men were weak and the choices were flawed. It soon transpired that Haynsworth had not always displayed the highest standards of ethics, having presided in cases in which he had a personal interest. His rejection by the Senate was followed by the President's comment that Haynsworth's integrity was unimpeachable! Carswell, a bitter opponent of civil rights, and a defender of white supremacy, also had the dubious distinction of having had more of his decisions overturned by the Courts of Appeal *on points of law* than any other federal judge. When he, too, was rejected by the Senate the President again praised the character and honesty of his nominees (yet more examples of President Nixon's penchant for offering praise of men with dubious values).

A second category of rejection concerns those the Senate will not confirm because of stands on constitutional matters or, as some would have it, because of political philosophies. Most recently, President Reagan's nominee, Robert Bork, an eminent jurist, proved unacceptable to the Senate because of his advocacy of judicial restraint, of a strict construction of the Constitution. Such construction ran counter to much of the *liberal* tradition of the previous quarter of a century, and offended many of the Democrats in the Senate. Bork would certainly have attempted to use his position to reverse many of the liberal decisions which marked the Warren Court, and even part of the Burger Court; but some, even those of liberal disposition, were led to question the propriety of a rejection which appeared to be motivated purely by political considerations, for neither the candidate's ethics nor his knowledge of the law was in question. Such questioning has of course been countered by Senators who have argued that, as Presidents have constantly used the appointive power to put people onto the Court because of their political views, they, as partners with the President in the appointive process, are perfectly entitled to use their position to reject on the selfsame grounds. (We should note that, at an earlier time, President Nixon had even suggested that the senatorial role was basically a formality:

> what is centrally at issue in ... [the nomination process] is the constitutional responsibility of the President to appoint members of the Court — and whether this responsibility can be frustrated by those who wish to substitute their own philosophy or their own subjective judgment for that of *the one person* entrusted by the Constitution with the power of appointment. ... If the Senate attempts to substitute its judgment as to who shall be appointed, the traditional constitutional balance is in jeopardy.[3]

It is, of course, a strange and hardly acceptable reading of the Constitution that makes the President the one person entrusted with the appointive power.)

While Presidents will usually complain when their nominees are rejected — few though those occasions may be — there have been times when they must have wished that the Senate had been tougher, for, as suggested earlier, there have been instances where they have been disappointed by those they put on to the Court. Thorough investigation of a candidate's stance on certain issues, or knowledge of his past political background cannot always ensure a Justice whose decisions will reflect the President's preferences or prejudices.

President Theodore Roosevelt, for example, is reported as saying of Oliver Wendell Holmes Jr, an eminent legal scholar, after he had taken an anti-government line in an anti-trust case, that he could carve a man with more backbone out of a banana. Half a century later, President Eisenhower, having appointed Earl Warren, a former Republican governor of California and candidate for the Vice-Presidency of the United States, to the Chief Justiceship, was shocked, if not appalled, by the 'liberal' decisions the Court handed down under Warren's leadership. He described the appointment as one of the biggest damned mistakes of his presidency. President Nixon, who had the unusual bonus of being in a position to appoint four Justices, and thereby, he hoped, to make the Court over in his own image, was greatly disappointed when this supposedly 'conservative' Court liberalized the law with regard to abortion, and required the bussing of school children across district lines in the attempt to secure racial balance in the schools. Worse still, so far as he was concerned, his presidency was effectively brought to an end when the Court ruled that he should hand over the tapes which were to reveal his part in the 'Watergate' affair.

While the power to appoint Justices is important, as asserted earlier, we must recognize that it is not always of immediate importance to the President making the appointments. Of course, if the Justices are fairly evenly divided, ideologically, the retirement or death of one, if followed by the appointment of someone of different persuasion, may quickly have a significant effect upon the outcome of cases (a five to four vote being sufficient to decide a case). For instance, in 1990 William Brennan, the outstanding liberal Justice, (and Eisenhower's other self-confessed 'mistake') announced his retirement. President Bush was thus given his first opportunity to appoint a Justice, and it was hoped by those on the right of the political spectrum that his nominee to fill the vacancy, David Souter, would provide the necessary conservative addition to produce a six to three majority for the reassertion of conservative viewpoints largely muted since Roosevelt's later years, and particularly since the accession to the Chief Justiceship of Earl Warren.

More often than not, however, it will take two or three changes in the Court personnel before an ideological shift can take place. It will usually be several years before a President can effect such a change, as Justices hold their posts during good behaviour and can only be removed by impeachment — never successfully moved against a Supreme Court Justice. Thus, a President's influence on the Court is likely to be most significant after he has left office. Future administrations are more likely to be affected rather than their own. As Alexander Bickel put it: 'To the extent that they are instruments of decisive change, Justices are time bombs, not warheads that explode on impact'.[4]

The 'time-bomb' effect of judicial appointments has often occasioned conflict between President and Court, and such conflict was perhaps best exemplified in the early years of the Franklin Roosevelt presidency. Roosevelt, elected during the depths of the Great Depression, launched a series of initiatives designed to mitigate the worst of the economic disaster. He was faced, however, by a Court largely appointed by Presidents whose *laisser-faire* attitude towards the economy was strongly at variance with that of Roosevelt. These Justices reflected those conservative views and accordingly declared a large part of the New Deal programme unconstitutional. Roosevelt was so incensed by this opposition that, after his re-election in 1936, he introduced what has come to be known as his court-packing plan. Attempting to gloss over his real intent, he argued that the Court needed help, particularly as some of the Justices were getting old, and he proposed therefore to increase the size of the Court, up to a maximum of fifteen, adding one new member for every Justice over the age of seventy. Although he had been overwhelmingly supported in the November election, Roosevelt's blatantly political attempt to interfere with the independence of the Court encountered tremendous opposition (even though the Court itself was similarly acting in a blatant political fashion) and the plan failed. But if the battle was lost, it did appear that the war was won, for in early 1937 the Court suddenly found constitutional justification for acts it had so recently deemed unconstitutional. This was what has been called 'the switch in time which saved nine', for one of the Justices at least may well have suspected that further recalcitrance might have led to another plan which might have been better received.

Roosevelt's successor, Harry Truman, did not have the same initial problems with his Court. Roosevelt had managed, before he died, to appoint eight Justices of relatively liberal hue. Yet when Truman sought to take over the steel mills during an industrial dispute, to maintain supplies of steel vital for the war effort in Korea, his action was deemed to be unconstitutional.

At the present time, when the White House since 1968 has been held by the Republicans for all but the four Carter years, and when most of the Court, from Nixon appointee, now Chief Justice, Rehnquist[5] down reflect the conservative leanings of those who appointed them, any Democrat who happened to win the presidency would be faced by a body of Justices probably unsympathetic to his goals.

While the Court has been involved at some time or another in most of the major political issues in American history, we should note its self-denial in one particular aspect. From the very earliest days, the Court has declined to be drawn directly into the political process, refusing to give advisory opinions concerning the constitutionality of proposed action. It has insisted that its role was limited to deciding proper cases, brought by parties with standing, which had come to it through the appropriate legal channels. In this way, the Court would never be in the position of passing judgement on a law in the making of which it had had some part. This collective refusal of the Court has not, however, applied to the Justices as individuals. Since George Washington's day, a number of Justices have been engaged in giving political advice to Presidents, although Scigliano suggests that only nine have been more than minimally involved: John Jay, Roger B. Taney, Louis D. Brandeis, William Howard Taft, Felix Frankfurter, William O. Douglas, James F. Byrnes, Fred M. Vinson, and Abe Fortas.[6]

Much of what Presidents seek to do will, of course, never become a matter for judicial resolution, while much of what the Court does is concerned with the interpretation or reinterpretation of existing laws, federal or state. The President may well have strong feelings about some of the matters upon which the Court rules, but the rulings in themselves may not touch directly upon his own declared policies. Furthermore, one must recognize the importance of judicial self-restraint. Justices have often declined to rule in certain cases on the grounds that the matters involved are political in character and therefore best left to the elected politicians. While an admirable restraint, some would argue, the problem with this concept of 'political' is that it appears to mean what the Justices themselves would have it mean, and it can and does change from one Court to the next. Again, in the relatively modern era, the Court appears to have adopted an attitude which, so far as non-civil liberty matters are concerned, deems the government innocent until proven guilty beyond all reasonable doubt, while with regard to questions relating to the area of civil liberties the burden of proof has usually been put on the other foot.

If, however, the Court now appears to act in circumspect fashion in so far as challenges to presidential authority and action in domestic matters are concerned, its judgements with regard to that authority in the foreign field have been of a much more positive nature. Indeed, a number of commentators have suggested that in many respects the Court has in reality become an arm of the executive branch. While the case of *United States* v. *Curtiss-Wright Export Corporation* (1936), which we have already cited (see pp.111–12), was the most explicit statement by the Court of the special powers of the President in this area, the Court has generally fought shy of imposing limits upon presidential actions, even though at times they might appear to involve an unconstitutional denial of civil rights. Thus, during the American Civil War, although Chief Justice Taney had issued an order calling upon the President to release John Merryman, who was being held without a trial — an order which was ignored — the Court generally gave its imprimatur (if only through a refusal to act) to other denials of civil rights. In the Second World War, people of Japanese ancestry were excluded from the three Western seaboard states, as well as part of Arizona, and were sent to detention camps for the duration of the war. There were some 70,000 American citizens among this group of 112,000 who lost their freedom, their jobs and often most of their possessions. In the major case relating to this unprecedented denial of civil rights on such a scale, *Korematsu* v. *United States*, the Court accepted the government's position that unspecified persons among the group might be sympathetic to any possible Japanese invaders, and the injustice was allowed to continue.[7]

During the nineteenth century the Court, in a number of decisions, had enshrined the constitutional edict that only Congress could initiate war, although it accepted that the President, as Commander-in-Chief, could take action to repel sudden attacks against the United States. However, the 1936 Curtiss-Wright case, with its declaration that the President is the 'sole organ of foreign affairs', established a spirit that has since tended to permeate most judicial decisions relating to the President's constitutional authority in that area. The war in Vietnam provides a classic example of this judicial expansion of presidential authority. When America entered that conflict, cases were brought challenging the legality of the action, for many doubted the authority of the President to commit American citizens and American money to the conflict in the absence of a formal declaration of war by Congress. However, in spite of this failure to observe the constitutional proprieties, the Supreme Court proved reluctant to check by judicial decree 'actions by the President for which Congress did not choose to cut off funds',[8] and generally it refused to hear such cases. Rather, it maintained a position which implied agreement with a decision ultimately handed down in the US Court of Appeals, Second Circuit, which argued:

> the Vietnamese war has been constitutionally authorized by the mutual participation of Congress and the President [and] we must recognize that those two coordinate branches of government — the Executive by military action and the Congress, by not cutting off appropriations that are the wherewithal for such action — have taken a position that is not within our power, even if it were our wish, to alter by judicial decree.[9]

This position taken by the Courts did, therefore, sanction actions taken outside the constitutional procedures laid down by the Founding Fathers. In case of sudden attack upon the United States, the need for immediate response could well justify, as we have noted, warlike action without a formal declaration, although, in fact, following the attack upon Pearl Harbour, the proper processes were followed. But so far as the Vietnamese situation was concerned there was no such attack, ample time existed for Congress to act in the constitutionally prescribed fashion, and yet Presidents involved the United States in what was undoubtedly a war. Of course, the Justices, in their refusal to pronounce on the constitutionality of this action, were recognizing political realities, for one must ask the question: what if the Court had found the war to be unconstitutional? Would the President have been subject to impeachment? If so, would a Congress which had voted funds to sustain an unconstitutional conflict have successfully prosecuted such an impeachment? What about the financial questions — money illegally spent; damages for those who had been sent to fight and sustained injury or death? The potential ramifications were considerable.

The Court's failure to involve itself, grounded though it may have been in a recognition of what was politically feasible, does, nevertheless, demonstrate the limitations of the constitutional constraints upon the President if the other actors on the political stage concur in his actions. Indeed, the Court has gone even further than this and has enunciated the principle that failure by the Congress to act with regard to a presidential act can be taken as agreement with that action. Justice Rehnquist asserted in 1981 that, by its silence, Congress had acquiesced in an executive agreement entered into by the President. The idea of an 'implicit' congressional approval was thereby introduced to sustain an agreement which, according to Fisher, the Court 'could not possibly overturn ... given the foreign policy implications'.[10] While the Court sought to limit the application of this decision to the specific case, a precedent has been established. The question for the future, as Fisher suggests, is whether or not it will be accepted as 'precedent for further expansions of presidential power'.

If the Court recognizes that there are certain decisions it cannot reach because of the 'policy implications', we must also give due recognition to that other great possible constraint upon judicial action, the absence of a judicial power of enforcement. The Court, while having the authority to hand down judgements, has no power to execute those judgements, as President Andrew Jackson purportedly noted in 1832 when he declined to send federal troops to force Georgia's compliance with a Court ruling: 'John Marshall has made his decision, now let him enforce it'.[11] The Justices are dependent upon others, in particular the executive branch, headed by the President, for implementation. Of course, the Court's decisions have acquired such an authority that, generally speaking, compliance and/or implementation are forthcoming, with differing degrees of grace. Thus, as mentioned above, when the Court ruled that President Truman did not have the authority to seize the steel mills in 1952,[12] he accepted the judgement and did not attempt to invoke once more his position as Commander-in-Chief to justify his action. Again, when President Nixon was ordered to hand over the incriminating tapes he, too, complied, although in this case refusal to do so might simply have hastened the onset of impeachment procedures.[13]

Particularly unpopular decisions may, naturally, encounter a considerable and prolonged resistance from affected parties which Presidents may be loath to tackle, either for personal or for political reasons. For instance, following the Court's decisions in *Brown* v. *The Board of Education*,[14] which ruled that segregation based upon the 'separate but equal' doctrine — that the Fourteenth Amendment does not outlaw segregation so long as equal facilities are provided for each race (enunciated by the Court in 1896 in *Plessy* v. *Ferguson* 163 US 537) — was a denial of the equal protection of the laws supposedly guaranteed by the Fourteenth Amendment, the states of the Deep South did everything they could to avoid compliance. Legislators, governors, school boards, even some Federal judges at the district level, were all involved in the fight to keep the schools segregated. President Eisenhower reluctantly intervened by sending in troops when Governor Faubus of Arkansas took an openly belligerent stance on the steps of Little Rock High School in 1957. Two years earlier, the President, who had no love of the *Brown* decision, had indicated that he would not use troops to enforce it, and this pronouncement may have given comfort to the hard-line segregationists and encouraged their resistance.

Eisenhower's intervention dealt with the immediate problem of Little Rock, but it did little to secure acquiescence elsewhere in the South: five years later, President Kennedy sent federal troops to secure the desegregation of the University of Mississippi. Indeed, a decade after the *Brown* decisions the number of black elementary and secondary students going to school with any whites in eleven southern states was still only 2.25 per cent.[15] It was a much more activist President, Lyndon Johnson, encouraging his Department of Health, Education and Welfare to use its 'power to withhold funds from school districts which refused to desegregate',[16] who got the ball rolling in effective manner towards an acceptable level of integration.

Many, in recent decades, have expressed concern about the degree to which the Justices have apparently arrogated power to themselves by entering fields which are the proper realm of Congress or of the President. Schlesinger's opprobrious term for the presidency, 'imperial', has even been applied by some to the Court. That some kind of clash should occur between elected representatives of the people and those charged with the exposition of the fundamental law is hardly to be wondered at, for disputes are bound to arise when the latter overturn the work of the former or interpret the law in such a way as to suggest that they are invading the realm of those charged with the enactment or execution of legislation. This is particularly so when it is quite apparent that Justices are not political castrati but carry to the Court in their intellectual baggage a whole host of political and social aims and prejudices. As Felix Frankfurter has written: 'the simple truth of the matter is that decisions of the Court denying or sanctioning the exercise of federal power . . . largely involve a judgement about practical matters and not at all any esoteric knowledge of the Constitution'.[17]

David Truman has suggested that the Constitution 'has lived to magnificent maturity largely because it has so readily admitted of discretionary interpretation by its guardians'[18] but, for many, Corwin's comment, that 'judicial review has contributed to the survival of the Constitution . . . largely by displacing it', is more apposite. As Corwin continued:

> the amended document of 1787 . . . has become little more than a taking-off ground; the journey out and back occurs in a far different medium, of selected precedents, speculative views regarding the nature of the Constitution and the purposes designed to be served by it, and *unstated judicial preferences.*[19]

Morris Cohen perhaps best captured this line of thinking when he declared: 'the whole system is fundamentally dishonest in its pretensions, pretending to say what the Constitution lays down when they [the Justices] are in fact deciding what [they think] is good for the country'.[20] Thus, when they created, from the well-recognized and understood concept, 'due process', a new and alien concept of 'substantive due process'[21] in order to provide the means to sustain the particular ends their prejudices demanded, or when they discovered 'a right to privacy', nowhere mentioned in the Constitution, in order to attain other ends, they demonstrated what many would describe as a totally cynical approach to the whole question of constitutional exegesis.

But powerful as the Court may appear, intrusive as its actions have at times been, it rarely offers prolonged resistance to a popular President. Franklin Roosevelt's first term did provide an example of an uncommon persistence of Court versus President, but when FDR went on to the offensive with the Court-packing plan which followed his 1936 re-election, the Court, as we have noted, quickly backed down. To have continued to frustrate a demonstrably popular President might well have had serious repercussions for the status of the Court. In 1952, on the other hand, both President Truman and the war in Korea were unpopular and the Court was therefore on much firmer ground when it found against the President in the Steel Seizure case. And in 1974, President Nixon's popularity had sunk to such a low that had he refused to obey the Court order to hand over the tapes, a move which he had apparently contemplated, impeachment proceedings would almost certainly have followed.

Direct confrontation between Court and President may not have occurred too frequently, but, as we have already noted, Presidents have at times been disappointed with Courts which, while not directly challenging the chief executives, have handed down decisions which do not accord with their preferences. Thus, President Eisenhower did not approve of the decisions in the *Brown* cases, but they were not a challenge to his authority and he did, ultimately, take steps to enforce the Court's rulings. Other Presidents have been variously disturbed by decisions relating to flag-saluting and morning prayers in schools; the rights accorded the accused in criminal cases; bussing, to achieve racial balance in schools; and abortion, and have on occasion spoken out strongly against them. Rarely, though, since the 1930s, has the Court, *as an institution*, been subject to attack for its pronouncements. The Warren Court did arouse the enmity of the South because of its segregation rulings, and of the extreme right as a result of its decisions in a number of civil liberties cases, and calls were made for institutional changes in the Court and for the impeachment of the Chief Justice, the more intemperate calling for the hanging of Earl Warren. But, generally speaking opposition to a decision has been expressed in more measured terms, with opponents committed to using the normal legal processes to secure a reversal.

The nine unelected Justices of the Supreme Court (and to a lesser degree the judges of the inferior Federal Courts) are then in a pivotal position with regard to the distribution and exercise of power within the American political structure. They may frustrate the wishes of the nationally elected chief executive or they may legitimize his actions or extend his authority. Thus, the President may be circumscribed as in the Steel Seizure case, or he may be given almost plenary foreign affairs authority as in *Curtiss-Wright* (interestingly, by the same Court which had given Roosevelt so much trouble over his New Deal programme). Indeed, in this latter area, 'acting as an arm of the executive branch, the Court has done much to undermine [the] collective decision-making and shared powers' prescribed by the Constitution,[22] thereby effecting a radical change in the balance of responsibilities attempted by the Founding Fathers.

That the Court has a high opinion of its role in expounding the law is evidenced in *Cooper* v. *Aaron*,[23] in which a unanimous Court declared that 'the federal judiciary is supreme in the exposition of the law of the Constitution', but such an assertion is by no means universally accepted by all the actors in the political process, and Presidents have indicated, from time to time, that they did not accept Supreme Court interpretations on particular issues. Three of America's greatest Presidents — Jefferson, Lincoln, Franklin D. Roosevelt — have asserted their 'right to interpret the Constitution' for themselves and have refused 'to accept an interpretation placed upon it by judges when ... convinced that they are wrong'. To deny this position, to accept without reservation the *Cooper* v. *Aaron* view, 'would, as Jefferson and Lincoln and others have pointed out, place the chief executive and everyone else under a judicial despotism'. As Scigliano also observes, 'Judges are neither infallible nor the constitutional superiors of Presidents and congressmen' and 'it is the Constitution that the President swears to support, and not what the Court says about the Constitution'.[24] So, while Presidents will generally accord due deference to Court rulings, in the final analysis they have their own obligation to protect the

Constitution. On the other side of the coin, while judges may accept the judgement of their forebears in the 1958 decision, and believe in that ultimate right, they do, nevertheless, at times proceed very cautiously in their approach to certain fundamental questions which may arise. For instance, as Chase and Ducat suggest, in the *Da Costa* v. *Laird* case 'the U.S. Court of Appeals, Second Circuit, handled the issues with all the care attributed to porcupines making love'.[25] They are, after all, heirs of Marshall, and conscious of the fact that the handing down of a decision is but one part of the whole process of making a Constitution work. It does not take place in a political vacuum. The co-operation of the other participants in the governmental network is also necessary. That such co-operation has generally been forthcoming over the two hundred years of the Republic's history is testament to the skill with which Justices, 'possessed of the powers of neither purse nor sword' (to paraphrase Hamilton), have played the political as well as the judicial game. The legitimacy which the courts, and in particular the Supreme Court, have acquired in these two areas is, of course, of great advantage to the judges when their decisions may be under attack. America, possibly the most litigious nation in the world, is accustomed to the resolution of its problems in the courts of law. Voters write to their Congressman but it is to the courts that they turn in vast numbers for redress of grievances which will range from the picayune to the great constitutional principle. And, unless the President is outstandingly popular, they also take pleasure in seeing the highest elective officer held in check — a symbol of the supremacy of the law under which they all live.

Baum has written that 'the Supreme Court should be viewed as a legal institution as well as a political one,[26] and the balance in this statement neatly captures the manner in which the Court has developed over the last two hundred years. As we have noted, it is, in so many matters, a political body and politics will largely determine its relations with the President: relations which may range from the comfortable to the uneasy. A President may be lucky enough to be blessed with a Court which shares his political and social philosophies, or may have the opportunity, through appointments, to shape it in his particular image. On the other hand, he may labour hard in the face of a Court determined, when cases arise, to obstruct his efforts, and his opportunities for making his own appointments may come too late to benefit himself or may not even come at all.

The Constitution may have separated the institutions of government but the relations between the President and the Court demonstrate once more the truth in Neustadt's observation about the sharing of the power of the state. It is interesting to reflect upon the fact that while it is the Congress which possesses the legislative power of the nation, it is to the President and to the Supreme Court, as we noted earlier, and not to the Congress, that different commentators have at times applied the epithet 'imperial'.

Notes

1. *The Federalist*, no. LXXVIII.
2. *Marbury* v. *Madison* 1 Cr. 137 (1803).
3. Quoted by Robert J. Sickels, *The Presidency* (Englewood Cliffs, NJ: Prentice Hall, 1980), pp. 250–1. My italics.
4. Alexander Bickel, *The Least Dangerous Branch* (Indianapolis: Bobbs-Merrill, 1962), p.31.
5. Once a speech writer for Barry Goldwater, a right-wing Republican.
6. Robert Scigliano, *The Supreme Court and the Presidency* (New York: The Free Press, 1971), pp. 69–70.
7. 323 US 214 (1944).
8. E.S. Corwin, *The Constitution and What it Means Today*, revised by Harold W. Chase and Craig R. Ducat (Princeton: PUP 1978 edn), p.158.
9. *Da Costa* v. *Laird*, 471 F. 2d. (1973). Quoted in Corwin, loc.cit.
10. *Dames & Moore* v. *Reagan* (453 US 1981), cited by David Gray Adler 'Foreign Policy & The Separation of Powers:The Influence of the Judiciary', in Michael W. McCann and Gerald L. Houseman (eds), *Judging the Constitution* (Glenview Ill.: Scott, Foresman, 1989), pp.163–4. See also Louis Fisher, *Constitutional Conflicts Between Congress and the President* (Princeton: PUP, 1985), pp. 276–7.
11. The case was *Worcester* v. *Georgia*, 6 Peters 515 (1832).
12. *Youngstown Sheet and Tube Co.* v. *Sawyer*, 343 US 579 (1952).
13. *United States* v. *Nixon*, 418 US 683 (1974).
14. *Brown* v. *Board of Education, Topeka Kansas*, 347 US 483 (1954) and 349 US 294 (1955).
15. See Laurence Baum, *The Supreme Court* (Washington, DC: Congressional Quarterly Press, 1981), p.187.
16. Ibid. p.205.
17. Felix Frankfurter, *Law and Politics*, edited by Archibald Macleish and E.F. Prichard Jr, (New York: Harcourt, Brace, 1939), p.12.

18. David Truman, *The Governmental Process*, 2nd edn (New York: Knopf, Borzoi Books, 1971), p.480.
19. E.S. Corwin, *Court Over Constitution* (Gloucester, Mass.: Peter Smith, by arrangement with PUP, 1957), p.126. My italics.
20. Quoted by Raoul Berger, Government by Judiciary (Cambridge, Mass.: Harvard University Press, 1977), p.416.
21. Through the creation of 'substantive due process', the Justices turned a concept long recognized as relating to proceedings in Courts of Law (e.g. fair trials for accused persons) into a means of checking the legislative initiatives of Congress.
22. Adler, op. cit. p.177.
23. *Cooper* v. *Aaron*, 358 US 1 (1958).
24. Scigliano, op. cit. pp.56 and 55.
25. Chase and Ducat, op. cit. p.158.
26. Baum, op. cit. p.2.

Conclusion

Our study of the presidency of the United States offers considerable evidence of the paradox that, as Denton and Hahn have suggested, 'the office always seems too strong or too weak'.[1] The sight of a President on his own authority mobilizing vast armed forces and sending them into conflict or potential conflict situations in the Middle East speaks of massive strength. On the other hand, the image of the same President forced by Congress into protracted negotiations and, ultimately, compromises over his budget, shouts of considerable weakness. When *Time* magazine grudgingly accorded President Bush its accolade of Man of the Year,[2] it presented him as two men, the one resolute in foreign policy, the other wavering, confused and hamstrung in domestic policy. Abroad he offers leadership to the nation and to a large part of the world; at home he seems to offer drift.

While the 'two presidencies' thesis, discussed at greater length earlier in the book (see pp.107–8), does provide the most clearcut examples, we must recognize that the paradox of the stong/weak presidency does exist even within the domestic sphere: that while Congress generally appears able to obstruct Presidents, there have been occasions when some chief executives have managed to dominate the legislative branch — for example, during the New Deal period — although such dominance has not usually been long-lived. But if our study demonstrates a paradox of the presidency, we must also recognize that it demonstrates something fundamental about the nature of government in the United States — that it is more generally characterized by inertia than by progress, for the leadership which is so often denied the President cannot be provided by the Congress.

Quite obviously, central to the problems of the presidency in particular and of the government in general is that albatross of American politics, the Constitution. That document, which, as we have noted, emerged as a series of compromises among the fears and prejudices of the Founding Fathers — whether of democratic excesses or of executive tyranny — established the conditions in which conflict rather than co-operation among the various actors was likely to prevail. Institutions were separated and powers were shared, but no formal mechanisms were created which might assist the emergence of harmony between the executive and the legislature. Rather than a constitution under which government might flourish, this was, in Mezey's term, 'a constitution against government',[3] one more likely to produce stalemate than action. The Constitution probably represented the strongest commitment which could be obtained from those disparate and often suspicious states and might well have been suitable for the conditions of the eighteenth century, for in those days little was expected of government, as a perusal of the functions given to the Congress in Article I, section 8 of the constitution demonstrates. But that circumscribed role of the federal government is a thing of the past. Today, there are few areas where the federal government has no input. The problems of the economy and of society, the responsibilities which have been assumed, the expectations which have developed, all demand a responsible leadership and effective government. And yet, as the twentieth century draws to a close, leadership and government still remain, in large part, inhibited by the outmoded divisions which sprang from those eighteenth-century suspicions.

What is apparent from the history of the United States presidency is the fact that the power a President wields is much more a function of his own personal commitment, of the particular goals he is pursuing and of the readiness of other political actors — Congressmen, bureaucrats, judges — to accept his leads, than of any formalized grant of power by the Constitution. Indeed, it might be said that he leads despite, rather than because of the Constitution. Of course, during the last two hundred years a variety of men, with a variety of aspirations, have reached the White House. For some, attainment of the highest office has been in itself the ultimate goal, and they have been quite content to play a quiet executive role. There have been others with quite a different vision of the office, but whose attempts at leadership have been thwarted by Congressmen jealous of their own rights or by judges concerned to protect the Constitution against expansive chief executives. Yet others have been able to pursue a variety of adventures abroad while still facing opposition to policies relating to the domestic front. Finally, very occasionally, crisis has permitted Presidents, for a brief period, to rule unchecked, as the other institutions have abdicated in favour of the 'strong man'. However, what is most apparent is that successful leadership has been very much a sporadic occurrence, something which Presidents have never been assured of achieving, and something which Americans could never rely on receiving.

The Constitution is no longer, of course, just as the Founding Fathers created it. It has changed over the years, fleshed out by amendments, by statutes, by judicial decisions and by practice. But little has been done which might encourage greater co-operation between the two major arms of government. Indeed, when, on occasion, Congress and President have taken steps which might improve their working relationships — for example, the legislative veto — the Supreme Court has stood ready to denounce any provision it considered a breach of the institutional separation provided by the Constitution. Even political parties, which one might have expected to provide the means of mitigating the effects of the Founding Fathers' biases against action, have not developed in such a way as to be the agencies of positive government.

Political parties are crucial to systems of government which lay claim to the democratic criteria of being both representative and responsible. They represent the means whereby the electorate may make informed choices among rival philosophies or candidates for office, and the means whereby those who have held office may be held responsible for their use of the powers of the state. Most significantly, perhaps, organized, hierarchical party systems, such as those found, for example, in the United Kingdom, are the structures which allow for that conjunction of the executive and legislative powers of the state necessary for responsible and effective government.

Political parties in the United States have not provided that conjunction and have failed to undo that legacy of the Founding Fathers, have failed to bridge the constitutional divide which was central to the eighteenth-century idea of limited government. In their earliest days, when 'King Caucus' was dominant, when the legislative members of a party, as we have seen, chose their presidential candidates, parties did offer a means of overcoming the separation, albeit at the expense of making Congressmen the 'kingmakers'. But the Jacksonian 'revolution' and the democratization of presidential selection processes greatly weakened the congressional/presidential link. Furthermore, while the national conventions which were created at that time became the symbols of united, national parties, they were in fact mere shells disguising the reality that the parties were weak, disjointed local creatures whose representatives in Washington had little incentive to follow the leads of the President. Matters have not improved since the nineteenth century and, indeed, are probably worse. The parties have floundered during this century, losing much in the way of committed support, as the number of declared independents has grown, and, with the extension of the primary system, abdicating much of their responsibility for candidate selection. Candidates for congressional office are now all too often independents bearing a party label, owing little allegience to their nominal party or to a President, and dependent for election and re-election upon their own efforts and their own record. This almost anarchic situation effectively denies the electorate an opportunity to make an informed choice among candidates or to pass judgement on the use made of office. In such circumstances, the concept of responsible government cannot exist, for there is no collectivity to be held responsible. If there is any sense of 'responsibility' it is the responsibility of individuals for their own actions, not that of group members working for their version of the common good.

And what is true of candidates for Congress is even more true of the President. Today, as Patterson has noted, candidatures for the presidency 'are built upon the dismantling of the political party'.[4] Consequently, he who reaches the White House does so without the support in the legislature which might have been forthcoming had he been part of a national team, fighting a national election in party terms. As the focal point of government, a President may be blamed for the failure of Washington to deal with particular problems, but the truth of the matter may well be that, lacking a loyal party majority in the Congress, he is unable to take steps that he might recognize as necessary and desirable. While the sign that stood on President Truman's desk — 'the Buck

Stops Here' — may have represented his readiness to accept a blanket responsibility for the deeds or misdeeds of government, it did not reflect the true constitutional position, for so long as Congress acts as an independent legislative body, unwilling, automatically, to accept presidential initiatives, responsibility, like power, remains diffused.

Compounding the failure of the parties to act in a coherent fashion, Congress itself is so organized that the attempts to build majorities to support presidential initiatives encounter on-going difficulties. Power within the legislature is scattered among the profusion of committee and sub-committee jurisdictions, and this does not make for the easy emergence of the coalitions necessary for the passage of legislation. Consequently, while Congress may demand leads from the President it is slow to accept leadership. Congressional eyes are fixed firmly upon personal power, whether in relation to district or state, or to the Washington nexus. At times, presidential policies fit into their calculations, at others, they do not. Party leaders may attempt to put together majorities for their President, but unless they can demonstrate a coincidence between presidential and legislative goals, their task is difficult.

It has been argued that the mischief of the Founding Fathers, so far as the twentieth century is concerned, is that their creation provides no answer to the question, 'who should govern?' Concern over the nature of government and the absence of strong coherent leadership is not, as we noted earlier, a new phenomenon. There have long been those who have sought reform, with many of the proposals advanced being in the direction of a system more closely akin to a parliamentary style — as with Woodrow Wilson's advocacy of something approaching Cabinet-style government, or with the American Political Science Association's study, *Towards a More Responsible Two-Party System*. Coherent and responsible government demands that leadership should be fixed, and fixed, it is suggested, in the one person who is elected as the representative of the whole nation, the President. To achieve these ends, some have argued that institutional change would be sufficient, others that the main problem is attitudinal.

A number of suggestions have been made for institutional changes which might strengthen the presidential hand. For instance, some have argued that the Twenty-second Amendment (should be repealed, since, by denying a President a third elective term, it effectively renders him a 'lameduck' during his second term. As he will not be running in the next presidential race, there will be no 'coat-tails' effect (if ever there is one) to assist candidates for Congress. Consequently, it is suggested, Congressmen will feel no necessity to consider his needs. However, it seems highly unlikely that such a move would have any significant impact upon Congressmen, particularly in light of their remarkably high success rate in their re-election races and of the apparent readiness of a large part of the electorate to split its vote among candidates of the different parties rather than vote a straight party ticket.

Others have argued that a greater sense of unity between President and Congress would be created if the calendar of elections to the various offices coincided more, and they have proposed that the term for the House of Representatives should be extended to four years, and that for the Senate to eight years (with half retiring every four years). In the past, when it was highly unusual for a President to be elected without a majority for his party in the House of Representatives, and when it was the mid-term elections which might cause the President to lose his nominal majority in Congress, such a proposal might well have had some appeal, but now that we have seen the regular occurrence of Republican Presidents elected at the same time as Democratic Houses, the argument for change does not seem to carry much weight. Nevertheless, some would argue that such an extension of Congressmen's terms would render them less dependent upon their constituencies and parochial issues. They would then be in a position to adopt more statesmanlike attitudes towards national problems.

Yet others have argued for a direct increase in presidential power through the introduction of the item veto, something possessed by most state governors. This could undoubtedly prove a valuable addition to the President's armoury in negotiating with Congress — he would no longer be put in the position of having to accept items of which he disapproved in a bill whose general purposes he desired. But even this would be a mere tinkering with a situation which some believe to be much more intractable.

For some, real change in the nature of government in the United States will only come when attitudes change, when Congress accepts John Stuart Mill's dictum that a numerous assembly is ill-fitted for the task of legislation, and instead accepts that its role should be that of representation rather than legislation.[5] Acceptance of such a role would, of course, involve considerable self-denial by other actors in the political process. Congressmen would need to be prepared to surrender their personal positions of power in order to subscribe to the President's conception of a greater good. Chairmanships of committees and sub-committees, rather than being the means whereby their holders enhanced their own prestige and authority, would become the means whereby presidential goals were attained, subject to the oversight functions which are the usual and appropriate functions of a legislative body. There does, however, appear to be little reason why those with power should abandon it in favour of a President whose policies may or may not prove beneficial in the home district or state. Elections for the Congress are largely concerned with matters parochial rather than national or international, and Congressmen standing for re-election receive little credit for supporting a President's policies if those policies work to the disadvantage of the district or state.

It is possible, some have argued, that the necessary changes in attitude by Congressmen might occur if the political parties were to reassert themselves as the appropriate agencies through which office is attained. If they were to resume their role in the selection and promotion of candidates for the presidency and for Congress, abandoning a system which in effect leaves offices as prizes to be seized by opportunists acting largely outside the parties, then links between the executive and the legislature might be strengthened. A sense of common purpose might then develop, and parties could become the means whereby power was exercised and responsibility measured.

While the presidential/congressional axis represents the most visible manifestation of weak, uncoordinated government there is yet another branch of government which, as we have seen, contributes to the weakness of presidential leadership: the bureaucracy. The complexity of America's administrative processes, the vast number of issue networks in which bureaucrats, chairmen of congressional committees and sub-committees, and representatives of interest groups interact, creates a situation in which decisions derive more often from the outcome of complex negotiations among the various parties than from presidential fiat. The President may, constitutionally, head the vast bureaucratic machine, but in reality his edict does not run far. His desires or goals are but one element in the calculations that go into the determination of policy. Those who would seek to retrieve power for the presidency from such entrenched networks (to which, at times, the epithet 'iron triangles' has been applied)[6] will face considerable opposition from those for whom the existing arrangements provide undoubted advantage.

The attainment of a more coherent system of leadership in the United States through attitudinal changes is then dependent in large part on the different participants in the processes of government. First, and foremost perhaps, those who would be President would need to surrender their rights to campaign for candidacy and presidency as their own agents rather than as representatives of party interests. Such a move might be a first step in the direction of strengthening links with party members in Congress. However, many would see such a development as representing a threat to their ambitions, restoring, as it would, the power of the party brokers. Change would also require that others be prepared to sacrifice their present power in favour of the President: to exchange power for mere influence. At the moment there appear to be few incentives for such self-denial. It is, of course, possible that a major crisis might induce change, with the electorate demanding leadership rather than drift and reacting against the undue influence of vested interests within the system. But there is little evidence in American history that, should such change occur, it would be permanent. Indeed, on the contrary, it would appear that periods of strong presidential leadership in the past have tended to produce a reaction, a reassertion by the other branches of their authority. If one relies upon attitudinal changes to produce the kind of government that is sought, one must recognize that while attitudes can and do change over time they are capable of changing in many directions. Perhaps, after all, what is needed, if responsible leadership is to be achieved, is a constitutional overhaul which does give real power to the President, subject to an ultimate congressional oversight. Such change, while it might not be able to guarantee the co-operation which is essential if any system of government is to work properly, could then at least provide an answer to the question, *who should govern*?

Finally, however, we must enter one important caveat concerning much of the above discussion. While there are many Americans who have called for the changes which might result in stronger government, there are many others who are happy to see power diffused. There is still a considerable body of opinion which rejects an Anglo-centric approach, which distrusts strong central government and which welcomes the fact that Congressmen, elected from local communities, are able to check the plans and policies of the person elected nationwide. They value the protection that can thereby be given to local interests, even if (or because) it is at the expense of national interests or programmes. Such attitudes have, of course, a long pedigree, dating back to the Founding Fathers themselves. They have been reinforced by the cult of the individual which developed in the opening up of the West and the creation of new states, and by the *laissez-faire*, social Darwinist philosophy that stressed the baleful effects of government interference.

Bearing in mind these conflicting attitudes, we should hesitate before we rush to judgement on the American presidency or, by extension, the whole system of government. We should rather accept that what many may perceive as weakness others may see as strength. Considering the size of the United States, the diversity of its population and the complexity of its economic and social interests, we might perhaps simply muse, paraphrasing Dr Samuel Johnson, that governing America 'is like a dog walking on his hinder legs. It is not done well; but you are surprised to find it done at all'.

Notes

1. Robert E. Denton Jr. and Dan F. Hahn, Presidential Communication (New York: Praeger, 1986), p.XI.
2. *Time*, 7 January 1991.
3. Michael L. Mezey, *Congress, The President and Public Policy* (Boulder, Colo.: Westview Press, 1989), p.18.
4. T.E. Patterson, *The Mass Media Election* (New York: Praeger, 1980), p.179.
5. See Mezey's arguments, op. cit. p.201.
6. Hinting at the strength of the connections.

Appendix I

The Constitution of the United States of America

We the People of the United States, in Order to form a more perfect Union, establish Justice, insure domestic Tranquility, provide for the common defence, promote the general Welfare, and secure the Blessings of Liberty to ourselves and our Posterity, do ordain and establish this Constitution for the United States of America.

Article I

Section 1.   All legislative Powers herein granted shall be vested in a Congress of the United States, which shall consist of a Senate and House of Representatives.

Section 2.   The House of Representatives shall be composed of Members chosen every second Year by the People of the several States, and the Electors in each State shall have the Qualifications requisite for Electors of the most numerous Branch of the State Legislature.

No Person shall be a Representative who shall not have attained to the age of twenty-five Years, and been seven Years a Citizen of the United States, and who shall not, when elected, be an Inhabitant of that State in which he shall be chosen.

Representatives and direct Taxes shall be apportioned among the several States which may be included within this Union, according to their respective Numbers, which shall be determined by adding to the whole Number of free Persons, including those bound to Service for a Term of Years, and excluding Indians not taxed, *three-fifths of all other persons.*[1] The actual Enumeration shall be made within three Years after the first Meeting of the Congress of the United States, and within every subsequent Term of ten Years, in such Manner as they shall by Law direct. The Number of Representatives shall not exceed one for every thirty Thousand, but each State shall have at Least one Representative: and until such enumeration shall be made, the State of New Hampshire shall be entitled to chuse three, Massachusetts eight, Rhode-Island and Providence Plantations one,

---

1.   Italics indicate passages altered by subsequent amendments. This was revised by the Sixteenth (apportionment of taxes) and Fourteenth (determination of persons) Amendments.

185

Connecticut five, New-York six, New Jersey four, Pennsylvania eight, Delaware one, Maryland six, Virginia ten, North Carolina five, South Carolina five, and Georgia three.

When vacancies happen in the Representation from any State, the Executive Authority thereof shall issue Writs of Election to fill such Vacancies.

The House of Representatives shall chuse their Speaker and other Officers; and shall have the sole Power of Impeachment.

Section 3. The Senate of the United States shall be composed of two Senators from each State, *chosen by the Legislature thereof,*[2] for six Years; and each Senator shall have one Vote.

Immediately after they shall be assembled in Consequence of the first Election, they shall be divided as equally as may be into three Classes. The Seats of the Senators of the first Class shall be vacated at the Expiration of the second Year, of the Second Class at the Expiration of the fourth Year, and of the third Class at the Expiration of the sixth Year, so that one-third may be chosen every second year; *and if Vacancies happen by Resignation, or otherwise, during the Recess of the legislature of any state, the Executive thereof may make temporary Appointments until the next Meeting of the Legislature, which shall then fill such Vacancies.*[3]

No Person shall be a Senator who shall not have attained to the Age of thirty Years, and been nine Years a Citizen of the United States, and who shall not, when elected, be an Inhabitant of the state for which he shall be chosen.

The Vice President of the United States shall be President of the Senate, but shall have no Vote, unless they be equally divided.

The Senate shall chuse their other Officers, and also a President pro tempore, in the Absence of the Vice President, or when he shall exercise the Office of President of the United States.

The Senate shall have the sole Power to try all Impeachments. When sitting for that Purpose, they shall be on Oath or Affirmation. When the President of the United States is tried, the Chief Justice shall preside: And no Person shall be convicted without the Concurrence of two-thirds of the Members present.

Judgment in Cases of Impeachment shall not extend further than to removal from Office, and disqualification to hold and enjoy any Office of honour, Trust or Profit under the United States; but the Party convicted shall nevertheless be liable and subject to Indictment, Trial, Judgment and Punishment, according to Law.

Section 4. The Times, Places and Manner of holding Elections for Senators and Representatives, shall be prescribed in each State by the Legislature thereof; but the Congress may at any time by Law make or alter such Regulations, except as to the Places of chusing Senators.

The Congress shall assemble at least once in every Year, and such

2. Revised by Seventeenth Amendment.
3. Revised by Seventeenth Amendment.

Meeting shall be *on the first Monday in December,*[4] unless they shall by Law appoint a different Day.

Section 5.   Each House shall be the Judge of the Elections, Returns and Qualifications of its own Members, and a Majority of each shall constitute a Quorum to do Business; but a smaller Number may adjourn from day to day, and may be authorized to compel the Attendance of absent Members, in such Manner, and under such Penalties as each House may provide.

Each House may determine the Rules of its Proceedings, punish its Members for disorderly Behavior, and, with the Concurrence of two-thirds, expel a Member.

Each House shall keep a Journal of its Proceedings, and from time to time publish the same, excepting such parts as may in their Judgment require Secrecy; and the Yeas and Nays of the Members of either House on any question shall, at the Desire of one-fifth of those Present, be entered on the Journal.

Neither House, during the Session of Congress, shall, without the Consent of the other, adjourn for more than three days, nor to any other Place than that in which the two Houses shall be sitting.

Section 6.   The Senators and Representatives shall receive a Compensation for their Services, to be ascertained by Law, and paid out of the Treasury of the United States. They shall in all Cases, except Treason, Felony and Breach of the Peace, be privileged from Arrest during their Attendance at the Session of their respective Houses, and in going to and returning from the same, and for any Speech or Debate in either House, they shall not be questioned in any other Place.

No Senator or Representative shall, during the Time for which he was elected, be appointed to any civil Office under the Authority of the United States, which shall have been created, or the Emoluments whereof shall have been encreased during such time; and no Person holding any Office under the United States, shall be a Member of either House during his Continuance in Office.

Section 7.   All Bills of raising Revenue shall originate in the House of Representatives; but the Senate may propose or concur with Amendments as on other Bills.

Every Bill which shall have passed the House of Representatives and the Senate, shall, before it become a Law, be presented to the President of the United States; if he approve he shall sign it, but if not he shall return it, with his Objections to that House in which it shall have originated, who shall enter the Objections at large on their Journal, and proceed to reconsider it. If after such Reconsideration two thirds of that House shall agree to pass the Bill, it shall be sent, together with the Objections, to the other House, by which it shall likewise be reconsidered, and if approved by two thirds of that House, it shall becomes a Law. But in all such Cases the Votes of both Houses shall

4.   Revised by Twentieth Amendment.

be determined by Yeas and Nays, and the Names of the Persons voting for and against the Bill shall be entered on the Journal of each House respectively. If any Bill shall not be returned by the President within ten Days (Sundays excepted) after it shall have been presented to him, the Same shall be a Law, in like Manner as if he had signed it, unless the Congress by their Adjournment prevent its Return, in which Case it shall not be a Law.

Every Order, Resolution, or Vote to which the Concurrence of the Senate and House of Representatives may be necessary (except on a question of Adjournment) shall be presented to the President of the United States; and before the Same shall take Effect, shall be approved by him, or being disapproved by him, shall be repassed by two-thirds of the Senate and House of Representatives, according to the Rules and Limitations prescribed in the Case of a Bill.

Section 8.   The Congress shall have Power To lay and collect Taxes, Duties, Imposts and Excises, to pay the Debts and provide for the common Defence and general Welfare of the United States; but all Duties, Imposts and Excises shall be uniform throughout the United States;

To borrow Money on the credit of the United States;

To regulate Commerce with foreign Nations, and among the several States, and with the Indian Tribes;

To establish an uniform Rule of Naturalization, and uniform Laws on the subject of Bankruptcies throughout the United States;

To coin Money, regulate the Value thereof, and of foreign Coin, and fix the Standard of Weights and Measures;

To provide for the Punishment of counterfeiting the Securities and current Coin of the United States;

To establish Post Offices and post Roads;

To promote the Progress of Science and useful Arts, by securing for limited Times to Authors and Inventors the exclusive Right to their respective Writings and Discoveries;

To constitute Tribunals inferior to the Superior Court;

To define and punish piracies and Felonies committed on the high Seas, and Offences against the Law of Nations;

To declare War, grant Letters of Marque and Reprisal, and make Rules concerning Captures on Land and Water;

To raise and support Armies, but no Appropriation of Money to that Use shall be for a longer Term than two Years;

To provide and maintain a Navy;

To make Rules for the Government and Regulation of the land and naval Forces;

To provide for calling forth the Militia to execute the Laws of the Union, suppress Insurrections and repel Invasions;

To provide for organizing, arming, and disciplining, the Militia, and for governing such Part of them as may be employed in the Service of the United States, reserving to the States respectively, the Appointment of the Officers, and the Authority of training the Militia according to the discipline prescribed by Congress;

To exercise exclusive Legislation in all Cases whatsoever, over such District (not exceeding ten Miles square) as may, by Cession of particular States, and the Acceptance of Congress; become the Seat of the Government of the United States, and to exercise like Authority over all Places purchased by the Consent of the Legislature of the State in which the Same shall be, for the Erection of Forts, Magazines, Arsenals, dock-Yards, and other needful Buildings; — And

To make all Laws which shall be necessary and proper for carrying into Execution the foregoing Powers, and all other Powers vested by this Constitution in the Government of the United States, or in any Department or Officer thereof.

Section 9. The Migration or Importation of such Persons as any of the States now existing shall think proper to admit, shall not be prohibited by the Congress prior to the Year one thousand eight hundred and eight, but a Tax or duty may be imposed on such Importation, not exceeding ten dollars for each Person.

The Privilege of the Writ of Habeas Corpus shall not be suspended, unless when in Cases of Rebellion or Invasion the public Safety may require it.

No Bill of Attainder or ex post facto Law shall be passed.

No Capitation, or other direct, Tax shall be laid, unless in Proportion to the Census or Enumeration herein before directed to be taken.[5]

No Tax or Duty shall be laid on Articles exported from any State.

No Preference shall be given by any Regulation of Commerce or Revenue to the Ports of one State over those of another; nor shall Vessels bound to, or from, one State, be obliged to enter, clear, or pay Duties in another.

No Money shall be drawn from the Treasury, but in Consequence of Appropriations made by Law; and a regular Statement and Account of the Receipts and Expenditures of all public Money shall be published from time to time.

No title of Nobility shall be granted by the United States: And no Person holding any Office of Profit or Trust under them, shall, without the Consent of the Congress, accept of any present, Emolument, Office, or Title, of any kind whatever, from any King, Prince, or foreign State.

Section 10. No State shall enter into any Treaty, Alliance, or Confederation; grant Letters of Marque and Reprisal; coin Money; emit Bills of Credit; may any Thing but gold and silver Coin a Tender in Payment of Debts; pass any Bill of Attainder, ex post facto Law, or Law impairing the Obligation of Contracts, or Grant any Title of Nobility.

No State shall, without the Consent of the Congress, lay any Imposts or Duties on Imports or Exports, except what may be absolutely necessary for executing its inspection Laws: and the net Produce of all Duties and Imposts, laid by any State on Imports or Exports, shall be for the Use of the Treasury of the United States; and all such Laws shall be subject to the Revision and Controul of the Congress.

---

5. Revised by Sixteenth Amendment.

No State shall, without the Consent of Congress, lay any Duty of Tonnage, keep Troops, or Ships of War in time of Peace, enter into any Agreement or Compact with another State, or with a foreign Power, or engage in War, unless actually invaded, or in such imminent Danger as will not admit of delay.

Article II

Section 1. **The executive Power shall be vested in a President of the United States of America.** *He shall hold his Office during the Term of four Years,*[6] **and, together with the Vice President, chosen for the same Term be elected as follows:**

Each State shall appoint, in such Manner as the Legislature thereof may direct, a Number of Electors, equal to the whole Number of Senators and Representatives to which the State may be entitled in the Congress but no Senator or Representative, or Person holding an Office of Trust or Profit under the United States, shall be appointed an Elector.

The Electors shall meet in their respective States, and vote by Ballot for two Persons, of whom at least one shall not be an Inhabitant of the same State with themselves. And they shall make a List of all the Persons voted for, and of the Number of Votes for each; which List they shall sign and certify, and transmit sealed to the Seat of the Government of the United States, directed to the President of the Senate. The President of the Senate shall, in the Presence of the Senate and House of Representatives, open all the Certificates, and the Votes shall then be counted. The Person having the greatest Number of Votes shall be the President, if such Number be a Majority of the whole Number of Electors appointed; and if there be more than one who have such Majority, and have an equal Number of Votes, then the House of Representatives shall immediately chuse by Ballot one of them for President; and if no person have a Majority, then from the five highest on the List the said House shall in like Manner chuse the President. But in chusing the President, the Votes shall be taken by States, the Representation from each State having one Vote. A quorum for this purpose shall consist of a Member or Members from two-thirds of the States, and a Majority of all the States shall be necessary to a Choice. In every Case, after the Choice of the President, the Person having the greatest Number of Votes of the Electors shall be the Vice President. But if there should remain two or more who have equal Votes, the Senate shall chuse from them by Ballot the Vice President.[7]

The Congress may determine the Time of chusing the Electors, and the Day on which they shall give their Votes; which Day shall be the same throughout the United States.

No Person except a natural born Citizen, or a Citizen of the United States, at the time of the Adoption of this Constitution, shall be eligible to the Office of President; neither shall any Person be eligible to that

6. See Twenty-second Amendment.
7. Superseded by Twelfth Amendment.

Office who shall not have attained to the Age of thirty-five Years, and been fourteen Years a Resident within the United States.

In case of the Removal of the President from Office, or of his Death, Resignation, or Inability to discharge the Powers and Duties of the said Office, the Same shall devolve on the Vice President, and the Congress may by Law provide for the Case of Removal, Death, Resignation or Inability, both of the President and Vice President, declaring what Officer shall then act as President, as such Officer shall act accordingly, until the Disability be removed, or a President shall be elected.[8]

The President shall, at stated Times, receive for his Services, a Compensation which shall neither be encreased nor diminished during the Period for which he shall have been elected, and he shall not receive within that Period any other Emolument from the United States, or any of them.

Before he enter on the Execution of his Office, he shall take the following Oath or Affirmation — 'I do solemnly swear (or affirm) that I will faithfully execute the Office of President of the United States, and will to the best of my Ability, preserve, protect and defend the Constitution of the United States.'

Section 2. The President shall be Commander in Chief of the Army and Navy of the United States, and of the Militia of the several States, when called into the actual service of the United States; he may require the Opinion, in writing, of the principal Officer in each of the executive Departments, upon any Subject relating to the Duties of their respective Offices, and he shall have Power to grant Reprieves and Pardons for Offences against the United States, except in Cases of Impeachment.

He shall have Power, by and with the Advice and Consent of the Senate, to make Treaties, provided two-thirds of the Senators present concur; and he shall nominate, and by and with the Advice and Consent of the Senate, shall appoint Ambassadors, and other public Ministers and Consuls, Judges of the supreme Court, and all other Officers of the United States, whose Appointments are not herein otherwise provided for, and which shall be established by Law: but the Congress may by Law vest the Appointment of such inferior Officers, as they think proper, in the President alone, in the Courts of Law, or in the Heads of Departments.

The President shall have Power to fill up all Vacancies that may happen during the Recess of the Senate, by granting Commissions which shall expire at the End of their next Session.

Section 3. He shall from time to time give the Congress Information of the State of the Union, and recommend to their Consideration such Measures as he shall judge necessary and expedient; he may, on extraordinary Occasions, convene both Houses, or either of them, and in Case of Disagreement between them, with Respect to the Time of Adjournment, he may adjourn them to such Time as he shall think proper; he shall receive Ambassadors and other public Ministers, he

---

8. Revised by Twenty-fifth Amendment.

shall take Care that the Laws be faithfully executed, and shall Commission all the Officers of the United States.

Section 4. The President, Vice President and all civil Officers of the United States, shall be removed from Office on Impeachment for, and Conviction of Treason, Bribery, or other high Crimes and Misdemeanors.

Article III

Section 1. The judicial Power of the United States, shall be vested in one supreme Court and in such inferior Courts as the Congress may from time to time ordain and establish. The Judges, both of the supreme and inferior Courts, shall hold their Offices during good Behaviour, and shall, at stated Times, receive for their Services, a Compensation, which shall not be diminished during the Continuance in Office.

Section 2. The judicial Power shall extend to all Cases, in Law and Equity, arising under this Constitution, the Laws of the United States, and Treaties made, or which shall be made, under their Authority; — to all Cases affecting Ambassadors, other public Ministers and Consuls; — to all Cases of admiralty and maritime Jurisdiction; — to Controversies to which the United States shall be a Party; — to Controversies between two or more States; — *between a State and Citizens of another State;*[9] — between Citizens of different States; — between Citizens of the same State claiming Lands under Grants of different States, *and between a State or the Citizens thereof, and foreign States, Citizens, or Subjects.*[9]

In all cases affecting Ambassadors, other public Ministers and Consuls, and those in which a State shall be Party, the supreme Court shall have original Jurisdiction. In all the other Cases before mentioned, the supreme Court shall have appellate Jurisdiction, both as to Law and Fact, with such Exceptions, and under such Regulations as the Congress shall make.

The Trial of all Crimes, except in Cases of Impeachment, shall be by Jury; and such Trial shall be held in the State where the said Crimes shall have been committed; but when not committed within any State, the Trial shall be at such Place or Places as the Congress may by Law have directed.

Section 3. Treason against the United States, shall consist only in levying War against them, or in adhering to their Enemies, giving them Aid and Comfort. No Person shall be convicted of Treason unless on the Testimony of two Witnesses to the same overt Act, or on Confession in open Court.

The Congress shall have Power to declare the Punishment of Treason, but no Attainder of Treason shall work Corruption of Blood, or Forfeiture except during the Life of the person attainted.

Article IV

Section 1. Full Faith and Credit shall be given in each State to the public Acts, Records, and judicial Proceedings of every other State. And the

9. Revised by Eleventh Amendment.

Congress may by general Laws prescribe the Manner in which such Acts, Records, and Proceedings shall be proved, and the Effect thereof.

Section 2. The Citizens of each State shall be entitled to all Privileges and Immunities of Citizens in the several States.

A Person charged in any State with Treason, Felony, or other Crime, who shall flee from Justice, and be found in another State, shall on Demand of the executive Authority of the State from which he fled, be delivered up, to be removed to the State having Jurisdiction of the Crime.

No person held to Service or Labour in one State, under the Laws thereof, escaping into another, shall, in Consequence of any Law or Regulation therein, be discharged from such Service or Labour, but shall be delivered up on Claim of the Party to whom such Service or Labour may be due.[10]

Section 3. New States may be admitted by the Congress into this Union; but no new State shall be formed or erected within the Jurisdiction of any other State; nor any State be formed by the Junction of two or more States, or Parts of States, without the Consent of the Legislatures of the States concerned as well as of the Congress.

The Congress shall have Power to dispose of and make all needful Rules and Regulations respecting the Territory or other Property belonging to the United States; and nothing in this Constitution shall be so construed as to Prejudice any claims of the United States, or of any particular State.

Section 4. **The United States shall guarantee to every state in this Union a Republican Form of Government, and shall protect each of them against Invasion; and on Application of the Legislature, or of the Executive (when the Legislature cannot be convened) against domestic Violence.**

Article V

The Congress, whenever two-thirds of both Houses shall deem it necessary, shall propose Amendments to this Constitution, or, on the Application of the Legislatures of two-thirds of the several States, shall call a Convention for proposing Amendments, which, in either Case, shall be valid to all Intents and Purposes, as Part of this Constitution, when ratified by the Legislatures of three-fourths of the several States, or by Conventions in three-fourths thereof, as the one or the other Mode of Ratification may be proposed by the Congress; Provided that no Amendment which may be made prior to the Year one thousand eight hundred and eight shall in any Manner affect the first and fourth Clauses in the Ninth Section of the first Article; and that no State, without its Consent, shall be deprived of its equal Suffrage in the Senate.

Article VI

All Debts contracted and Engagements entered into, before the Adoption of this Constitution, shall be as valid against the United States under this Constitution, as under the Confederation.[11]

10. Superseded by Thirteenth Amendment.
11. See Fourteenth Amendment, Section 4.

This Constitution, and the Laws of the United States which shall be made in Pursuance thereof; and all Treaties made, or which shall be made, under the Authority of the United States, shall be the supreme Law of the Land; and the Judges in every State shall be bound thereby, any Thing in the Constitution or Laws of any State to the Contrary notwithstanding.

The Senators and Representatives before mentioned, and the Members of the several State Legislatures, and all executive and judicial Officers, both of the United States and of the several States, shall be bound by Oath or Affirmation, to support this Constitution; but no religious Test shall ever be required as a Qualification to any Office or public Trust under the United States.

Article VII

The Ratification of the Conventions of nine States, shall be sufficient for the Establishment of this Constitution between the States so ratifying the Same.

Done in Convention by the Unanimous Consent of the States present the Seventeenth Day of September in the Year of our Lord one thousand seven hundred and eighty-seven and of the Independence of the United States of America the twelfth. In witness whereof We have hereunto subscribed our Names.

. . .

ARTICLES IN ADDITION TO, AND AMENDMENT OF, THE CONSTITUTION OF THE UNITED STATES OF AMERICA, PROPOSED BY CONGRESS, AND RATIFIED BY THE SEVERAL STATES, PURSUANT TO THE FIFTH ARTICLE OF THE ORIGINAL CONSTITUTION.
(Ratification of the first ten amendments was completed 15 December, 1791.)

Amendment I

Congress shall make no law respecting an establishment of religion, or prohibiting the free exercise thereof; or abridging the freedom of speech, or of the press; or the right of the people peaceably to assemble, and to petition the Government for a redress of grievances.

Amendment II

A well-regulated Militia, being necessary to the security of a free State, the right of the people to keep and bear Arms, shall not be infringed.

Amendment III

No Soldier shall, in time of peace be quartered in any house, without the consent of the Owner, nor in time of war, but in a manner to be prescribed by law.

Amendment IV

The right of the people to be secure in their persons, houses, papers, and effects, against unreasonable searches and seizures, shall not be violated, and no Warrants shall issue, but upon probable cause, supported by Oath or affirmation, and particularly describing the place to be searched, and the persons or things to be seized.

Amendment V

No person shall be held to answer for a capital, or other infamous crime, unless on a presentment or indictment of a Grand Jury, except in cases arising in the land or naval forces, or in the Militia, when in actual service in time of War or public danger; nor shall any person be subject for the same offence to be twice put in jeopardy of life or limb; nor shall be compelled in any criminal case to be a witness against himself, nor be deprived of life, liberty, or property, without due process of law; nor shall private property be taken for public use, without just compensation.

Amendment VI

In all criminal prosecutions, the accused shall enjoy the right to a speedy and public trial, by an impartial jury of the State and district wherein the crime shall have been committed, which district shall have been previously ascertained by law, and to be informed of the nature and cause of the accusation; to be confronted with the witnesses against him; to have compulsory process for obtaining witnesses in his favor, and to have the Assistance of Counsel for his defence.

Amendment VII

In Suits at common law, where the value in controversy shall exceed twenty dollars, the right of trial by jury shall be preserved, and no fact tried by a jury, shall be otherwise reexamined in any Court of the United States, than according to the rules of the common law.

Amendment VIII

Excessive bail shall not be required, nor excessive fines imposed, nor cruel and unusual punishments inflicted.

Amendment IX

The enumeration in the Constitution, of certain rights, shall not be construed to deny or disparage others retained by the people.

Amendment X

The powers not delegated to the United States by the Constitution, nor prohibited by it to the States, are reserved to the States respectively, or to the people.

Amendment XI (8 January 1798)

The Judicial power of the United States shall not be construed to extend to any suit in law or equity, commenced or prosecuted against one of the United States by Citizens of another State, or by Citizens or Subjects of any Foreign State.

Amendment XII (25 September 1804)

The Electors shall meet in their respective states and vote by ballot for President and Vice President, one of whom, at least, shall not be an inhabitant of the same state with themselves; they shall name in their ballots the person voted for as President, and in distinct ballots the person voted for as Vice President, and they shall make distinct lists of all persons voted for as President and of all persons voted for as Vice President, and of the number of votes for each, which lists they shall sign and certify, and transmit sealed to the seat of the government of the United States, directed to the President of the Senate; — The President of the Senate shall, in the presence of Senate and House of Representatives, open all the certificates and the votes shall then be counted; — The person having the greatest number of votes for President, shall be the President, if such number be a majority of the whole number of Electors appointed; and if no person have such majority, then from the persons having the highest numbers not exceeding three on the list of those voted for as President, the House of Representatives shall choose immediately, by ballot, the President. But in choosing the President, the votes shall be taken by states, the representation from each state having one vote; a quorum for this purpose shall consist of a member or members from two-thirds of the states, and a majority of all the states shall be necessary to a choice. And if the House of Representatives shall not choose a President whenever the right of choice shall devolve upon them, *before the fourth day of March next following*,[12] then the Vice President shall act as President, as in the case of the death or other constitutional disability of the President. — The person having the greatest number of votes as Vice President shall be the Vice President, if such number be a majority of the whole number of Electors appointed, and if no person have a majority, then from the two highest numbers on the list, the Senate shall choose the Vice President; a quorum for the purpose shall consist of two-thirds of the whole number of Senators, and a majority of the whole number shall be necessary to a choice. But no person constitutionally ineligible to the office of President shall be eligible to that of Vice President of the United States.

Amendment XIII (18 December 1865)

Section 1. Neither slavery nor involuntary servitude, except as a punishment for crime whereof the party shall have been duly convicted, shall exist within the United States, or any place subject to their jurisdiction.

12. Revised by the Twentieth Amendment.

Section 2.   Congress shall have the power to enforce this article by appropriate legislation.

Amendment XIV (28 July 1869)

Section 1.   All persons born or naturalized in the United States, and subject to the jurisdiction thereof, are citizens of the United States and of the State wherein they reside. No State shall make or enforce any law which shall abridge the privileges or immunities of citizens of the United States; nor shall any State deprive any person of life, liberty, or property, without the process of law; nor deny to any person within its jurisdiction the equal protection of the laws.

Section 2.   Representatives shall be apportioned among the several States according to their respective numbers, counting the whole number of persons in each State, excluding Indians not taxed. But when the right to vote at any election for the choice of electors for President and Vice President of the United States, Representatives in Congress, the Executive and Judicial officers of a State, or the members of the Legislature thereof, is denied to any of the male inhabitants of such State, being twenty-one years of age, and citizens of the United States, or in any way abridged, except for participation in rebellion, or other crime, the basis of representation therein shall be reduced in the proportion which the number of such male citizens shall bear to the whole number of male citizens twenty-one years of age in such State.

Section 3.   No person shall be a Senator or Representative in Congress, or elector of President and Vice President, or hold any office, civil or military, under the United States, or under any State, who, having previously taken an oath, as a member of Congress, or as an officer of the United States, or as a member of any State legislature, or as an executive or judicial officer of any State, to support the Constitution of the United States, shall have engaged in insurrection or rebellion against the same, or given aid or comfort to the enemies thereof. But Congress may by a vote of two-thirds of each House, remove such disability.

Section 4.   The validity of the public debt of the United States, authorized by law, including debts incurred for payment of pensions and bounties for services in suppressing insurrection or rebellion, shall not be questioned. But neither the United States nor any State shall assume or pay any debt or obligation incurred in aid of insurrection or rebellion against the United States, or any claim for the loss or emancipation of any slave; but all such debts, obligations, and claims shall be held illegal and void.

Section 5.   The Congress shall have power to enforce, by appropriate legislation, the provisions of this article.

Amendment XV (30 March 1870)

Section 1.   The right of citizens of the United States to vote shall not be denied or abridged by the United States or by any State on account of race, color, or previous conditions of servitude.

Section 2.   The Congress shall have power to enforce this article by appropriate legislation.

Amendment XVI (25 February 1913)

The Congress shall have power to lay and collect taxes on incomes, from whatever source derived, without apportionment among the several States, and without regard to any census or enumeration.

Amendment XVII (31 May 1913)

The Senate of the United States shall be composed of two Senators from each State, elected by the people thereof, for six years; and each Senator shall have one vote. The electors in each State shall have the qualifications requisite for electors of the most numerous branch of the State legislatures.

When vacancies happen in the representation of any State in the Senate, the executive authority of such State shall issue writs of election to fill such vacancies: *Provided*, That the legislature of any State may empower the executive thereof to make temporary appointments until the people fill the vacancies by election as the legislature may direct.

This amendment shall not be so construed as to affect the election or term of any Senator chosen before it becomes valid as part of the Constitution.

Amendment XVIII (29 January 1919)

Section 1.   After one year from the ratification of this article the manufacture, sale, or transportation of intoxicating liquors within, the importation thereof into, or the exportation thereof from the United States and all territory subject to the jurisdiction thereof for beverage purposes is hereby prohibited.

Section 2.   The Congress and the several States shall have concurrent power to enforce this article by appropriate legislation.

Section 3.   This article shall be inoperative unless it shall have been ratified as an amendment to the Constitution by the legislatures of the several States, as provided in the Constitution within seven years from the date of the submission hereof to the States by the Congress.[13]

Amendment XIX (26 August 1920)

The right of citizens of the United States to vote shall not be denied or abridged by the United States or by any State on account of sex.

Congress shall have power to enforce this article by appropriate legislatioin.

Amendment XX (6 February 1933)

Section 1.   **The terms of the President and Vice President shall end at noon on the 20th day of January, and the terms of Senators and Representatives at noon on the 3rd day of January, of the years in which such terms would have ended if this article had not been ratified; and the terms of their successors shall then begin.**

13. Repealed by the Twenty-first Amendment.

Section 2. The Congress shall assemble at least once in every year, and such meeting shall begin at noon on the 3rd day of January, unless they shall by law appoint a different day.

Section 3. If, at the time fixed for the beginning of the term of the President, the President elect shall have died, the Vice President elect shall become President. If a President shall not have been chosen before the time fixed for the beginning of his term, or if the President elect shall have failed to qualify, then the Vice President elect shall act as President until a President shall have qualified; and the Congress may by law provide for the case wherein neither a President nor a Vice President elect shall have qualified, declaring who shall then act as President, or the manner in which one who is to act shall be selected, and such person shall act accordingly until a President or Vice President shall have qualified.

Section 4. The Congress may by law provide for the case of the death of any of the persons from whom the House of Representatives may choose a President whenever the right of choice shall have devolved upon them, and for the case of the death of any of the persons from whom the Senate may choose a Vice President whenever the right of choice shall have devolved upon them.

Section 5. Sections 1 and 2 shall take effect on the 15th day of October following the ratification of this article.

Section 6. The article shall be inoperative unless it shall have been ratified as an amendment to the Constitution by the legislatures of three-fourths of the several States within seven years from the date of its submission.

Amendment XXI (5 December 1933)

Section 1. The eighteenth article of amendment to the Constitution of the United States is hereby repealed.

Section 2. The transportation or importation into any State, Territory, or possession of the United States for delivery or use therein of intoxicating liquors, in violation of the laws thereof, is hereby prohibited.

Section 3. This article shall be inoperative unless it shall have been ratified as an amendment to the Constitution by conventions in the several States, as provided in the Constitution, within seven years from the date of the submission hereof to the States by the Congress.

Amendment XXII (26 February 1951)

Section 1. No person shall be elected to the office of the President more than twice, and no person who has held the office of President, or acted as President, for more than two years of a term to which some other person was elected President shall be elected to the office of president more than once. But this Article shall not apply to any person holding the office of President when this Article was proposed by the Congress, and shall not prevent any person who may be holding the office of President, or acting as President, during the term within which this Article becomes operative from holding the office of President or acting as President during the remainder of such term.

Section 2.   This Article shall be inoperative unless it shall have been ratified as an amendment to the Constitution by the legislatures of three-fourths of the several States within seven years from the date of its submission to the States by the Congress.

Amendment XXIII (29 March 1961)

Section 1.   The District constituting the seat of Government of the United States shall appoint in such manner as the Congress may direct:

A number of electors of President and Vice President equal to the whole number of Senators and Representatives in Congress to which the District would be entitled if it were a State, but in no event more than the least populous State; they shall be in addition to those appointed by the States, but they shall be considered, for the purposes of the election of President and Vice President, to be electors appointed by a State; and they shall meet in the District and perform such duties as provided by the twelfth article of amendment.

Section 2.   The Congress shall have power to enforce this article by appropriate legislation.

Amendment XXIV (23 January 1964)

Section 1.   The right of citizens of the United States to vote in any primary or other election for President or Vice President, for electors for President or Vice President, or for Senator or Representative in Congress, shall not be denied or abridged by the United States or any state by reason of failure to pay any poll tax or other tax.

Section 2.   The Congress shall have the power to enforce this article by appropriate legislation.

Amendment XXV (10 February 1967)

Section 1.   In case of the removal of the President from office or of his death or resignation, the Vice President shall become President.

Section 2.   Whenever there is a vacancy in the office of the Vice President, the President shall nominate a Vice President who shall take office upon confirmation by a majority vote of both Houses of Congress.

Section 3.   Whenever the President transmits to the President pro tempore of the Senate and the Speaker of the House of Representatives his written declaration that he is unable to discharge the powers and duties of his office, and until he transmits to them a written declaration to the contrary, such powers and duties shall be discharged by the Vice President as Acting President.

Section 4.   Whenever the Vice President and a majority of either the principal officers of the executive departments or of such other body as Congress may by law provide, transmit to the President pro tempore of the Senate and the Speaker of the House of Representatives their written declaration that the President is unable to discharge the powers and duties of his office, the Vice President shall immediately assume the powers and duties of the office as Acting President.

Thereafter, when the President transmits to the President pro tempore of the Senate and the Speaker of the House of Representatives his written declaration that no inability exists, he shall resume the powers and duties of his office unless the Vice President and a majority of either the principal officers of the executive departments or of such other body as Congress may by law provide, transmit within four days to the President pro tempore of the Senate and the Speaker of the House of Representatives their written declaration that the President is unable to discharge the powers and duties of his office. Thereupon Congress shall decide the issue, assembling within forty-eight hours for that purpose if not in session. If the Congress, within twenty-one days after receipt of the latter written declaration or, if Congress is not in session, within twenty-one days after Congress is required to assemble, determines by two-thirds vote of both Houses that the President is unable to discharge the powers and duties of his office, the Vice President shall continue to discharge the same as Acting President; otherwise, the President shall resume the powers and duties of his office.

Amendment XXVI (30 June 1971)

Section 1.   The right of citizens of the United States, who are eighteen years of age or older, to vote shall not be denied or abridged by the United States or any state on account of age.

Section 2.   The Congress shall have the power to enforce this article by appropriate legislation.

Appendix II

1988 Election Timetable

January
14	Michigan county conventions (R)
29–30	Michigan state convention (R)

February
1	Kansas caucus begins (R)
4	Hawaii precinct caucuses (R)
8	Iowa precinct caucuses (D and R)
16	New Hampshire presidential primary
18	Nevada caucus (R)
20	Kansas congressional district conventions (R)
23	Minnesota precinct caucuses (D and R)
	South Dakota presidential primary
26–28	Maine municipal caucuses (R)
27	Alaska caucus begins (R)
28	Maine municipal caucuses (D)

March
1	Vermont non-binding presidential primary
5	Kansas state convention
	South Carolina presidential primary (R)
	Wyoming caucus
	Wyoming county conventions (D and R)
8	Known as 'Super Tuesday'; presidential primaries in:

Alabama
Arkansas
Florida
Georgia
Kentucky
Louisiana
Maryland

Massachusetts
Mississippi
Missouri
North Carolina
Oklahoma
Rhode Island
Tennessee
Texas
Virginia

Also:

Hawaii precinct caucuses (D)
Idaho county caucuses (D)
Nevada precinct caucuses (D)
Texas Democratic precinct caucuses
Washington precinct caucuses (D and R)
American Samoa caucus (D)
10	Alaska precinct caucuses (D)
15	Illinois presidential primary
19	Kansas county caucuses (D)
20	Puerto Rico presidential primary
22	Democrats Abroad presidential mail-in primary
26	Michigan caucus (D)
29	Connecticut presidential primary

April

2	Virgin Islands district conventions (D)
4	Colorado precinct caucuses (D and R)
5	Wisconsin presidential primary
16	Arizona legislative district caucuses (D)
18	Delaware caucuses (D)
19	New York presidential primary
	Vermont caucus
19–20	Democratic House and Senate super-delegates selected
24	Guam caucus (D and R)
25	Utah caucus
26	Pennsylvania presidential primary

May

3	District of Columbia presidential primary
	Indiana presidential primary
	Ohio presidential primary
10	Nebraska presidential primary
	West Virginia presidential primary
17	Oregon presidential primary
24	Idaho presidential primary

June
7	California presidential primary
	Montana presidential primary
	New Jersey presidential primary
	New Mexico presidential primary
14	North Dakota presidential primary

July
18–21   Democratic national convention (Atlanta)

August
15–18   Republican national convention (New Orleans)

November
8   Election day

Appendix III

Presidents and Vice-Presidents of the United States

Presidents and party		Vice-Presidents	Term
1. George Washington (1732–1799)	F	John Adams	1789–1797
2. John Adams (1735–1826)	F	Thomas Jefferson	1797–1801
3. Thomas Jefferson (1743–1826)	D–R	Aaron Burr (to 1805) George Clinton	1801–1809
4. James Madison (1751–1836)	D–R	George Clinton (to 1813) Elbridge Gerry	1809–1817
5. James Monroe (1758–1831)	D–R	D.D. Tompkins	1817–1825
6. John Quincy Adams (1767–1848)	D–R	John C. Calhoun	1825–1829
7. Andrew Jackson (1767–1845)	D	John C. Calhoun (to 1833) Martin Van Buren	1829–1837
8. Martin Van Buren (1782–1862)	D	R.M. Johnson	1837–1841
9. William H. Harrison (1773–1841)	W	John Tyler	1841
10. John Tyler (1790–1862)	W		1841–1845
11. James K. Polk (1795–1849)	D	George M. Dallas	1845–1849
12. Zachary Taylor (1784–1850)	W	Millard Fillmore	1849–1850
13. Millard Fillmore (1800–1874)	W		1850–1853
14. Franklin Pierce (1804–1869)	D	William R. King	1853–1857

15. James Buchanan (1791–1868)	D	J.C. Breckinridge		1857–1861
16. Abraham Lincoln (1809–1865)	R	H. Hamlin Andrew Johnson		1861–1865
17. Andrew Johson (1805–1875)	U			1865–1869
18. Ulysses S. Grant (1822–1885)	R	S. Colfax (to 1873) H. Wilson		1869–1877
19. Rutherford B. Hayes (1822–1893)	R	W.A. Wheeler		1877–1881
20. James A. Garfield (1831–1881)	R	Chester A. Arthur		1881
21. Chester A. Arthur (1830–1886)	R			1881–1885
22. Grover Cleveland (1837–1908)	D	A. Hendricks		1885–1889
23. Benjamin Harrison (1833–1901)	R	Levi P. Morton		1889–1893
24. Grover Cleveland (1837–1908)	D	Adlai E. Stevenson		1893–1897
25. William McKinley (1843–1901)	R	G.A. Hobart (to 1901) Theodore Roosevelt		1897–1901
26. Theodore Roosevelt (1858–1919)	R	C.W. Fairbanks (from 1905)		1901–1909
27. William H. Taft (1857–1930)	R	J.S. Sherman		1909–1913
28. Woodrow Wilson (1856–1924)	D	T.R. Marshall		1913–1921
29. Warren G. Harding (1865–1923)	R	Calvin Coolidge		1921–1923
30. Calvin Coolidge (1872–1933)	R	Charles G. Dawes (from 1925)		1923–1929
31. Herbert Hoover (1874–1964)	R	Charles Curtis		1929–1933
32. Franklin D. Roosevelt (1882–1945)	D	John N. Garner Henry Wallace (from 1941) Harry Truman (from 1945)		1933–1945
33. Harry S. Truman (1884–1972)	D	Alben W. Barkley (from 1949)		1945–1953
34. Dwight D. Eisenhower (1890–1969)	R	Richard M. Nixon		1953–1961

35. John F. Kennedy (1917–1963)	D	Lyndon B. Johnson		1961–1963
36. Lyndon B. Johnson (1908–1973)	D	Hubert Humphrey (from 1965)		1963–1969
37. Richard M. Nixon (b.1913)	R	Spiro Agnew[1] Gerald Ford (from 1973)[2]		1969–1974
38. Gerald Ford (b.1913)	R	Nelson Rockefeller		1974–1977
39. Jimmy Carter (b.1924)	D	Walter F. Mondale		1977–1981
40. Ronald Reagan (b.1911)	R	George Bush		1981–1989
41. George Bush (b.1924)	R	Dan Quayle		1989–

F = Federalist; DR = Democratic-Republican; D = Democratic; W = Whig; R = Republican; U = Union.

[1] Spiro Agnew resigned from the Vice-presidency after admitting charges of income tax evasion.

[2] Gerald Ford was the first Vice-President to be appointed under the terms of the 25th Amendment. Until then, if the Vice-Presidency became vacant it stayed vacant until the next presidential election. Ford went on to become President when Richard Nixon became the first President to resign the office.

Bibliography

The books listed in this section are but a sample of the works which have been written about the presidency in its various roles, and they are intended to supplement the works cited in the text and to provide the interested reader with some idea of what is available for further study. Three points need to be made. First, no articles are listed, and they do abound in the various academic journals which may with profit be consulted. Secondly, while I have attempted to place the books into relevant sections, this exercise has its limitations, for many books fall into two or more categories. Readers seeking to study some particular aspect should, then, be prepared to look at other sections for books which may be of value. Finally, with one or two exceptions, I have excluded the welter of books which relate to specific presidencies, but, again, reading some of them may well prove rewarding.

General

Bailey, Harry A. and Shafritz, Jay (eds), *The American Presidency: Historical and Contemporary Perspectives* (Chicago: Dorsey, 1988).

Barber, James D., *Presidential Character* (Englewood Cliffs, NJ: Prentice Hall, 1977).

Berman, Larry, *The New American Presidency* (Boston: Little Brown, 1987).

Corwin, Edward S., *The President: Office and Powers, 1787–1957* (New York: New York University Press, 1957).

Cronin, Thomas, *The State of the Presidency*, 2nd edn (Boston: Little Brown, 1980).

Cronin, Thomas, *Rethinking the Presidency* (Boston: Little Brown, 1982).

Franck, Thomas M. (ed.), *The Tethered Presidency* (New York: Columbia University Press, 1981).

Goldstein, J., *The Modern American Vice-Presidency* (Princeton: Princeton University Press, 1983).

Hart, John, *The Presidential Branch* (New York: Pergammon Press, 1987).

Hinckley, Barbara, *Problems of the Presidency* (Glenview, Ill.: Scott, Foresman, 1985).

Hodgson, Godfrey, *All Things To All Men* (Harmondsworth: Penguin Books, 1984).

Kearney, Edward (ed.), *Dimensions of the Modern Presidency* (St Louis, M.: Forum Press, 1981).

King, Gary and Ragsdale, L., *The Elusive Executive* (Washington DC: Congressional Quarterly, 1988).

Koenig, Louis W., *The Chief Executive*, 5th edn (San Diego: Harcourt Brace Jovanovich, 1986).

Laski, Harold, *The American Presidency* (London: Allen & Unwin, 1940).

Light, P., *Vice-Presidential Power* (Baltimore: Johns Hopkins University Press, 1984).

Lowi, Theodore, *The Personal President* (Ithaca NY: Cornell University Press, 1985).

Nelson, Michael (ed.), *The Presidency and the Political System*, 3rd edn (Washington, DC: Congressional Quarterly Press, 1990).

Neustadt, Richard, *Presidential Power*, revised edn (New York: Wiley 1980).

Pfiffner, James, *The Strategic Presidency* (Chicago: Dorsey Press, 1988).

Pious, Richard M., *The American Presidency* (New York: Basic Books, 1979).

Reedy, George E., *The Twilight of the Presidency* (New York: World, 1970).

Rossiter, Clinton, *The American Presidency*, 2nd edn (New York: Harcourt, Brace & World, 1960).

Salamon, Lester and Lund, Michael (eds) *The Reagan Presidency and the Governing of America*, (Washington DC: The Urban Institute, 1984).

Schlesinger, Arthur M. Jr, *The Imperial Presidency* (New York: Popular Library, 1974).

Shaw, Malcolm (ed.), *Roosevelt to Reagan: The Development of the Modern Presidency* (London: Hurst, 1987).

Sickels, Robert J., *The Presidency* (Englewood Cliffs, NJ: Prentice Hall, 1980).

Tugwell, Rexford G. and Cronin, Thomas E. (eds), *The Presidency Reappraised* (New York: Praeger, 1974).

Watson, Richard A. and Thomas, Norman, *The Politics of the Presidency* (New York: Wiley, 1983).

Wilson, Woodrow, *Constitutional Government in the United States* (New York: Columbia University Press, 1908).

Background

Borden, Morton (ed.), *The Anti-Federalist Papers* (East Lansing: Michigan State University Press, 1965).

Farrand, Max (ed.), *The Records of the Federal Convention of 1787* (New Haven, Conn.: Yale University Press, 1911).

Farrand, Max, *The Framing of the Constitution of the United States* (New Haven, Conn.: Yale University Press, 1913).

Kelly, Alfred H. and Harbison, Winfred A., *The American Constitution: Its Origins and Development* 4th edn (New York: Norton, 1963).

Mason, Alpheus T., *The States' Rights Debate: Anti-Federalism and the Constitution* (Englewood Cliffs, NJ: Prentice Hall, 1964).

Rossiter, Clinton, *Alexander Hamilton and the Constitution* (New York: Harcourt, Brace & World, 1963).

Thach, Charles C., *The Creation of the Presidency 1775–1789* (Baltimore: Johns Hopkins University Press, 1923).

Warren, Charles, *The Making of the Constitution* (Cambridge, Mass.: Harvard University Press, 1928. Reprinted edn, New York: Barnes & Noble, 1967).

Selection, election and parties

Alexander, Herbert, *Spending in the 1984 Elections* (Lexington, Mass.: Lexington Books, 1987).

Asher, H., *Presidential Elections and American Politics* (Homewood, Ill.: Dorsey, 1976).

Bickel, Alexander, *The New Age of Political Reform: The Electoral College, the Convention & the Party System* (New York: Harper & Row, 1968).

Blumenthal, Sidney, *The Permanent Campaign* (Boston: Beacon, 1980).

Croty, William and Jacobson, Gary, *American Parties in Decline* (Boston: Little Brown, 1980).

Huckshorn, Robert J., *Political Parties in America* (Scituate, Mass.: Duxbury, 1980).

Kessel, J., *Presidential Campaign Politics*, 2nd edn (Homewood, Ill.: Dorsey, 1984).

King, A. (ed.), *The New American Political System* (Washington, DC: AEI, 1978).

Kirkpatrick, J., *Dismantling the Parties* (Washington, DC: AEI, 1979).

Kirkpatrick, J., Malbin, M. et al., *The Presidential Nominating Process: Can it be Improved?* (Washington, DC. AEI, 1980).

Lipset, Seymour Martin (ed.), *Emerging Coalitions in American Politics* (San Francisco: Institute for Contemporary Studies, 1978).

Longley, Lawrence and Braun, Alan, *The Politics of Electoral College Reform* (New Haven: Yale University Press, 1975).

Matthews, Donald (ed.), *Perspectives on Presidential Selection* (Washington DC: Brookings, 1972).

Patterson, Thomas E., *The Mass Media Election: How Americans Choose Their President* (New York: Praeger, 1980).

Pierce, Neil R., *The People's President* (New York: Simon & Schuster, 1968).

Polsby, Nelson and Wildavsky, A., *Presidential Elections*, 7th edn (New York: Scribner's, 1988).

Ranney, Austin, *Curing the Mischiefs of Faction* (Berkeley: University of California Press, 1975).

Sorauf, Frank, *Money in American Elections* (Glenview, Ill.: Scott, Foresman, 1988).

Watson, Richard A., *The Presidential Contest*, 2nd edn (New York: Wiley, 1984).

Wayne, Stephen, *The Road to the White House* (New York: St. Martin's Press, 1984).

White, Theodore, *The Making of the President 1960* (and volumes for subsequent presidential elections) (New York: Atheneum, 1961 et al.).

Witcover, Jules, *Marathon: The Pursuit of the Presidency* (New York: Viking, 1977).

Cabinet and administration

Anderson, P., *The President's Men* (Garden City: Doubleday, 1968).

Fenno, Richard, *The President's Cabinet* (Cambridge, Mass.: Harvard University Press, 1959).

Hess, Stephen, *Organizing the Presidency*, 3rd edn (Washington, DC: Brookings, 1987).

Johnson R., *Managing the White House* (New York: Harper & Row, 1974).

Kirkpatrick, J., *The New Presidential Elite* (New York: Russell Sage, 1976).

Meltsner, Arnold J. (ed.), *Politics and the Oval Office* (San Francisco: Institute for Contemporary Studies, 1981).

Nathan, R., *The Plot that Failed* (New York: Wiley, 1975).

Nathan, R., *The Administrative Presidency* (New York: Wiley, 1983).

President and Congress

Adler, David, *The Constitution and the Termination of Treaties* (New York: Garland Publishing, 1986).

Berger, Raoul, *Executive Privilege: A Constitutional Myth* (Cambridge, Mass.: Harvard University Press, 1974).

Bond, Jon R. and Fleisher, Richard, *The President in the Legislative Arena* (Chicago: University of Chicago Press, 1990).

Bowles, Nigel, *The White House and Capitol Hill* (Oxford: Clarendon Press, 1987).

Crabb, C. and Holt, P., *Invitation to Struggle*, 2nd edn (Washington, DC: Congressional Quarterly Press, 1984).

Edwards, George C. III, *Presidential Influence in Congress* (San Francisco: Freeman, 1980).

Fisher, L., *Constitutional Conflicts Between Congress and the President* (Princeton: Princeton University Press, 1985).

Fisher, L., *The Politics of Shared Power: Congress and the Executive* 2nd edn (Washington DC: Congressional Quarterly Press, 1987).

Huntington, Samuel P., *The Common Defense* (New York: Columbia University Press, 1963).

Hyland, William (ed.), *The Reagan Foreign Policy* (New York: New American Library, 1987).

King, A. (ed.), *Both Ends of the Avenue: The Presidency, the Executive Branch and Congress in the 1980s* (Washington, DC: AEI, 1983).

Mansfield, Harvey, Snr (ed.), *Congress Against the President* (New York: Praeger, 1975).

Mayhew, David P., *Congress: The Electoral Connection* (New Haven: Yale University Press, 1974).
Nathan, James and Oliver J.K., *Foreign Policy Making and the American Political System* (Boston: Little Brown, 1983).
Oleszek, W.J., *Congressional Procedures and the Policy Process* 2nd edn (Washington DC: Congressional Quarterly Press, 1984).
Ornstein, Norman J. (ed.), *President and Congress* (Washington, DC: AEI, 1982).
Polsby, Nelson, *Congress and the Presidency*, 4th edn (Englewood Cliffs, NJ: Prentice Hall, 1986).
Pyle, Christopher and Pious, Richard (eds), *The President, Congress and the Constitution* (New York: Free Press, 1984).
Spanier, John and Uslaner, Eric, *American Foreign Policy Making and the Democratic Dilemmas* (New York: Holt, Rhinehart & Winston, 1985).
Tatalovich R. and Daynes, Byron, *Presidential Power in the United States* (Monterey: Brooks/Cole Publishing, 1984).
Wayne, Stephen, *The Legislative Presidency* (New York: Harper & Row, 1986).

Leadership and policy-making

Burns, James MacGregor, *Roosevelt: the Lion and the Fox* (New York: Harcourt, Brace, 1956).
Burns, James MacGregor, *The Power to Lead: The Crisis of the American Presidency* (New York: Simon & Schuster, 1984).
Destler, I., *Making Foreign Economic Policy* (Washington, DC: Brookings, 1981).
Edwards, George C. III and Wayne, Stephen J., *Presidential Leadership: Politics and Policy Making*, 2nd edn (New York: St Martin's Press, 1990).
Greenstein, Fred (ed.), *Leadership in the Modern Presidency* (Cambridge, Mass.: Harvard University Press, 1988).
Hargrove, Erwin and Nelson, Michael, *Presidents, Politics and Policy* (New York: Knopf, 1984).
Heclo, Hugh and Salamon Lester, *The Illusion of Presidential Government* (Boulder: Westview, 1981).
Heclo, Hugh, *A Government of Strangers* (Washington, DC: Brookings, 1987).
Kellerman, Barbara, *The Political Presidency: Practice of Leadership* (New York: OUP, 1984).
Kessell, J., *The Domestic Presidency* (Scituate, Mass.: Duxbury, 1975).
Light, Paul, *The President's Agenda* (Baltimore: Johns Hopkins University Press, 1982).
Lynn, Laurence E. Jr, *Managing Public Policy* (Boston: Little Brown, 1987).
Mezey, Michael L., *Congress, the President and Public Policy* (Boulder: Westview, 1989).
Porter, Roger B., *Presidential Decision Making* (Cambridge: CUP, 1980).

Rockman, Bert, *The Leadership Question: The Presidency and the Political System* (New York: Praeger, 1984).

Roosevelt, Theodore, *The Autobiography of Theodore Roosevelt* (Charles Scribner's Sons, 1913).

Schlesinger, Arthur M. Jr, *A Thousand Days* (New York: Fawcett, 1965).

Stockman, David, *The Triumph of Politics* (New York: Harper & Row, 1986).

Sundquist, James, *Politics and Policy: The Eisenhower, Kennedy and Johnson Years* (Washington, DC: Brookings, 1968).

Taft, William Howard, *Our Chief Magistrate and his Powers* (New York: OUP, 1916).

Wildavsky, A., *The Politics of the Budgetary Process* (Boston: Little Brown 1984).

Presidents and the judiciary

Abraham, Henry J., *Justices and Presidents* (New York: OUP, 1985).

Berger, Raoul, *Government by Judiciary* (Cambridge, Mass.: Harvard University Press, 1977).

Bickel, Alexander, *The Least Dangerous Branch* (New Haven, Conn.: Yale University Press, 1962).

Choper, Jesse, *Judicial Review and the National Political Process* (Chicago: University of Chicago Press, 1980).

Corsi, Jerome R., *Judicial Politics* (Englewood Cliffs, NJ: Prentice Hall, 1984).

Craig, Barbara, *Chadha: The Story of an Epic Constitutional Struggle* (New York: OUP, 1988).

Murphy, Walter F. and Pritchett, C. Herman (eds), *Courts, Judges and Politics*, 4th edn (New York: Random House, 1986).

Rossiter, C., *The Supreme Court and the Commander in Chief*, expanded edn (Ithaca, NY: Cornell University Press, 1976).

Schubert, Glendon A. Jr, *The Presidency in the Courts* (Minneapolis: University of Minnesota Press, 1957).

Scigliano, Robert, *The Supreme Court and the Presidency* (New York: Free Press, 1971).

Presidents and the media

Barber, James D., *The Pulse of Politics: Electing Presidents in the Media Age* (New York: Norton, 1980).

Cornwell, Elmer E., *Presidential Leadership of Public Opinion* (Bloomington, Ind.: Indiana University Press, 1965).

Graber, Doris A., *Mass Media and American Politics* (Washington, DC: Congressional Quarterly Press, 1980).

Graber, Doris A. (ed.), *The President and the Public (Philadelphia: Institute for Study of Human Issues, 1982)*.

Grossman, Michael and Kumar, Martha, *Portraying the President: the White House and the News Media* (Baltimore: Johns Hopkins University Press, 1981).

Porter, William E., *Assault on the Media: The Nixon Years* (Ann Arbor: University of Michigan Press, 1976).

Thompson, Kenneth W. (ed.), *The Media: the Credibility of Institutions, Policies and Leadership* (Lanham, Md.: University Press of America, 1985).

Index